The Unions and the Democrats

THE UNIONS and THE DEMOCRATS

An Enduring Alliance

Updated Edition

TAYLOR E. DARK

ILR Press
an imprint of
Cornell University Press
ITHACA AND LONDON

For my parents

First published 1999 by Cornell University Press
First printing, Cornell Paperbacks, 2001

Printed in the United States of America

Library of Congress Cataloging-in-Publication Data

Dark, Taylor E.
The unions and the Democrats : an enduring alliance / Taylor E. Dark, III.
p. cm.
Includes bibliographical references and index.
ISBN 0-8014-3576-5 (cloth : alk. paper) 0-8014-8733-1 (paper : alk. paper)
1. Trade-Unions—United States—Political activity—History—20th century. 2. United States—Politics and government—20th century. 3. Democratic Party (U.S.)—History. 4. AFL-CIO—History. I. Title.
HD6510.D37 1998
322'.2'09730904—dc21 98-30400

Cornell University Press strives to use environmentally responsible suppliers and materials to the fullest extent possible in the publishing of its books. Such materials include vegetable-based, low-VOC inks and acid-free papers that are recycled, totally chlorine-free, or partly composed of nonwood fibers.

Cloth printing 10 9 8 7 6 5 4 3 2 1

Paperback printing 10 9 8 7 6 5 4 3 2 1

Contents

Preface to the Cornell Paperbacks Edition

The thesis of this book is that labor union political power in recent decades has been significantly underestimated by most observers. In particular, the resiliency of the alliance between organized labor and the Democratic party has been overlooked. While there is much in the pages that follow that supports such an interpretation, one fascinating piece of evidence was revealed only in the political maneuvers following the Monica Lewinsky scandal, which erupted in January 1998. By the spring of that year, the survival of Bill Clinton as president had grown uncertain as Republican members of Congress—and even a few Democrats—openly contemplated impeaching the president or at least forcing his early resignation. The cause of the contretemps was, of course, the revelation that Clinton had apparently lied under oath about his affair with the young White House intern. As Independent Counsel Kenneth Starr closed in on the president, Democrats in Washington grew increasingly anxious about the possible political impact of the president's misdeeds.

It was at this crucial moment, as described by the *Washington Post*'s Peter Baker, that John J. Sweeney, president of the AFL-CIO, played a decisive role in discouraging any Democratic attempts to encourage Clinton to resign. As Baker recounts, Harold M. Ickes, Clinton's deputy chief of staff in his first term and a key figure in the reelection campaign of 1996, was deeply worried about the effects of the scandal on the party's fortunes in the upcoming congressional elections—not to mention the presidential election of 2000. Ickes began approaching key players within the party about the possibility of a Clinton resignation, which would place Vice President Gore in the White House and could salvage the party's fortunes in 2000. Baker writes:

> One of the power players that Ickes met with was John J. Sweeney, president of the AFL-CIO, still perhaps the single most dominant force within the Dem-

> ocratic Party even after decades of decline. Ickes and Sweeney got together over breakfast at the Washington Hilton Hotel, and the former White House aide presented his case. Sweeney listened but was not yet ready to abandon Clinton.
>
> "Let's wait and see, Harold," he said. "Let's see how this unfolds."[1]

With these words, the tide was turned: talk of resignation would go by the wayside, and Ickes ended his covert wanderings among Washington's political elites. Without Sweeney's support, bringing along other party figures would be a nearly hopeless task.

How could this be? How could it still be the case that, after decades of declining union representation in the workforce, the labor movement was "still perhaps the single most dominant force within the Democratic Party" and its top leader the most crucial figure in holding back a potential crisis of party unity? Hadn't the last rites already been performed over a dying U.S. labor movement at some point during the 1980s?

This book provides the answers to these and other questions, explaining how organized labor still managed to generate valuable resources for exchange with elected officeholders in national politics. Contrary to some interpretations, I find that the level of workforce representation is not the crucial issue for the near-term potency of the labor movement in politics. Rather, what matters is the intensity of resource mobilization—how well labor does in generating votes, volunteers, propaganda, and money—and the overall unity of the movement as it interacts with Washington policymakers. In a special postscript to this edition, these factors are considered once more in the context of the 2000 election and the last years of Clinton's presidency. I conclude that labor's success at generating new resources bodes well for the maintenance of the labor movement as an influential force in national politics, albeit a force much weaker than union leaders and their sympathizers would like. John J. Sweeney—or his successor—will continue to be a major player in the Washington community.

TAYLOR DARK

Kyoto, Japan

[1] Peter Baker, "The Breach: White House Unhinged," *Washington Post* Sept. 18, 2000. See also Peter Baker, *The Breach: Inside the Impeachment and Trial of William Jefferson Clinton*. New York: Scribner, 2000.

Acknowledgments

Portions of this book were written while the author was living in Russia, Ukraine, and Japan, in addition to sojourns in Washington, D.C., and Berkeley. The result is a long trail of debts that is hard to accurately recall, much less properly acknowledge. At a minimum, though, I must extend my thanks to the following institutions for their generous financial support: the Governmental Studies Program at the Brookings Institution, the Graduate Division of the University of California at Berkeley, the Everett C. Dirksen Center for Congressional Research, and the Walter P. Reuther Library for Urban Affairs at Wayne State University. More recently, the Graduate School of American Studies at Doshisha University in Kyoto, Japan, provided an ideal location for bringing this work to completion.

At an early stage in this project, graduate students and professors in the Department of Political Science at UC Berkeley kindly provided much commentary, support, and assistance. Professors Michael Rogin, Judith Gruber, and Martin Sanchez-Jankowski were especially helpful.

On a personal note, I am deeply indebted to my parents for both their financial and their emotional support over the many years I worked on this book. I thank Nina for her limitless patience and understanding.

Sections of this book were previously published as articles, which have since seen considerable revision. Portions of Chapter 5 appeared in "Organized Labor and Party Reform: A Reassessment," *Polity* Vol. 28, No. 4 (Summer 1996): 497–520. An early version of Chapter 6 was published as "Organized Labor and the Carter Administration: The Origins of Conflict," in *The Presidency and Domestic Policies of Jimmy Carter*, ed. Herbert Rosenbaum and Alexej Ugrinsky (Westport, Conn.: Greenwood Press, 1994), 761–82. A section of Chapter 7 appeared as "Organized Labor and the Presidential Nominating Process," *Presidential Studies Quarterly* Vol. 26, No. 2 (Summer 1996): 391–401. Much of Chapter 8 was published as "Organized Labor and the Congressional Democrats," *Political Science Quarterly* Vol. 111 (Spring 1996): 83–104.

Introduction: The Continuing Significance of Labor Politics

Anyone who begins a study of labor unions in contemporary American politics soon encounters a stereotypical image that guides the thinking of most observers. The story goes something like this: labor unions were economically secure and politically vigorous from the late 1930s to roughly the mid-1970s, after which time their power in all areas dramatically declined. Although unions had by the end of World War II effectively consolidated their hold in the great mass-production industries at the core of the American economy, and had routinized access to the most important of national policymakers, this success was fragile and fleeting. The decline of mass-production industries, problems of inflation and lowered productivity, and the rise of conservative politicians and ideologies all contributed to a marked change in labor's fortunes. Economic change quickly exceeded the capacities of unions to adjust, and union membership figures took a downward slide that continued unimpeded for decades to come. As a result, labor's political power virtually collapsed. The Democratic Party turned its back on the unions, denying them the access and support that had once been commonplace. The Republican Party became more anti-union than ever, abandoning any pretense of even-handedness in relations between labor and capital. Thus, from the mid-1970s onward, it was all downhill for American unions. By the 1990s, they were shadows of their former selves, condemned to beg for merely symbolic assurances from Washington elites in both parties who regarded unions as little more than privileged dinosaurs, the Jurassic remnants of an earlier stage of economic and political development.

The thesis of this book is that much of this conventional wisdom is in error. The evidence presented here will show that unions have actually been remarkably successful in holding on to political power, despite having to cope with a marked decline in union representation in the workforce, the Republican resurgence, and other hostile conditions. The relationship of union leaders and lobbyists with Democratic Party officeholders, especially in Congress, remains very strong and has influenced important public policy outcomes into the 1990s. Presidents Jimmy Carter and Bill Clinton both maintained close ties to the labor movement and tried to advance union interests in a wide variety of ways. Although unions have had their share of conflicts with Democratic presidents and members of Congress, these conflicts are not qualitatively new and are very much in keeping with long-standing historical patterns. In short, I will argue for a surprising degree of continuity in labor's overall position in national politics.

None of this, of course, is meant to deny that many of the economic and political developments in recent decades posed new difficulties for organized labor, and that some were downright harmful. Yet an emphasis on decline alone misses an important part of the story. Although there is no doubt that many unions lost members and faced extraordinary economic adversity, it is also the case that some unions, especially those based in the public sector, have done very well, experiencing large increases in membership and newly acquired political influence. At the same time, unions under economic stress and with dwindling membership rolls have often greatly expanded their political activities, raising more money for campaigns and organizing their members more effectively for political action. Reforms in Congress and the presidential nominating process have created new avenues for the pursuit of political power that many unions have eagerly pursued (though some academics have claimed that these reforms are inherently inimical to the exercise of union power). The result of all these factors is that unions not only remain major players in the politics of the Democratic Party but have even enhanced their power in certain areas. Consequently, any analysis of the Democratic Party that ignores the continuing role of organized labor will have serious inadequacies.

Such findings are of considerable importance for several reasons. First, unions can generate impressive amounts of both economic and political power. It is no exaggeration to say that union activity can lead to violence, and even death—sometimes at the hands of striking workers, but at times from hostile employers or government authorities. American history is replete with examples of how unions have provoked intense conflict, and have brought about major reorderings of political and economic power.[1] At a minimum, it is clear that the capacity to disrupt economic production makes unions exceptional: only they, or management itself, can bring important sectors of the economy to a virtual standstill. As recently as March 1996, for instance, a strike by only three thousand members of the United Auto Workers employed in just two plants completely immobilized the production lines of General Motors, the world's largest corporation. Before the seventeen-day strike ended, twenty-seven of GM's twenty-nine assembly plants in North America had been shut down, 177,000 workers had been laid off, and the auto giant was sustaining losses of up to $50 million *a day*.[2] As this case suggests—and a large academic literature confirms—there is no doubt that union collective bargaining can have major effects on the distribution of income, the rates of economic growth and inflation, and the material well-being of large numbers of employees, whether unionized or not.[3]

It is also universally acknowledged that the rise of industrial unionism was crucial in laying the foundation for the Democratic Party's electoral success and legislative accomplishments from the New Deal onward. Unions were key players in promoting the expansion of the welfare state and the adoption of neo-Keynesian economic policies. Indeed, there are few major domestic policies endorsed by the Democratic Party since the 1930s that do not in some way reveal the hand of organized labor, whether the issue be civil rights or federal funding of education, health care or the war on poverty. But the activity of unions is far from purely historical. In 1996 the AFL-CIO alone spent well over $35 million to secure the reelection of Bill Clinton and help Democrats in their bid to regain control of Congress. This is simply an extraordinary sum of money for a single interest group to wield in national politics. Moreover, that figure does not take into account the spending of the separate national unions, or the role of unions in mobilizing their members and their families to work on campaigns and vote on election day. Such electoral activity alone justifies far closer consideration of union political involvement than has typically been the case.

Nor should the unusual ideological baggage associated with union activity be forgotten. It was not only Marxism in its various forms that depicted unions and other working-class organizations (properly guided by the correct ideology, of course) as forces endowed with a unique historical role derived from their special place in the process of production. Social democrats and American liberals have at various points also viewed organized labor as the linchpin in their programs of social reconstruction. The very term "working-class hero," often referenced in both literary and popular discussions, evokes not only the image of the individual employee defiantly expressing his or her own dignity and autonomy but also a collective actor (once called the proletariat) reshaping society as a whole. These visions have little resonance today, either in the United States or in other advanced industrial countries. But shorn of their utopian pretensions, these perspectives can still help us identify something important about unions—namely, that in a society dedicated to market-oriented individualism, they stand for collective solidarity. It is for just this reason that unions have often had great difficulty fitting into American culture; but like the Catholic Church, with which they have often been aligned, unions continue to fulfill social functions and promote values that few other organizations even take seriously. As the United States experiences growing income inequality and a difficult transition to new forms of economic production, there is good reason to think that unions can have an important, and beneficial, role to play.

Perhaps the most important reason for a reconsideration of union political activity can be found in the dramatic changes in the top leadership of the American Federation of Labor–Congress of Industrial Organizations (AFL-CIO). The election in October 1995 of John J. Sweeney as the new AFL-CIO president—an outcome achieved through a truly circuitous set of political maneuvers—was a startling event for anyone familiar with the politics of the labor federation. Since the merger of the AFL and CIO some forty years earlier, the AFL-CIO had known only two presidents. Moreover, there had never been a contested election for the federation presidency. Thus, Sweeney's efforts—first to remove Lane Kirkland and then to run against Kirkland's interim successor, Tom Donahue, for the presidency—brought an air of excitement and debate into the federation's lackluster political culture. Sweeney campaigned on a platform that called for the AFL-CIO to be much more active in union organizing and political mobilization, taking a role that would include reaching out to liberal constituencies long estranged from the labor movement. The scale of Sweeney's subsequent victory therefore signaled a major change in the federation's internal politics. The consequences will be discussed in Chapter 8, but suffice it to say here that the new regime achieved much during its first years in power, not the least of which was the raising of vast sums of money for a campaign to dislodge the Republican majority from Congress. Although the long-term significance of Sweeney's tenure remains unclear, especially as it relates to the goal of reversing the decline in the percentage of the workforce belonging to unions, its immediate importance for the political role of American labor should not be underestimated.

Additionally, I hope that this study will also offer much to political scientists and others interested in the changing character of national politics. By the late 1970s, political scientists had begun to talk of a "new American political system," referring to an interrelated set of reforms in both Congress and the presidential nominating process that opened the door to new constituencies and created a less predictable political environment. Although the claims of newness can be exaggerated (much, of course, did not change at all), the importance of these institutional renovations is indisputable, and they have generated a large scholarly literature assessing their consequences.[4] This book offers one of the few accounts that explicitly compares the situation of an interest group both before and after the reforms of the late 1960s and 1970s. Therefore, it should be valuable to anyone concerned with the effects of institutional change on interest group behavior, alliance formation, and the balance of power in national politics.

Boundaries

My analysis concentrates mainly on those unions (and their leaders) that devote substantial resources to affecting national-level political outcomes.

This criterion necessarily curtails any serious discussion of the involvement of unions in state and local politics. Although activity by unions at these levels of the political system is of growing importance, and clearly insufficiently studied by political scientists and labor historians, it is impossible for a single individual to examine the role of unions in the arena of national politics over an extended period of time, and in any detail, while still doing justice to the complexities of local and state involvement. A natural companion piece to the present volume, therefore, would be a thorough analysis of union activity at the grassroots, exploring in greater detail the demographic changes and tactical innovations that have in recent years transformed the face of many unions.

For now, though, we will be occupied exclusively with the crucial terrain of national politics, where issues of vast importance for the health and future of the labor movement are raised, debated, and resolved. Here we are immediately confronted with a difficult question of scope, for the number of U.S. unions active in national politics is surprisingly large (in fact, much larger than in other advanced industrial countries), and a full appreciation of all their activities is a formidable task indeed. In 1998 well over one hundred labor organizations existed in the United States, seventy-five of which were affiliated with the AFL-CIO, the only national labor federation. Since that number includes almost all of the large and powerful unions, a student of union political activity might find it tempting to concentrate research exclusively on the headquarters of the federation, which, after all, has the unique organizational mandate to represent the entire labor movement in national politics.

To make this decision would, however, be a mistake—primarily because the AFL-CIO has been in the past and remains today a weakly disciplined organization that in most respects cannot command the compliance of its union affiliates. As its name implies, it is not a mass membership organization; rather, it is a *federation* of independent national unions whose constituent units are determined to guard their autonomy and distinct rights and privileges vis-à-vis the central headquarters. One result of this decentralization is that the articulation of political demands by the federation is not formally binding on the affiliated unions. This fact is crucial, for the national unions generate immense political resources that they can and do wield independently. Indeed, the total budgets of several affiliated unions exceed that of the AFL-CIO, and the massive size and marbled foyers of their Washington headquarters reflect their affluence. Clearly, an analytical focus on the AFL-CIO alone will entirely overlook a major portion of the labor movement's political involvement.

Therefore, this study deals with a wide range of national unions as they become politically relevant actors at the national level. That is not as unmanageable a task as it might first appear, for despite the large number of unions in the United States, the main pattern of political activity has been set by a much smaller group, all of which influence one another's programs and strategies. As Jack Joyce, the long-serving president of the International Union of Bricklayers, has noted, "There are probably only about ten or twelve unions within the AFL-CIO that are politically effective."[5] Among these powerhouses must be included such organizations as the United Auto Workers, United Steelworkers of America, Communication Workers of America, International Association of Machinists and Aerospace Workers, Service Employees International Union, United Food and Commercial Workers, the International Brotherhood of Teamsters, such public employee unions as the American Federation of State, County, and Municipal Employees and the American Federation of Teachers, and such smaller but very active unions as the Laborers' International Union of North America, United Brotherhood of Carpenters and Joiners, and Hotel Employees and Restaurant Employees International Union. These key organizations, along with the federation itself, are my focus.

The time span chosen for analysis—the mid-1960s to the mid-1990s—is appropriate for two reasons. First, this period is commonly viewed as encompassing both the high and low points of labor union power in national politics since the end of World War II. At the height of the Great Society, AFL-CIO President George Meany noted: "To a greater degree than ever before in the history of this country, the stated goals of the Administration and of Congress, on one hand, and of the labor movement, on the other, are identical."[6] In contrast, Meany's successor, Lane Kirkland, concluded in 1984 that "no President or conservative block of anti-labor Senators has ever so threatened the very existence of our unions and the laws and programs that protect our members."[7] The views of these union leaders also correspond closely to the judgments of scholars who have studied unions in politics over this period. Any interpretation of the role of unions in American politics therefore ought to be able to account for the key changes that took place over these years.

Second, the historical approach used here provides a set of case studies examining labor's role at different points in time. A comparative methodology provides a more precise rendering of the continuities and discontinuities in labor's position. With the close of the first Clinton administration, it is now possible to compare the activities of three different Democratic presidents over this period. As a result, we are in a much better position to generate and to test various hypotheses about the sources and nature of political change. These techniques will make it possible to dispense with the simplistic dichotomy according to which unions are viewed as exercising a high degree of political power in the 1960s and before, and virtually none afterward. We can substitute instead a more nuanced appreciation of the ways in which unions have adapted to changes in their political, economic, and ideological environment.

Overview

Chapters 1 and 2 describe the major substantive and theoretical issues that will concern us throughout the book. Chapter 1 sets the stage by exploring the debates over the extent and causes of union membership decline, as well as its impact on the political agenda of labor and its alliance with the Democratic Party. I argue that the concept of decline, although seemingly straightforward, is actually quite complex and of limited value in understanding the changing fortunes of the labor movement. Measuring a decline in power can be quite difficult, and the large number of unions and the diversity of issues on their agendas makes accurate generalization a challenge. Thus, what is needed is a more subtle, disaggregated, and empirically detailed analysis of the *actual* role that unions play in the political system during a time of economic adversity.

Chapter 2 formulates a theoretical approach designed to avoid the problems that have weakened many existing analyses of union political involvement. This approach begins with the assumption that both union leaders and elected officeholders are rational actors who seek to maintain their leadership roles. They do so in part through political bargaining, whereby unions provide resources that politicians find valuable, and politicians in turn support pro-union legislation and policy implementation. In this process, unions tap a wide range of their own economic and political resources, and they utilize different mixes of these resources as their internal and external environments change. The success of such efforts will depend, however, on the degree to which national policymakers actually need union resources. If other interest groups can meet their needs, or if the costs of meeting union demands are too high, then politicians may go elsewhere. Alliances between unions and politicians will also depend on the institutional conditions prevailing both inside the labor movement and in the broader political system. If the union movement is highly decentralized or disunited—or, similarly, if power in Washington is widely dispersed within Congress or between the executive and legislative branches—then it will be more difficult to foster ongoing, high-trust relationships between union leaders and national-level politicians.

This framework is applied in the ensuing chapters to analyze the evolving role of unions in national policymaking and the course of their alliance with Democratic officeholders. Chapter 3 examines the context for political bargaining in Washington during the presidency of Lyndon Johnson. Through a process of mutual accommodation, President Johnson and key union leaders were able to construct an unusually cooperative and jointly beneficial relationship. The origins of this relationship were found not just in the pleasantly high rates of economic growth and public spending of the 1960s but also in the relatively high level of unity within the labor movement, on the one hand, and the high concentration of power within Washington in the person of President Johnson, on the other. Despite the best efforts of the AFL-CIO and the White House, though, their cooperation remained profoundly limited by institutional constraints that neither side could overcome. A crucial handicap was Johnson's inability to fully gain control over a Congress where much power remained lodged in the hands of conservative committee chairs, and where liberal legislation could be regularly blocked in the Senate by filibusters. These institutional procedures gave a potent advantage to the traditional "conservative coalition," composed of Republicans and southern Democrats opposed to the enhancement of union power. Equally important was the inability of AFL-CIO President George Meany to control the collective bargaining behavior of the various affiliated national unions—a weakness that took on great significance as inflation worsened in the late 1960s. Thus, while both Meany and Johnson exercised an unusual degree of power within their respective domains, their ability to control some of their most crucial assets remained circumscribed.

Notwithstanding the limitations on their power, by the late 1960s both Meany and Johnson came to be viewed as dangerously autocratic figures, holding themselves above accountability to the constituencies that they putatively represented. As divisive new issues arose (most notably the Vietnam War), pressures grew within both the political system and the labor movement for greater participation and a wider diffusion of decision-making power. These pressures led to a wide-ranging crisis of representation, described in Chapter 4, wherein discontented actors and emergent groups demanded and achieved major procedural reforms. Within Congress and the presidential nominating process, power was dispersed to a larger number of individuals, thereby reducing the capacity of any small set of leaders to make and keep any deals that they might strike with interest groups (including organized labor). Within the labor movement, a set of conflicts over political goals and tactics fostered much greater political engagement on the part of individual national unions, in contrast to the previous near-hegemony of the AFL-CIO bureaucracy. Bargaining capacity was redistributed from the central AFL-CIO leadership to a more fractious set of national union chiefs. By the mid-1970s, then, the exchange relationships between national politicians and union leaders had become much less tidy and predictable.

The consequences of these fragmentations became fully apparent only during the Carter administration, when the labor movement proved unable to sustain the patterns of political bargaining established during the Johnson years. Chapter 5 examines the origins of conflict between the Carter administration and the unions, and explains why nearly half of the nation's union leaders eventually supported Senator Edward M. Kennedy's candidacy in 1980 against the Democratic incumbent. The effects of severe economic problems at this time—especially the constant rise in the rate of inflation—were deeply exacerbated by the power splits within the labor movement as well as the Washington community. Both George Meany and Jimmy Carter soon discovered that in this altered environment they were less able to deliver on their promises to one another than either had expected. As Meany found it increasingly difficult to maintain his influence over individual national union leaders, Carter was forced to confront a more obstreperous Congress where the levers of power were harder to grasp. This unstable situation resulted in a mutual scapegoating that brought relations between the AFL-CIO and the White House to a postwar low.

One lesson that unions leaders drew from this experience was that they needed to be more actively and directly involved in the postreform presidential nominating process. The days of determinative vetoes of potential candidates, exercised behind closed doors and among long-standing political allies, were lost forever. Thus, union leaders chose to enter more aggressively into Democratic primaries and the formal structure of the national Democratic Party. The AFL-CIO realized this goal when it ensured the selection of former vice president Walter Mondale as the Democratic nominee for president in 1984, as well as when it coordinated union involvement in the 1988 and 1992 campaigns. By analyzing these developments, Chapter 6 shows that unions retained an important capacity for political bargaining both in the nominating process and in the general election, even if the techniques and locations of that bargaining had changed considerably. A significant cost still would be paid by Democratic presidential candidates who alienated organized labor, and most carefully avoided doing so.

Such bargaining also persisted in the relationship between organized labor and Democrats in Congress, though here too there were major changes. Chapter 7 describes the persistence of a virtually symbiotic relationship between labor lobbyists and the Democratic congressional leadership, especially in the House of Representatives. Despite some developments in Congress that would seem to lessen their clout, labor unions possessed resources that reelection-minded politicians, operating under conditions of considerable uncertainty, found quite valuable. To the extent that members of the Democratic leadership sought to unify the congressional party around a legislative program, the lobbying support of organized labor was useful within the legislative process itself. Moreover, trends toward recentralizing power within Congress, most clearly visible during the tenure of Speaker Jim Wright, facilitated a cooperative relationship between organized labor and the congressional leadership. The weakening of conservative southern Democrats after the 1960s opened up new avenues for unions to exercise power, thus belying the claims of some authors that the contemporary Congress was a markedly more hostile terrain for the advancement of labor's demands than it had been previously.

Chapter 8 shows how the experience of the first Clinton administration recapitulated many of the patterns found during previous Democratic presidencies. Like both Presidents Johnson and Carter, Clinton would support at least some pro-union changes in the labor law, only to find reform blocked in the Senate by the conservative coalition using the filibuster. Still (and again like his predecessors), Clinton was able to make pro-union appointments to the National Labor Relations Board, the Department of Labor, and other federal departments and agencies. Clinton's handling of issues of union access and consultation was also highly adept, and more reminiscent of LBJ's skillful techniques than Jimmy Carter's less successful approach. The administration turned to the unions for support in passing its social welfare agenda—with positive results when it came to the family and medical leave legislation and several other policies, but with much less success on the administration's bold health care proposal. Although the formal structure of the administration/labor alliance on health care was very similar to that used by LBJ to help pass Medicare in 1965, this time the weight of their alliance in a hyperpluralistic Washington community was insufficient. The most notable area of conflict between the unions and the president concerned trade policy, manifested in the intense battles over GATT (the General Agreement on Tariffs and Trade) and NAFTA (the North American Free Trade Agreement). But these conflicts were temporary and had no long-term consequences for the health of the labor/Democrat alliance. Indeed, in the aftermath of the 1994 takeover of Congress by the Republican Party, the alliance grew even stronger, as unions became central to the Democratic attempt to retake Congress and retain the presidency in 1996. The defeat of fast-track trade legislation in the fall of 1997, which was the logical result of these developments, registered the growing sway of labor in the congressional party.

Finally, the conclusion assesses the aspects of change and continuity in labor's role in national politics since the 1960s. The persistence of union influence within the Democratic Party reveals the need for a reconsideration of recent efforts to periodize contemporary labor and political history around the rise and fall of a "New Deal" or "Democratic" political order. These approaches claim to demarcate distinct eras in political history when the prevailing relationships between ideas, interests, and institutions are decisively favorable or unfavorable for particular interest groups, including organized labor. Such interpretations cite the rise of organized labor as a key element in constructing the New Deal political order and, on this basis, predict that the "end" of that order should end or severely reduce union influence. In contrast, my analysis emphasizes the persistence of historical patterns. In the unsettled politics at the end of the twentieth century, unions are still included in the American political system on roughly the same terms that they were fifty years ago.

Part One

BEYOND THE IMAGE OF DECLINE

1 *The Debate about Decline*

Have labor unions lost political power? If so, has the long-standing alliance between Democratic Party politicians and the union movement suffered a corresponding deterioration? Surprisingly, neither the academic world nor contemporary journalism provides much in the way of clear answers to these questions. According to one common view, "the Democratic Party"—an entity regularly described in almost monolithic terms—consciously abandoned a dying labor movement during the 1970s, lured away by the siren songs of a revitalized business community and masses of conservative suburban voters. *Washington Post* reporter Thomas Byrne Edsall concluded in 1984: "There is no chance that Democratic elected officials in the foreseeable future will permit a declining labor movement with little public support to regain the influence and stature it had in Congress in the mid-1960s." Similarly, political scientist David Vogel argued in 1989 that "not only has union membership been declining steadily but, even more important, ties between trade unions and the Democratic party have measurably weakened." *New Left Review* editor Mike Davis surmised in 1986 that congressional Democrats had become "increasingly reliant upon business PACs and middle-class interest groups" and that power in the party now lay with "younger neo-liberals with scant loyalty to labor or minorities."[1] These views were echoed by many others who saw a major and irreversible deterioration in labor's bargaining position vis-à-vis Democratic officeholders.[2]

The above claims clearly represent the conventional wisdom on the subject. Yet numerous studies reach opposite conclusions, emphasizing instead the extent to which unions have adapted to changes in their political environment, and thus have maintained a good bargaining relationship with Democratic politicians. According to historian Ronald Radosh, writing in 1996, "More and more, the one constituency group with money for Democrats is the one they have been counting on since the FDR era: the AFL-

CIO." Radosh predicts that in the future, "public employee unions and the Hollywood liberal elite will likely be the main backers of the Democratic party—and it will be to these elements that any would-be candidates will have to turn for support."[3] So, too, sociologist William Form sees a fundamental continuity in the labor/Democrat relationship over recent decades: "Mutually dependent, labor and the party seemed permanently locked in an uncomfortable embrace." On his account, after a period of rising conflict in the 1970s, union leaders and Democratic politicians "settled into a fluctuating pattern of symbiotic cooperation."[4] And three scholars of industrial relations argue, on the basis of quantitative measurements of union campaign spending and congressional legislative outcomes during the 1980s, that "the labor-Democratic party alliance has remained strong."[5]

Such divergent claims give rise to fundamental questions: What does it mean to say that the labor movement has declined, especially in terms of its political power? How do we know "decline" when we see it, and what are its causes and consequences? To provide answers, this chapter unpacks the idea of decline, first by identifying the degree and causes of the decline in unionization, and then by evaluating the literature that purports to chart the political consequences of that decline. This review will establish that most accounts of a sudden or precipitous decline in union political power assume more than they show, adopt vague or inconsistent measures of union power, and leave large areas of contemporary union political involvement unexamined. Consequently, the whole idea of decline needs to be recast with greater nuance and precision, and its empirical indicators must be specified more clearly.

The Decline of Unions as Collective Bargaining Agents

The single most significant—and startling—fact about the situation of unions in American society is that union density (the percentage of the workforce enrolled in unions) has been declining since the mid-1950s. At that time, in the aftermath of two decades of fairly steady union growth, unions reached a historic high point in their penetration of the labor market, representing nearly 33 percent of the nonagricultural workforce (table 1.1). This was a remarkable accomplishment, especially given the status of unions at the beginning of the Great Depression, when a very weak labor movement had succeeded in capturing only 13 percent of the workforce. For scholars, politicians, and unionists alike, the increased membership decisively confirmed the phenomenal expansion of organized labor's political and economic power during the New Deal and World War II. With the core mass-production industries now organized, a mature and lasting solution to the "labor question" that had haunted American politics since the late nineteenth century seemed, at last, to have been found. The new membership

Table 1.1. Union Membership as a Proportion of Nonagricultural Labor Force, 1930–97

Year	Percentage Union	Year	Percentage Union	Year	Percentage Union
1930	12.7	1953	32.5	1976	27.9
1931	13.4	1954	32.3	1977	26.2
1932	14.4	1955	31.8	1978	25.1
1933	14.7	1956	31.4	1979	24.5
1934	15.4	1957	31.2	1980	23.2
1935	13.5	1958	30.3	1981	22.6
1936	14.2	1959	29.0	1982	21.9
1937	18.4	1960	28.6	1983	20.7
1938	20.4	1961	28.5	1984	18.8
1939	21.2	1962	30.4	1985	18.0
1940	22.5	1963	30.2	1986	17.5
1941	23.9	1964	30.2	1987	17.0
1942	25.4	1965	30.1	1988	16.8
1943	27.5	1966	29.6	1989	16.4
1944	29.0	1967	29.9	1990	16.1
1945	30.4	1968	29.5	1991	16.1
1946	31.1	1969	29.5	1992	15.8
1947	32.1	1970	29.6	1993	15.8
1948	31.8	1971	29.1	1994	15.5
1949	31.9	1972	28.8	1995	14.9
1950	31.6	1973	28.5	1996	14.5
1951	31.7	1974	28.3	1997	14.1
1952	32.0	1975	28.9		

Sources: 1930–83: Leo Troy and Neil Sheflin, *Union Sourcebook* (West Orange, N.J.: Industrial Relations Data and Information Services, 1985), appendix; 1984–97: National Directory Series, Bureau of Labor Statistics, Department of Labor (website: ftp://146.142.4.23/pub/special.requests/collbarg/unmem.txt).

base reflected not only the dramatic emergence of imposing industrial unions, such as the United Auto Workers (1,260,000 members in 1955), International Ladies' Garment Workers (383,000), and United Steelworkers (980,000), but also the renewed growth of old but revamped craft unions, such as the United Brotherhood of Carpenters (750,000 members), International Association of Machinists (627,000), and United Association of Plumbers (200,000). The 1955 merger of the American Federation of Labor, with its mainly craft union base, and the upstart Congress of Industrial Organizations, composed of the new industrial unions, occurred precisely at the apex of this membership surge, further signaling the consolidation of labor's position in both politics and the economy.

Few would have predicted that organized labor's strong representation in the workforce—and its corresponding centrality in the nation's political economy—was to be only a transitory feature of postwar American society. But by 1997, a decades-long decline in union membership had produced another remarkable statistic: unions now represented only 14.1 percent of the workforce.[6] Indeed, union density was down to the diminished, even pathetic, level that preceded the passage of the National Labor Relations Act (NLRA) in 1935. Even in absolute numbers, the unions were in deep trouble, as membership declined from a peak of 20.2 million members in 1978 to only 16.4 million in 1995.[7] The drop was especially obvious among the energetic and ambitious industrial unions that had been so prominent during the New Deal and early postwar period. The flagship UAW (whose president, Walter Reuther, had once been a household name and the frequent target of conservative political attacks), shrank to 751,000 members by 1995—about half of its postwar peak of 1.4 million. The Steelworkers union, which had once presided over the core of the American economy, suffered similar losses, with only 403,000 members in 1995, down from a peak of 1,069,900 in 1973.[8] Even the skilled craft unions, with traditions dating back to the mid–nineteenth century, experienced major decline: the Carpenters dropped from 750,000 members in 1955 to 378,000 in 1995, and the Machinists, despite having evolved into a semi-industrial union based in the airlines industry, shrank to only 448,000 from a postwar high of nearly one million members. The Machinists' headquarters in Washington still carried a marble engraving boasting that the union was "a million strong" long after it was barely half that size.

Indeed, a few unions seemed on the verge of extinction. The American Federation of Musicians, ravaged by the rise of recorded music and by changing technology, contracted from 250,000 in the 1950s to only 35,000 by the mid-1990s. The International Ladies' Garment Workers Union (ILGWU) was reduced to 123,000 members, about a third of its size forty years earlier, while the other major textiles union, the American Clothing and Textile Workers Union (ACTWU), shrank by half to about 129,000 members. These unions, which had once provided two of the nation's most dynamic union leaders in ILGWU President David Dubinsky and ACTWU President Sidney Hillman, were now so threatened by membership loss that they chose in 1995 to merge, forming the new Union of Needletrades, Industrial, and Textiles Employees (UNITE). But this last-ditch effort seemed unlikely to reverse a process of decline deeply rooted in changing markets and technology. Even the United Mine Workers, which under the extraordinary leadership of John L. Lewis had played a crucial role in establishing the CIO and leading the New Deal revival of labor's fortunes, was by the 1990s a shrunken version of its former self, with only 70,000 members and much-reduced economic and political significance.

In startling contrast, unions representing public employees managed to grow dramatically during the same period, with important consequences for the balance of power within the labor federation. Most significant was the extraordinary expansion of the American Federation of State, County, and Municipal Employees (AFSCME), which ballooned from 99,000 members in 1955 to nearly 1.2 million by 1995. From virtual irrelevance in the 1950s, AFSCME became the second largest union in the AFL-CIO, close behind the

Teamsters (table 1.2). The American Federation of Teachers experienced similarly impressive growth, vaulting from 40,000 to 613,000 members between 1955 and 1995. The National Education Association (NEA), unaffiliated with the AFL-CIO, had also become gigantic, representing nearly two million of the nation's schoolteachers by the 1990s. In the view of many (and not just Republican presidential candidates), the NEA had become the most politically powerful union in the country. The American Federation of Government Employees, mainly representing federal workers, also expanded impressively, from 47,000 in 1955 to 153,000 forty years later. Because of the success of these unions, density in the public sector grew to 37.2 percent by 1997, far more than the negligible 9.8 percent organized in the private sector, and public sector members accounted for about 40 percent of the total number of union members in the United States.[9] It is hardly surprising that public employee unions also started to gain the upper hand within the AFL-CIO, a development reflected in the crucial role of AFSCME President Gerald McEntee in sponsoring John Sweeney, president of the Service Employees International Union (SEIU), in his successful campaign for the federation presidency in 1995.

Partially because of these public sector gains, the total membership of the AFL-CIO itself remained fairly stable, beginning at 12.6 million in 1955, peaking at 14 million in 1975, and falling back to 13 million in 1996 (table 1.3). Another factor was the reaffiliation during the 1980s of such unions as the UAW, Teamsters, and Mine Workers, all of which had left the AFL-CIO in earlier years. At the same time, many unions revealed an impressive capacity to maintain or even increase their organizational budgets, despite absolute declines in membership. Recent research shows that total real

Table 1.2. Membership of the Fifteen Largest Unions Affiliated with the AFL-CIO, 1995

Union	Membership
1. International Brotherhood of Teamsters	1,285,000
2. American Federation of State, County and Municipal Employees	1,183,000
3. Service Employees International Union	1,027,000
4. United Food and Commercial Workers	983,000
5. United Auto Workers	751,000
6. International Brotherhood of Electrical Workers	679,000
7. American Federation of Teachers	613,000
8. Communication Workers of America	478,000
9. International Association of Machinists and Aerospace Workers	448,000
10. United Steelworkers of America	478,000
11. United Brotherhood of Carpenters and Joiners	378,000
12. Laborers' International Union of North America	352,000
13. International Union of Operating Engineers	298,000
14. American Postal Workers Union	261,000
15. Hotel Employees and Restaurant Employees International Union	241,000

Source: AFL-CIO press release, November 1995.

Table 1.3. AFL-CIO Paid Membership, 1955–1995

Year	Members (in thousands)
1955	12,622
1957	13,020
1959	12,779
1961	12,553
1963	12,469
1965	12,919
1967	13,781
1969	13,005
1971	13,177
1973	13,407
1975	14,070
1977	13,542
1979	13,621
1981	13,602
1983	13,758
1985	13,109
1987	13,702
1989	13,556
1991	13,933
1993	13,299
1995	13,007

Source: AFL-CIO, *Executive Council Report, 1995* (Washington, D.C.: AFL-CIO, 1995), 223.

(inflation-adjusted) receipts among all private sector unions grew from $4.8 billion in 1960 to $10.4 billion in 1987—an increase of 115.7 percent at a time when the total membership among private sector unions declined from 14.6 million to 10.86 million.[10] Unions have kept their budgets in good condition by increasing dues and maximizing returns on their assets in the form of interest, dividends, and rental income. One innovation was the AFL-CIO's negotiation in 1996 of a new financial arrangement to offer credit cards to union members. Under the deal worked out with its credit card provider, the federation would receive an estimated $375 million over a five-year period.[11] Unions have also received substantial funds from the federal government, especially in the form of grants from the Department of Labor and the National Endowment for Democracy.[12] Overall, the growth in union income has provided a reasonably stable resource basis, enabling the federation and the national unions to construct effective political programs.

In assessing the changing situation of the unions, we must also place recent developments in a broader historical perspective. Unions have clearly faced far worse situations in American history, even during the twentieth century. Between 1920 and 1933, organized labor experienced not only a decline in density but a virtual hemorrhage in absolute membership. In the face of employer hostility, total union membership, which in 1920 had stood at over 5 million, fell to 3.5 million in 1923; the effect of the Great Depression reduced it to under 3 million in 1933.[13] Moreover, such major unions as the United Mine Workers and the International Ladies' Garment Workers Union almost collapsed as organizations, and several other unions, including the once 115,000-strong Seamen's union, disappeared completely. The labor movement remained powerful in only a few major industries, such as construction, coal, and railroads, while the dynamic new manufacturing sector (including auto and steel) was virtually devoid of collective bargaining. It seemed, as the eminent labor historian Irving Bernstein put it, that "the United States labor movement stood still as the main stream of American society swept by."[14]

Such catastrophic earlier losses warn against exaggerating the magnitude of the present crisis of organized labor. Nevertheless, the situation remains grim, especially for unions in the private sector. Despite their various countervailing efforts, the decline in density has been constant through the recessions and recoveries of the 1980s and 1990s, and over both Democratic and Republican administrations; it shows no signs of a reversal. It is entirely possible that the century will close with unions representing as little as 9 percent of the private sector workforce. Tellingly, evidence from National Labor Relations Board elections shows that unions were organizing far fewer new workers per year in the 1980s and 1990s than they had during the 1970s or earlier decades, although the total size of the workforce was constantly expanding.[15] In 1996, despite popular notions of a labor revival, growth in the AFL-CIO was insignificant—only 12,000 members.[16] Equally ominous, even the ability of unions to effectively engage in collective action deteriorated. In 1997 only 29 major work stoppages were recorded (idling 339,000 workers), the fewest since the Bureau of Labor Statistics began tracking in 1947 and a stark contrast with the high point reached in 1952, when 479 stoppages occurred and 2.7 million workers were involved in strikes or lockouts.[17]

The reasons for the decline in union density remain hotly debated. Indeed, outstanding scholars of industrial relations who have spent years researching this vexing question have reached nearly opposite conclusions.[18] Nevertheless, most specialists would at least agree on the relevant factors.[19] First, the shift from manufacturing to service sector industries has reduced in size the traditional union redoubts, replacing them with new workplaces and new kinds of workers that seem much less receptive to union organizing. Second, some firms have implemented new management techniques, often in response to growing foreign competition, that reduce the demand for union representation by providing better working conditions and more opportunities for employee participation. Third, and also in response to increasing competitive pressures, other firms have become much more aggressive in opposing unions, hiring professional anti-union consultants and sometimes even illegally firing pro-union employees. Fourth, government-mandated benefits, from workplace safety regulations to family and medical leave requirements, have provided what unions once promised, thus reducing the demand for union representation. Fifth, the unions themselves have been lax in seeking new members, preferring to advance the interests of their current membership over costly and risky new organizing drives. Sixth, the traditional hostility to unions in American political culture has reemerged in recent years, probably because the memory of the Great Depression is receding as fears of an adverse union impact on economic growth are growing. Seventh, the decentralized structure of American unionism has made it harder for unions to engage in the coordinated wage policies that many European labor movements have pursued, thus encouraging individual employers to fight ferociously to avoid unionization. And last, but far from least, the legal regime governing the process of union recognition has made it increasingly difficult for unions to organize new members or to protect their current membership from management predations.

This eighth factor deserves further discussion, for it is the most directly political of all the causes mentioned and has in fact had a major impact on the labor movement's legislative agenda in the postwar period. The legal framework governing labor relations is embodied in the National Labor Relations Act (enacted in 1935), the Taft-Hartley Act (1947), and the Landrum-Griffin Act (1959). Both the Taft-Hartley and the Landrum-Griffin Acts, approved by Congress during a period of rising public concern about excessive union power, involved many new restrictions on union activity.[20] Taft-Hartley completely banned the closed shop, in which an employer agrees to hire only union members. Furthermore, section 14(b) of the act allowed the states to enact so-called right-to-work legislation that bars union shops, in which workers must join the union (or at least pay union dues) within a designated time to retain their jobs. The act also restricted wildcat strikes, sit-down strikes, and slowdowns, and it established an employers' right to wage anti-union publicity campaigns aimed at their own workers. The Landrum-Griffin Act (formally known as the Labor-Management Reporting Disclosure Act of 1959), in addition to establishing new procedures to prevent union corruption, restricted secondary boycotts and "hot cargo" agreements, whereby one employer agrees not to handle the products of another company involved in a labor dispute. Together, these laws eliminated some of the more effective tools that unions had once used in pressuring intransigent employers; they also brought the federal government decisively into the collective bargaining relationship.

Defenders of these limitations claimed that the National Labor Relations Act (also known as the Wagner Act, after its chief congressional sponsor in 1935, Senator Robert Wagner of New York) had already put in place a set of adequate protections for union organizing. Although the NLRA was indeed intended to provide a framework that recognized and protected the legal right of workers to organize, most notably by establishing a formal procedure for official union recognition and certification under the auspices of the federal government, most unionists would argue today that it has become an obstacle to union growth. They focus their criticisms mainly on the complex and delay-prone procedures for union certification. In comparison to Canada, for example, the American process seems very slow and cumbersome. Unions in Canada are usually granted official certification immediately after evidence is presented that a majority of employees in a workplace have becoming dues-paying union members. In contrast, to gain recognition in the United States unions must prevail in an official election that is held only after organizers have obtained the signatures of 30 percent of the employees in an enterprise. This process, though superficially straightforward, allows hostile employers many opportunities to delay the election through legal and administrative challenges. Often, elections take place only months or even years after the initial petitions were signed, leaving much time for lengthy anti-union campaign by employers. As companies became more openly opposed to unions in the 1970s, they increasingly took advantage of these methods to delay and subvert existing labor law. At the same time, the NLRB itself grew more conservative, especially after the appointments made by President Ronald Reagan.[21] The result is a legal structure that throws many obstacles in the way of any group of employees seeking to organize or join a union.

In general, labor leaders have singled out the inadequacy of labor law as the most important factor in explaining union decline. Therefore, a major goal of the labor movement since the passage of the Taft-Hartley Act has been the repeal of section 14(b) and, perhaps more important, the passage of new legislation to ease the process of union recognition. Arguably, any future growth of the labor movement, especially in the private sector, will depend on such legislative success. Thus, we are confronted with the central question of this book: How has the decline in union density affected the political power of the unions?

Union Decline and the "Right Turn" in American Politics: The Conventional View

Although the decline in union density is crucial background for understanding the role of labor in national politics, in and of itself this fact tells us little about the actual power and position of unions in the political system. It bears repeating that there is no causal force *requiring* that declining union density should inevitably translate into declining union political power. Indeed, there is good reason to believe the opposite: faced with a deterioration of their position in collective bargaining, unions may actually increase the resources they devote to politics, potentially leading to an expansion rather than reduction in union power. What cannot be won in the economic market can, perhaps, be won in the political market. Because such a development is logically possible, we must keep an open mind in assessing the political consequences of declining union density. Although we may hypothesize about any number of possible causal links between declining membership and particular political outcomes, such hypotheses are little more than idle speculation in the absence of evidence about the actual role of unions in the political arena.

Nonetheless, most scholarly work to date has endorsed a connection between the decline in union density and a decline in the importance of unions in American politics, especially in comparison to their role in the 1960s and earlier.[22] The key dependent variable used is the content of American public policy. It is argued, first, that public policy shifted, especially after the mid-1970s, in a direction that was inimical to the interests of labor unions and their members and, second, that this change indicates a loss of union power. Most often cited is the situation of labor during the Reagan administration, when unions experienced assaults from the executive branch of a magnitude not seen since before the New Deal. In this view, President Reagan's firing of striking federal air traffic controllers in 1981 and the subsequent disbanding of their union was part of a deliberate effort to legitimate a new level of anti-union hostility in the private as well as public sector. Likewise, Reagan's appointments of pro-business conservatives to the National Labor Relations Board and to key posts within the Department of Labor, which had traditionally maintained close ties to the labor movement, were all part of a scheme to undermine unions. In another attack on labor, prevailing wage statutes, which guarantee relatively high wage levels for employees performing government contract work, were rendered less effective by administrative interpretations put forth by the Department of Labor. Funding for unemployment insurance, which strengthened the position of all workers vis-à-vis employers and was thus strongly supported by the labor movement, was cut back. Worker safety and health standards were lowered, and even those lower standards were only weakly enforced. Together, these changes constituted a deterioration in the protective ramparts that labor had constructed with the help of the federal government in previous decades.

Macroeconomic policy also became more unfavorable to the interests of unions, as the Reagan administration endorsed a tight monetary policy intended to wring inflation out of the economy the old-fashioned way: through a major constriction in demand and a corresponding downturn in production. Moreover, the administration's commitment to free trade, its support for a strong dollar in international currency markets, and its refusal to restrict hostile takeovers and leveraged buyouts all encouraged the restructuring of the economy away from unionized industries. The persistence of unemployment in the unionized sectors reduced the economic bargaining power of labor unions, easing the way for a decline in real wages. Thus, not

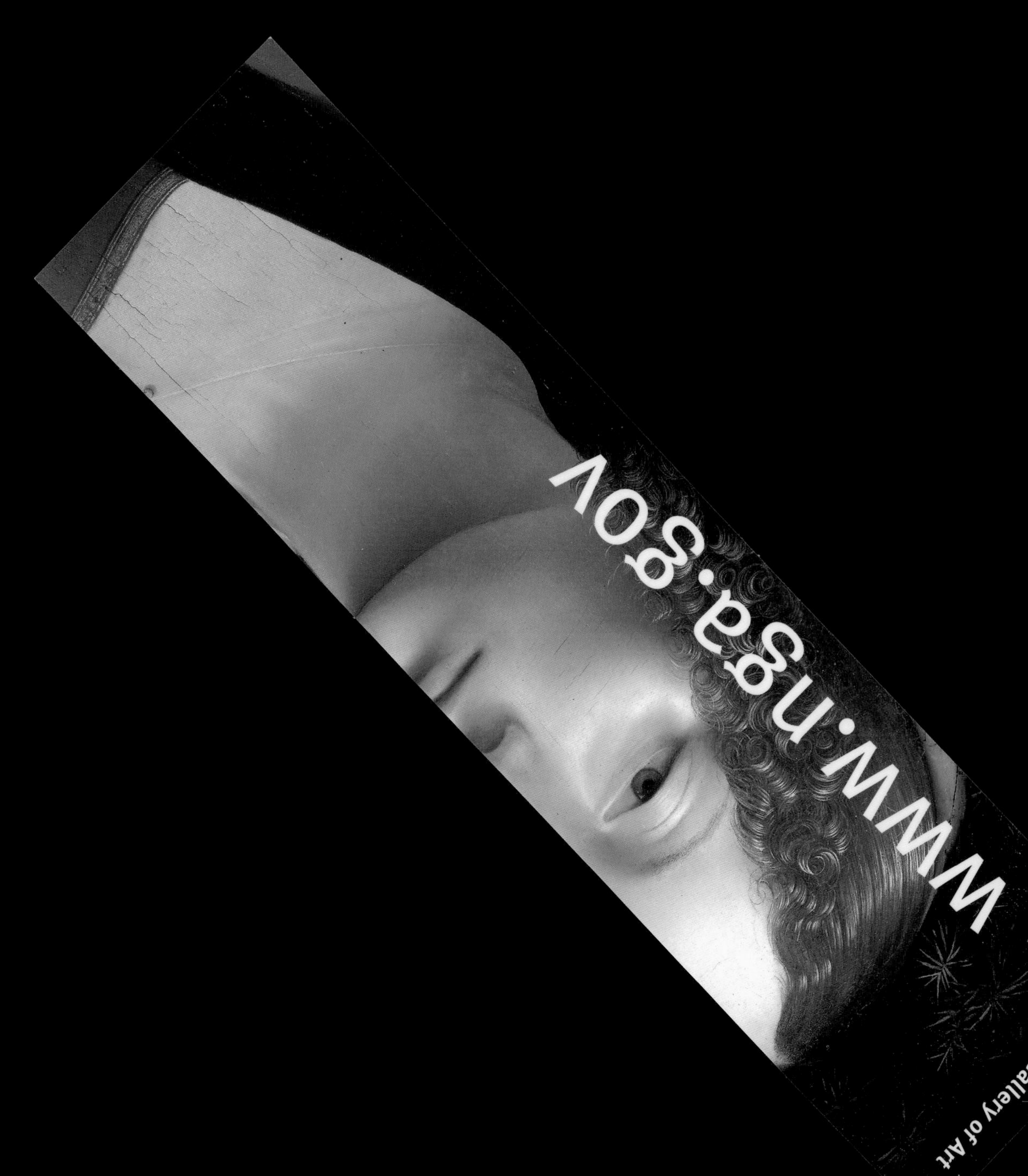
www.nga.gov
Gallery of Art

Information about the National Gallery of Art's comprehensive collection of more than 108,000 works may be found on the Gallery's Web site at **www.nga.gov**.

Leonardo da Vinci, *Ginevra de' Benci*, obverse, c. 1474, oil on panel, National Gallery of Art, Ailsa Mellon Bruce Fund

only did membership decline but so did the quality of the contracts negotiated in unionized industries.

The adverse effects of Republican economic policy were compounded by a set of budgetary and tax changes with regressive consequences, which were strongly opposed by the labor movement. The tax-cutting measures of the early 1980s redistributed income away from most union members and other employees, thereby exacerbating structural trends that were already generating an increasingly skewed distribution of income. Simultaneously, the budgets of the early 1980s reduced funding for several major social programs created in previous decades with the help of organized labor. These cuts in public service jobs programs, welfare, Medicaid, the food stamp program, and public housing expenditures now are cited as indicators of a declining union ability to protect the programs of the welfare state.

More generally, the tenor of political debate in the 1980s shifted to the right, in a manner detrimental to the goals enunciated by organized labor. Public discussion often centered on how to best cut taxes and spending, or how to most effectively reduce the regulatory burdens on business—themes that directed attention away from the redistributive proposals endorsed by the unions. The skepticism among political elites as well as much of the general public about the viability of Keynesian economics and the feasibility of a large welfare state constituted yet another barrier. These obstacles were reinforced by the intractability of large federal budget deficits that made any expansion of state expenditure seem impossible or, at best, foolhardy. The Reagan administration appears in this way to have come up with the perfect strategy: the creation of massive deficits that prevented expansion of the welfare state for many decades to come.

As the Republicans attacked, the Democratic Party also shifted in a more conservative direction. It is alleged that this first became clear during the presidency of Jimmy Carter, when the Democratic administration chose to pursue regressive tax cuts and budget reductions as part of an effort to fight inflation. The Carter administration and Democrats in Congress thereby initiated many of the public policy trends that are now usually associated with the Reagan years. Deregulation of airlines and trucking, which undermined union power in both sectors, as well as the relaxation of environmental and workplace safety standards all began in the late 1970s. The failure of the Carter administration to achieve passage of a major labor law reform proposal or a national health care initiative is also viewed as marking the decline of union power even when Democrats controlled both the executive and legislative branches. Labor unions especially needed the protection of the state during this period, because of the decline in union density, but the Democrats failed to pass any legislation that would help unions survive as organizations. Many critics see this as proof that labor's alliance with Democratic politicians was fundamentally misguided and unproductive.

It is also claimed that the Carter years were a major departure from the days of the Great Society, when President Lyndon Johnson was able to work effectively with Democratic majorities in Congress to expand the welfare state and protect the interests of workers. According to this analysis, because organized labor was able to set and enforce the agenda of Congress at this time, it was the most instrumental force in lobbying for the expansion of social programs. Unions had unique lobbying and electoral resources that members of Congress found useful as they sought to be reelected and see their policy goals translated into legislation. In a Washington community with far fewer interest groups than today, organized labor was one of the few groups that could consistently help Democratic politicians. The Johnson administration itself was highly receptive to the concerns of labor leaders, developing economic policy that took their interests into account. In fact, labor and the Democrats became so deeply integrated that some observers began to argue for the "partial equivalence" of this alliance to the ties between social democratic parties and unions in Western Europe.[23] All of this vanished like dust in the wind by the end of the Carter administration (or so it is claimed).

The Clinton administration is usually viewed as being even worse for labor than the Carter administration—the miserable end product of a long decline in the quality of the labor/Democrat relationship. In supporting new free trade agreements, the administration contributed directly to the decline of American unions and a diminished quality of life for their members. Beholden to Wall Street investment bankers and bond traders, President Clinton was more interested in reducing the federal budget deficit than in spending more on new infrastructural investments or other social services. He also endorsed the restrictive monetary policy pursued by the Federal Reserve Board and its chair, Alan Greenspan, whose tacit support was crucial for the advancement of Clinton's initial budget and tax proposals.[24] The failure of the striker replacement bill and the fact that no other labor law reform proposals made any headway are also seen as revelatory: the administration could not care less about the unions. President Clinton did not see his future or the future of the Democratic Party as dependent on maintaining this key constituency, and he was therefore unwilling to expend major political capital on projects for its protection or rejuvenation. In contrast, Clinton *was* willing to risk such expenditures in support of the causes of homosexuals and women.[25] On the whole, it is argued that the unions were not inside players during the Clinton years, and their status in the legislative and policymaking process was not comparable to that achieved during the 1960s.

In general, then, everyone seems to agree that virtually all the outcomes of any real importance in American politics since the time of the Great Society reveal a profound weakening, even collapse, of union political power, especially inside the Democratic Party. The *causes* are found in a multitude of debilitating developments. Most crucially, it is asserted, a major offensive by employers against unions and their liberal allies began in the late 1970s. Buffeted by increased foreign competition and by domestic environmental and safety regulations, employers were worried about declining profits and increasing government interference. Fearing the potential consequences of Democratic governance in the wake of Republican defeats in 1976, employers began to increase their political action committee (PAC) expenditures in campaign finance, as well as to beef up their Washington lobbying efforts. Any willingness to compromise with unions, environmentalists, and consumer groups was suppressed or at least downplayed. Groups like the Chamber of Commerce and the National Association of Manufacturers were revitalized, and business devoted new efforts to influencing public opinion—both through grants to Washington think tanks and through direct public relations efforts.

The offensive by the business community was, it is alleged, helped along by various changes within the Democratic Party in Congress. As more Democrats arrived from suburban congressional districts, hastened by the discrediting of the Republican Party after Watergate, they brought a new way of thinking into the party. The freshmen members, dubbed the "Class of '74," were younger than their predecessors and more skeptical of the economic and social policies of the New Deal and Great Society—and of the unions that had traditionally been these policies' main supporters. This change in the composition of the Democratic Party in Congress also reinforced reforms that had been underway since the late 1960s. These congressional reforms had several effects. Power was redistributed away from committee chairs and toward subcommittee chairs and individual members. More generally, power in the House and Senate came to be increasingly fragmented and diffused as traditional norms of deference and seniority were overwhelmed by new opportunities for individualized political entrepreneurship and media access. As a result, policy outcomes were less predictable, and party discipline deteriorated as members became fixated on the best means of ensuring their own reelection. Members could now vote as they pleased to a greater degree than ever before, even if their votes were contrary to the demands of key party constituencies.

Furthermore, legal reforms in the mid-1970s addressing federal campaign finance had the unintended effect of facilitating the efforts of the business community to establish political action committees. The Federal Election Campaign Act of 1974 and the 1975 Sun Oil decision by the Federal Election Commission made it possible for corporations to establish their own PACs, to which both management and employees could voluntarily donate. The ensuing vast increase in the number of corporate PACs in the 1970s and 1980s, and their outdistancing of union PACs in total campaign contributions, is said to have contributed to a decline of union influence in Congress. More broadly, the shift toward a more capital-intensive regime of electoral politics—driven by greater use of professional polling and public relations, campaign consultants, the broadcast media, direct mail, and phone banks—

is held to have reduced the competitive advantage of unions, which was seen to lie more in their organizational resources and human capital than in their financial capacities. The net effect of all these changes is to have made Congress a much more hostile place for unions than it was in the 1960s.

At the same time, an ambitious set of reforms in the Democratic Party's presidential nominating process also rendered labor unions less potent. After the intense conflict in 1968 over the Vietnam War and the selection of the Democratic Party's presidential nominee, the national party approved major changes in the procedures for selecting delegates to the national convention. Although these reforms took on a different procedural character in each state, their overall effect was to encourage a preexisting trend toward using primaries and caucuses to select delegates. Delegates to the national convention would now be allotted to various candidates on the basis of the candidate's percentage of the vote in a primary election or caucus open to all Democratic voters. By contrast, in the old system party leaders at the state and local level would choose party "regulars" as delegates, often bypassing primaries and caucuses altogether. In the old days the state delegation would be under the control of its leadership, which could then swing it behind a candidate at the convention after deals were made with other party leaders behind closed doors. The views of the unions would, it is claimed, be taken into account by the party leaders, who would be unlikely to select a candidate that would be offensive to so loyal and important a constituency.

A large academic literature now argues that party reform, and the resulting shift from elite bargaining to mass participation as a means for delegate selection, was very bad for labor unions.[26] Primaries, more than general elections, tend to be dominated by higher-income and better-educated voters. Furthermore, primaries aid single-issue interest groups and social movements that are capable of mobilizing a passionate faction behind a particular candidate. Critics allege that as a result, "white-collar" voters and factional interest groups have gained power over the nomination of Democratic presidential candidates, to the detriment of labor unions and working-class voters. The old system accorded unions de facto veto power; now, unions find it hard to push their favored candidate or stop those whom they dislike. The result, they argue, has been a weakening of union power, manifested most clearly in the nominations of Jimmy Carter and Bill Clinton, men who allegedly lacked much support from or experience with the labor movement prior to their selection as the nominee.

The weakening of labor's position within the nominating process is often related to a broader pattern of conflict between labor unions and the newer interest groups and social movements that emerged in the Democratic Party after the 1960s. It is argued that labor unions found it difficult to tolerate the rise of such competitors as environmentalists, consumer advocates, women, homosexuals, racial and ethnic minorities, and so on. Union leaders were supposedly alarmed by these groups that undercut their previously hegemonic position within the Democratic Party and posed a threat to their cultural and personal identity. These insurgent groups, in turn, saw the unions as led by crotchety old working-class white men who were extreme cold warriors and closet racists, sexists, and homophobes. The eruption of this conflict, and its apparent continuation during the incessant "cultural wars" of our times, is said to have contributed to the further marginalization of unions within the Democratic Party. The situation only worsened, many claimed, when the unions abandoned previous commitments to broad social reform in order to concentrate on simple organizational survival. This turn was manifested in support for trade protectionism and an increased commitment to fostering environmentally unsound industries. Thus, labor has become increasingly narrow and particularistic and has allowed the liberal alternative to be defined by groups to which labor has no ties, and to which it is often in opposition.

Of course, the fact underlying all these changes in the institutional and political environment has been the ongoing decline in union density. The shrinkage of the relative size of labor as a voting bloc, as well as the alleged decrease in union member voting cohesion, has supposedly reduced the weight of unions in the American electorate. Furthermore, the declining membership of unions has been seen as reducing their organizational capacity, lessening their ability to provide in-kind services to reelection-seeking politicians. Unions have also lost much of their popularity among the public at large, and union support today often constitutes an electoral liability for a candidate, not an asset (unlike some time in the past when things were supposedly different). Thus, at the same time that the political environment has grown much worse for unions, the resources that unions possess for political bargaining with politicians have diminished. Unions have less to offer politicians, and politicians find it increasingly convenient to go elsewhere for financial and organizational support. Hence, labor unions have lost and will continue to lose political power as union density declines, and the alliance with the Democratic Party will become more and more of a "barren marriage."[27]

Toward a Critique: The Trouble with "Decline"

Although focusing on the various new problems that have confronted organized labor has been quite valuable, the above-described literature has also either ignored or distorted much under its purview. The proponents of a comprehensive decline in union political power have yet to show convincingly that all of the cited changes in the political and economic environment have actually ruined labor's political strategy. Nor do they show that these developments have in fact effected a qualitative transformation in labor's role. There are numerous reasons for this failure. First, a decline in union power, which at first seems so straightforward, is quite difficult to accurately measure. There are numerous unions in the United States, and they work on a broad range of political issues. One union may enjoy political success, even as others experience devastating setbacks. And even when a union achieves some of its goals, other objectives may remain far out of reach. Therefore, any evaluation of union political power will reflect the particular issues and episodes chosen for examination. A single case, such as the failure of Congress to pass labor law reform in 1978, can easily be employed to definitively indicate union weakness. Conversely, the success of organized labor in a different struggle, such as plant-closing legislation in 1988 (or fast-track trade legislation in 1997), can just as easily be used to show the continuing vitality of union power. Without some criteria to discern the relative importance of the vast diversity of issues on which unions take positions, such choices become purely arbitrary. Developing such criteria is, however, a problem in itself, for unions differ greatly among themselves over what is most important. Consider, for example, the labor defeat on NAFTA: Does that episode provide an appropriate measure of the power of the public employee unions, which had no direct material interests at stake in the battle?

Second, quick and easy generalizations about the decline of union political power fail to take into account the fragmented nature of the American political system and the decentralized nature of our political parties. Because of the divided constitutional structure in the United States, it is quite possible for unions to gain power within one institutional location, even as they suffer dramatic losses in another. If the presidency falls into the hands of unfriendly Republicans, for example, unions may intensify their efforts to protect themselves in Congress, and vice versa. Similarly, if the federal judiciary becomes more hostile, unions may seek new legislation to restore their rights or limit the powers of the courts. In fact, unions did precisely these things during the 1980s, as their opponents sought to consolidate control over the executive branch and the federal judiciary. Thus conclusions based on a single issue, or on outcomes within a single institution in a divided and fragmented state, risk ignoring important countervailing trends. Similarly, the Democratic Party has been viewed in profoundly erroneous terms as a monolithic and unitary actor that makes decisions *as a party*, rather than as what it really is: an undisciplined hodgepodge of individual politicians loosely united under a single label. To avoid such errors we need to look at *actual* bargaining relationships between the individuals involved instead of theorizing about such imaginary monoliths as the "party," the "labor movement," or the "state."

A third problem is that the idea of decline has served in most writings as the exclusive conceptual lens for understanding how the role of unions in American politics in recent decades has changed. By fixating on a single (albeit crucial) variable—labor's influence over political outcomes—analysts have ignored changes in other aspects of labor's role in American politics. Thus, new developments in the political agenda of organized labor and in union political strategies have been overlooked in favor of broad generalizations about declining power; the qualitative changes in the kinds of relationships that unions forge with other actors in the political system have been ignored. Yet, as a large body of literature by political scientists has documented, the workings of the American political system have undergone significant alteration—both procedural and substantive—since the 1960s.

Fourth, unions are usually seen as almost completely passive victims of a changing and increasingly hostile environment. Seldom is any attention paid to how unions have sought to *adapt* to external forces by developing new political goals and strategies, and by creating new resources to deploy in the political marketplace. Although students of formal organizations commonly assume that organizations seek to survive by altering their behavior in response to their environment, recent analyses of the role of unions in American politics largely discount this possibility.[28]

Fifth, most analysts fail to clearly identify the time periods employed in their comparisons. This tendency makes the task of measuring decline all the more difficult, because evaluations always depend on the nature of the benchmark chosen and the relative accuracy with which it is described. If the benchmark is based not on a detailed understanding of a specific period in the past but rather on a set of loose impressions, then judgments about more recent developments cannot be trusted. Thus, the failure of labor law reform in 1978 seems less momentous when it is recognized that similar efforts at reform failed in an analogous fashion during the mid-1960s and late 1940s. So too the defections of congressional Democrats on liberal legislation during the 1970s and 1980s seem remarkable or new only when the obstructive power of the "conservative coalition" over much of the twentieth century is completely forgotten. Sentimental and unsubstantiated images of a day when unions "ruled Capitol Hill" certainly do not constitute an adequate baseline to ground interpretation of later events.

Finally, the standard accounts often implicitly assume that union political power is derived from one or two sources, such as the size of the total membership, the level of union density, or both. The question of power is, however, much more complicated, as mainstream pluralist theory insisted many decades ago.[29] The political power of an interest group is obviously not determined directly by the size of its membership. If political strength corresponded automatically to size, neither the American Jewish community nor the farm lobby (to cite just two examples) would have much influence in contemporary America. The same applies to labor.

Measuring Union Power

In light of these weaknesses, can we devise better ways of measuring union political power? A proper analysis should try to do the following: (1) Specify a historical benchmark clearly, and note the parameters of union power at that time. This task requires a consideration of union influence in different institutions in the American political system, outcomes on a wide range of issues on labor's political agenda, and differences in the rate of success experienced by different unions. (2) Measure the various resources available to unions for use in political bargaining as precisely as possible. Thus, quantitative measures of union member voting behavior, campaign expenditures, lobbying expenses, and the like should be used, as well as qualitative descriptions of union strategies, techniques of electoral mobilization and lobbying, and so on. (3) Examine the degree of interaction and coordination between individual politicians and union leaders, as measured in the number and the character of meetings and other contacts and their subsequent impact on behavior. (4) Trace the outcomes of similar policy battles over different times in order to determine the extent to which union political preferences are actually realized in different periods.

Using these guidelines, we should be able to better identify decline if and when it occurs. Unions would be in political decline if they were losing legislative battles that they once had won, if their political and economic resources were diminishing, if the level of access and coordination between union leaders and Democratic Party politicians was deteriorating, and if the demand among elected officeholders for union resources was decreasing.

There is one more measurement issue that should be addressed. It might be argued that it would be a sign of declining union political power if the demand by unions for legislation and other public policy benefits was *rising*, but the supply or output (in the form of desired public policy) remained *stable*. In other words, if unions needed government help more than before, but could only manage to maintain previous levels of access and influence, they would be deteriorating. This view suggests that a failure to obtain labor law reform in 1994 is much more serious than a corresponding failure in 1965, revealing decline even though labor had not prevailed on the issue previously.

The point is well-taken, but this kind of measure must be handled carefully. If we say that unions (or other interest groups) are in political decline because they cannot compel the government to step in to rescue them from their own economic problems, even if they could not compel the government to do so previously, then we are raising the bar for declaring a group powerful very high indeed. By this measure, one might claim that unions have been losing political power ever since 1935, when the last major piece of federal legislation expanding protections to unions as organizations was enacted. Thus, it might be better to simply identify the limits on union power, and then determine whether the *costs* of those limits have grown or decreased over time. In fact, I will argue in later chapters that while there are few new limits on labor's power, the old ones were bad enough and have prevented unions from gaining the government help needed to mitigate their economic decline.

With this approach in mind, then, we can start anew. But are these rough guidelines enough? Although they tell us how to better measure union political power, they give us few hints about the possible causes of the ups and downs in union influence. It is to this question that we turn in the next chapter.

2 *Labor Unions and Political Bargaining*

There are many conflicting assertions about what unions do in national politics, but all ultimately come down to a series of claims about the nature of the bargaining relationships that union leaders establish with elected officeholders. Are the union leaders weak or strong in these relationships? Are their demands parochial and narrow, or broad and universal? Do Democratic Party officeholders feel especially dependent on unions for support? Or are union leaders exploited by the Democrats? And perhaps the most interesting question of all: Why does bargaining between unions and Democrats sometimes produce splendid cooperation, while at other times only bitter conflict?

This chapter provides a framework for generating better answers to these questions. I begin with a straightforward observation: the process of political bargaining between union leaders and politicians involves an exchange of resources that each side finds valuable. The state can provide union leaders with governmental resources and policies that can enhance their position within the union organization and benefit their membership in various ways. Politicians, in turn, can gain from unionists the support needed to be elected and reelected, as well as the help needed to achieve their policymaking goals. For bargaining to work, each side must compromise and accept a limitation of its autonomy in return for the greater gains derived from the attainment of otherwise unobtainable benefits. All of this behavior is goal-oriented. Therefore, if we are to understand how these bargaining relationships play out, the first step is to identify the goals and priorities of both union leaders and politicians. After identifying the interests of each side, we will be in a better position to understand why unions are in politics, what resources union leaders and politicians bring to the table for political bargaining, and the conditions under which stable cooperation is likely to develop.

What Do Union Leaders Want?

The key figure in the analysis that follows is the union leader, especially the national president based at the union's headquarters and typically serving many years, perhaps decades, in office. Although the duties of union presidents vary considerably from union to union, the leaders are usually responsible for negotiating collective bargaining agreements, formulating the union's political agenda and strategy, supervising the administrative affairs of the union, appointing staff, and interpreting the union constitution. Because this position is well paid (in some cases, very well paid indeed), and carries with it considerable prestige and power, I assume that union presidents will want to be reelected and will therefore seek to deliver a package of benefits to internal constituencies with the power to affect their tenure.[1] Although the pursuit of job security cannot account for everything that union leaders and their agents (such as lobbyists and PAC directors) do in national politics, this goal is a confining condition that operates most of the time to structure leadership behavior. After all, the pursuit of any ancillary aim, such as a program of broad social reform, will require that union leaders stay in office; those who ignore this imperative are unlikely to remain on the national scene for very long.

Union leaders secure their organizational position through a variety of mechanisms, depending on the level of the labor movement and the kind of leadership selection process in place. In the case of a national union president, the typical means for selection is a vote by delegates at a national convention, usually held at two- or four-year intervals and composed of representatives elected by the membership of each union local. Although most unions have adopted this system of indirect election, a few allow for the election of the national president by a vote of the rank-and-file membership, typically held at four- or five-year intervals. The latter system is currently used in the Mine Workers, in the Steelworkers, and, because of the intervention of the U.S. Department of Justice, in the Teamsters union since 1991. But regardless of which system is in place, union presidents operate in a profoundly political context, and must pursue a methodical strategy to ensure their own reelection. Although the overthrow of a union president is a relatively rare event, it happens often enough to keep most union leaders looking over their shoulder at the preferences of both the rank-and-file membership and the local and regional leaders who serve as delegates to the national convention.[2]

To forestall challenges to their leadership, therefore, union presidents seek to deliver benefits to politically relevant internal constituencies. A tangible benefit of great and enduring popularity is a job working for the union—in other words, old-fashioned patronage. As industrial relations scholar Richard Lester once noted, "In many respects, a union resembles a political party."[3] It is thus not surprising that many union leaders have borrowed power-retaining techniques originally developed by political parties. Most notably, they frequently build political machines that operate on the basis of particularized benefits (i.e., patronage) distributed to key groups of supporters. Since union presidents sometimes control hundreds of internal appointed positions, the material basis for the construction of such a machine is readily available. In addition, within most unions the incumbent leadership's power is reinforced by its domination of key sources of information, internal communication structures, procedures for running the conventions and elections, and intra-union judicial procedures. The opposition, meanwhile, typically lacks the financial resources to wage an insurgent campaign, even if the membership should be ready to support one. Still, the construction of a political machine is no guarantee that a discontented membership, perhaps led by a dissident faction within the national leadership, cannot eventually remove an existing president. The stories of union presidents who grew too smugly satisfied, and then suddenly found themselves out of a job, are simply too common to believe otherwise.[4]

Consequently, to guarantee security the union leadership needs to deliver a broader range of benefits than just job patronage. In this respect, the most important single source of benefits remains the collective bargaining process itself. The initial purpose of any union, of course, is to extract resources (in the form of better pay, working conditions, pensions, etc.) from employers. For a long period in the history of the American labor movement, this was considered the only practicable, and sometimes even the only desirable, means for providing benefits to the membership. It was believed that the main alternative—pro-union public policy by federal, state, or local governments—was unattainable in the United States except at great cost, and was therefore not worth pursuing in a serious or systematic fashion. This doctrine of "voluntarism" has, however, long since been superseded by a substantial union commitment to extracting desirable policies from the state. Indeed, by the 1990s it seemed that in some ways it was easier to obtain benefits by procuring new legislation from Congress than by achieving a breakthrough in collective bargaining with employers. Union leaders now naturally turn to politics as a rich source of benefits that can help secure their organizational status.[5]

The diversity and scope of the benefits that unions can obtain from political action, which are quite impressive, are rarely fully recognized by outside observers. Most important is the protection for union organizing and collective bargaining that is available through federal and state-level labor law. Once unions become dependent on the law for their very survival, they must make constant efforts to preserve the legal framework against those interests seeking a rollback of existing protections. But this motivation hardly exhausts the range of interests on the agenda of labor leaders. In the post–New Deal era of big government, union leaders can also claim credit for a large array of material benefits.[6] Fiscal and monetary decisions, for example, determine the overall rate of economic growth and level of employment, and to the extent that union leaders influence these variables they can claim to have won both a more favorable collective bargaining environment and the generous contracts that follow. Regulation of foreign trade provides the benefit of well-paid jobs protected from international competition. Prevailing wage laws (such as the Davis-Bacon Act) ensure that union members working for government receive the same salaries as the best of their private sector colleagues. New public works or defense projects deliver yet more well-paid jobs. Federal grants to unions, in areas as diverse as foreign policy and job training, help generate new employment opportunities within the union itself, which easily become sources of patronage for union leaders. In addition to these material assets, politics also provides symbolic and ideological benefits, as seen in union support for civil rights or foreign policy initiatives. And access to policymakers reinforces the prestige and status of union officials, as it also encourages secondary leaders to channel their political demands through the incumbent national leadership. In all these ways, the state provides a deep well of material and symbolic benefits that national union leaders can tap in order to enhance their organizational status.

A similar logic operates at the level of the labor federation. Just as in the national unions, the AFL-CIO leadership is elected indirectly, by a convention held every two years and composed of delegates from each of the affiliated unions, represented in numbers proportional to each union's total membership. The top offices are the president, a secretary-treasurer, an executive vice president (since 1995), and an executive council composed of the most important and prestigious figures within the national labor leadership. Because the formal powers of the office of AFL-CIO president are quite limited, and reelection is required every two years (or, after changes approved in 1997, every four years), the president must actively work at maintaining internal support. To be sure, in the first forty years of its existence the federation had only two presidents—but not because there were no internal challenges to the national leadership. In fact, George Meany, AFL-CIO president from 1955 to 1979, spent much of his first ten years in office consolidating his own power and cutting off possible threats to his leadership on the part of his archrival, Walter Reuther of the Auto Workers. More recently, the overthrow of Lane Kirkland and his designated successor, Thomas Donahue, both in the space of one year, demonstrated to any doubters that there could indeed be a very competitive election for federation president.

One very effective means for the AFL-CIO president to increase job security and internal power is to expand the role of the federation as the main political voice of the labor movement. Since the national unions monopolize the process of collective bargaining, a central function of the federation has always been national-level political activity. As a result, the federation is capable of intervening in electoral and legislative processes, mainly through the

Department of Legislation, which handles lobbying, and the Committee on Political Education (COPE), which serves as a political action committee and a source of technical advice and assistance, both to candidates for elective office and to national unions. By effectively controlling these political operations, the federation president can make himself indispensable to other union leaders, thereby reducing the likelihood of a challenge to his leadership. George Meany, for example, dominated the channels of access between the labor movement and the national political system, especially whenever a Democratic president was in office. Other union leaders were forced to recognize that Meany was essential to obtaining many of the public policy outcomes they desired. In contrast (and as the fate of Lane Kirkland suggests), a federation president who becomes politically irrelevant in Washington will soon find his political position in the labor movement correspondingly diminished.

Thus the federation's top leader has numerous reasons to construct close ties with national politicians. Few labor leaders at the national level can hope to stay in power long without serious attention to public policy. How, then, can unions influence the elected officeholders who hold the keys to the various treasures that the state can provide?

Power Resources and Bargaining Capacity

The possible sources of interest group power have been long debated by social scientists, but most would agree that interest groups will have power if they can affect the likelihood that the electoral ambitions or policy goals of officeholders will be realized;[7] if a politician becomes completely dependent on a particular group, it will have a great deal of power indeed. If, in contrast, a politician can achieve his or her electoral and policy goals regardless of the actions or preferences of a group, then it is unlikely that the group will be able to consistently exercise much influence. Thus, in the language of Washington politics, unions will have "clout" when elected officeholders either fear the consequences of ignoring or opposing union demands, crave the resources and assistance that cooperation with unions may bring forth, or both. The more resources that unions have, and the more effectively they utilize them, the more likely they are to make politicians grateful, afraid, or some combination of the two.

In general, there are two principal types of resources that unions mobilize for exchange with elected officeholders; they can be categorized as *economic* or as *political* depending on whether they issue from labor's role in the workplace or from its role in electoral and legislative processes. *Economic resources*, as I conceive them, are based on the capacity of unions to alter economic outcomes and affect daily life through the effects of collective bargaining, strikes, slowdowns, and other disruptions of economic production.

These effects constitute bargaining chips insofar as politicians seek, for their own purposes, to either avoid or obtain them.[8] For example, if a president concerned about inflation desires union cooperation in restraining wage increases, union leaders may demand privileged access to the executive branch in return for their cooperation. Or if a president wants an early resolution of a strike that threatens to cripple the national economy, union leaders might ask for pro-union changes in public policy in return.[9] As these examples suggest, such power is distinct from electoral and lobbying activities—a sufficiently large or well-situated union may have considerable power even if it avoids electioneering and lobbying altogether. Thus, this resource can be viewed as having a "structural" component to the extent that it involves taking advantage of the unique capacity of labor unions to arrange the collective withholding of labor in a capitalist society with free labor markets.[10]

Political resources, in contrast, are based on the ability of labor unions to alter government policy through direct involvement in the electoral and legislative processes of the political system. The political resources utilized by labor unions typically include direct campaign contributions, independent spending, mobilization of members and nonmembers to register and vote, campaign rallies, grassroots and elite lobbying, and so on. Unions have also provided information to members of Congress about the content and implementation of public policy, the views of other members of Congress (especially regarding legislation), conditions in their home districts, and activities by other interest groups. In this manner, unions can help politicians get elected, stay in office, and achieve their policy goals by working on their campaigns, providing them with information, and helping them to pursue their legislative agenda.[11] When unions offer such help at lower costs or with greater effectiveness than their rivals (mainly other interest groups), their potential power increases. Unions, like other interest groups, also benefit if members of Congress know that the issues of concern to unions are likely to be salient in the future and the unions will be able to provide help in many forthcoming elections.[12] Thus, the availability of unions as allies over the long run, and on a wide range of issues, can itself constitute a source of power: it helps build relationships of trust, loyalty, and commitment that go much deeper than a simple calculation of how much money and energy was spent in the last election or lobbying campaign.

Together, these economic and political resources produce a versatile menu of possible instruments for advancing union interests (table 2.1). Naturally, the kinds of tools used by unions can change over time as conditions within and outside the unions evolve. When economic resources are weakened, perhaps due to declining union membership or adverse trends in collective bargaining, unions may try to enhance their political resources by contributing more money to campaigns, improving their lobbying apparatuses, and mobilizing members more effectively for political action. Conversely, a shrinking of political resources or fall in their effectiveness may encourage unions

Table 2.1. Sources of Union Bargaining Power in National Politics

Economic Resources
Effects of union activity on the rate of inflation
Effects of union activity on the rate of economic growth
Effects of strikes on government procurement (including defense production)
Effects of public employee unions on governmental operations, budgets, etc.
Effects of union activity on the preference of business and other elites
Effects of strikes, demonstrations, and protests on attitudes of general public
Political Resources—In the Electoral Process
Financial contributions to campaigns
In-kind assistance to campaigns
Electoral mobilization of union members
Mobilization of affiliated and allied constituencies
Public relations campaigns on behalf of the party's or candidate's issues
Assistance in developing of campaign strategy and tactics
Electoral mobilization of elite support among party influentials
Provision of information on constituency preferences
Political Resources—In the Legislative Process
Assistance in lobbying to secure passage of legislation
Facilitation of communication within legislative institutions
Provision of political intelligence on views of legislators
Mobilization of other interest groups and political actors
Provision of substantive information on policy issues and outcomes
Availability as an ally on a wide range of issues
Availability as an ally over a long period of time
Willingness to engage in logrolling and to make long-term deals

to use economic resources to intimidate intransigent state actors. Such resources can be usefully brought to bear even on politicians who are not dependent on labor for political support but who need union help to achieve certain policy ends, such as a lower rate of inflation. Presidents Nixon and Ford, for example, both sought union cooperation in wage restraint and granted labor leaders various concessions in return, including privileged access to the White House.[13]

However, the resources potentially available to union leaders will prove of little consequence if leaders cannot wield them. Even a very large and active labor movement, with the potential to wreak havoc in the economy and affect the outcomes of elections, will generate only limited bargaining power for its leaders if these leaders lack control over the actions of the membership and other elites in the organization. Similarly, the manifold resources available to politicians—such as influence over various laws, regulations, executive orders, and so forth—will not enhance their bargaining power unless they can credibly claim to control or at least significantly influence policy outcomes. In this sense, we can make a distinction between the resources to which union leaders and politicians may theoretically have access and their ability to actually provide those resources to those with whom they enter into bargaining relationships. It is this ability to deliver on one's promises or threats that I call *bargaining capacity*.

The concept of bargaining capacity allows us to develop a model of two ideal-typical "bargaining regimes" that may emerge in national politics: "centralized pluralism" and "fragmented pluralism." [14] In the first, bargaining capacity is centralized among a small number of elite actors who can reliably deliver on their promises, and who expect to be dealing with each other on a regular basis for a long time to come.[15] This system facilitates cooperation because trust is enhanced if there is a mutual expectation that promises made can actually be kept. Accordingly, we can expect that if bargaining capacity is concentrated, and if the national politicians invested with this capacity are Democrats, then a high and stable level of cooperation is likely to emerge between the labor leadership and top elected officeholders.[16] The two sides will coordinate their actions on behalf of common goals that have been agreed on through a process of mutual adjustment. I call this kind of bargaining regime "centralized pluralism" because it is, by American standards, relatively centralized, but it nevertheless remains typically "pluralist" in acknowledging and accepting autonomous power centers within both the labor movement and the state structure.[17]

The microfoundations of cooperation in these circumstances have been plausibly identified by rational choice theorists. In summarizing a large academic literature, Douglass C. North writes: "We usually observe cooperative behavior when individuals repeatedly interact, when they have a great deal of information about each other, and when small numbers characterize the group." [18] A bargaining regime of centralized pluralism enjoys all three of these prerequisites. When top union leaders and politicians are invested with a high degree of bargaining capacity, they can meet privately, in small numbers, with a credible expectation that they will continue to do so on many future occasions. In this environment, each side gains more information about the other, facilitating a higher level of trust. The result is more cooperation.

To see how centralized pluralism might work in practice, imagine the following scenario. Say that power in Washington is concentrated in the hands of a Democratic president, while the labor movement is united under strong and effective leadership, with the federation president speaking convincingly for labor as a whole. In this context, the two sides will be in a good position to make long-term plans, link many different issues on their agendas, and coordinate action on a wide front. With bargaining capacity more centralized, the preferences of each side will be determined through a process of mutual adjustment; labor will pursue or delay certain issues in response to its close ties to the executive branch, and the president will reciprocate. The expectation of a long-term, recurring relationship encourages each side to alter its behavior to avoid disruptive conflict. As each side proves successful in delivering the promised goods, trust deepens and the likelihood of further cooperation grows, making it possible to agree on ambitious strategies that might otherwise be considered too risky. As a result, unions and their leaders come to act less like pressure groups and more like partners in their dealings with national politicians. In this more partisan role, as unions help to aggregate and coalesce other interest groups in the Democratic Party, they start to take responsibility for the party as an institution.[19]

There are dangers, however. One emergent problem of this regime is that the actors invested with centralized bargaining capacity may come to be seen as unrepresentative both of their own members and of groups and individuals outside the bargaining process. That perception may produce a "crisis of representation," as consequential political actors conclude that the existing modes of representation and decision making cannot adequately address their needs.[20] As the crisis unfolds, excluded actors—perhaps other lawmakers, interest group and party leaders, or rank-and-file unionists—will mobilize to demand reform and will call for changes in institutional norms, rules, and procedures. We can imagine two outcomes: either political power will be dispersed outward and downward, to other players within the labor movement and the national policymaking process, or the centralized bargainers will be brought to heel by newly created mechanisms of accountability. In any case, we can identify a contradiction within centralized pluralism: the more power is centralized, the more likely it is that high-level cooperation will emerge—yet the more likely it is as well that other actors will mobilize in opposition. Especially if there are no formal procedures to legitimize the concentration of power in a few key players, centralized pluralism can easily stimulate its own set of centrifugal pressures.

A regime of "fragmented pluralism," in contrast, exists when bargaining capacity is diffused widely throughout the political system and the labor movement. When bargaining capacity is decentralized, high-trust relationships will be far more difficult to create and sustain. Promises may be made, but the goods are less likely to be delivered. For example, when the president or top congressional leaders count on labor for support, but labor fails to deliver, the likelihood of further cooperation is diminished. Conversely, if labor's expectations that the president or congressional leaders will implement certain policies are not met, union leaders are not likely to spend much time making ambitious plans for coordinated action. After several such disappointments, the relationship will degenerate; each player will withdraw, disillusioned and having few credible expectations of a mutually beneficial relationship. Following this deterioration, bargaining is likely to occur only intermittently, and only when the benefits exchanged are immediately and easily identifiable. A high degree of trust is no longer required because long-term commitments are weak or nonexistent, and those exchanges that do occur are discrete and easily verified rather than diffuse and ongoing. This kind of interaction is characterized by an "arm's-length" distance between the two sides, marked more by distrust than by close coordination.

In a regime of fragmented pluralism, unions will also find new bargaining partners in the outer reaches of the political system, reflecting a system where power has been flung outward from inner sanctums in the White House or Congress to an array of committee leaders and individual legislators. Simultaneously, the dispersal of bargaining capacity within the labor movement itself stimulates a diversification of union lobbying activity, as each national union independently sets up shop on Capitol Hill. In the resulting regime, bargaining capacity is spread widely, the number of players is increased, and the opportunities for strategic trade-offs are less common. We can therefore expect the opportunities to advance broad programs of social reform to shrink, as the labor movement finds it more difficult to build the congressional majorities needed for such initiatives and struggles to coordinate the involvement of a fragmented labor movement. In this context, the temptation grows to pursue rearguard actions on the margins of the political system, concentrating mainly on the defense of narrow, union-specific issues. In response, other interest groups in the Democratic Party become more independent, and they resist a central role for labor in aggregating interests and building coalitions.

These two ideal-typical regimes thus illustrate the importance of bargaining capacity in accounting for cooperation or discord. The degree of centralization or fragmentation, I argue, is determined both by institutional structure *and* by the quality of leadership.[21] With respect to the labor movement, institutional structures in the United States have always been very decentralized and far weaker than those in many other countries. The federation has no substantive role in collective bargaining and little capacity to direct the political behavior of even its own affiliates. The AFL-CIO president can only implore—and never command—the affiliated unions, at the national and local level, to endorse and support the federation's legislative and electoral initiatives. Because many of the most important economic and political resources of the individual unions remain beyond the president's formal control, he tends to have less capacity to bargain for the labor movement as a whole or to articulate and enforce political strategies that balance competing union interests.

Nevertheless, the actual power of the federation and of the AFL-CIO president has varied widely in response to leadership strategies and abilities. William Green, president of the AFL from 1924 to 1952, was notoriously weak in relation to the national union leaders and made little effort to consolidate his personal position as a power broker for the labor movement as a whole. In contrast, George Meany, labeled by one biographer the "unchallenged strong man of American labor," was generally recognized as having succeeded in establishing himself as a leader who could deliver a considerable portion of the power resources generated by the labor movement.[22] Thus, the degree to which the AFL-CIO president has a strong bargaining capacity will depend on that individual's political skills, the degree of unity within the labor movement, and the kinds of relationships constructed with national union leaders. Although institutions matter, so does leadership, and it may be possible for a skillful leader to concentrate power far more effectively than the formal rules or procedures might suggest.

On the side of the state, the structure of the American government has shaped the bargaining capacity of elected officeholders. The Constitution deliberately disperses power widely among the legislative, executive, and judicial branches, and between the states and the national government. The bargaining capacity of elected officeholders, such as the president and top congressional leaders, has been correspondingly diminished. Nevertheless, skillful presidents can partially overcome these constitutional barriers, and those who do so will be in a much better position to establish cooperative bargaining relationships with labor leaders. The same applies to the top congressional leadership in the House and Senate. Thus, closer cooperation is more likely when power is concentrated into the hands of politicians sympathetic or beholden to the labor movement (i.e., Democratic Party officeholders). As political scientists have long noted, one means of achieving such concentration is by disciplining and strengthening the Democratic Party, and we would therefore expect greater party unity to produce more cooperation and coordination between party leaders and labor leaders.[23] Thus effective leadership and disciplined parties can partially alleviate the deliberate fragmentation in the formal structure of the American state, laying the foundations for a more centralized version of pluralism.

On the basis of the foregoing analysis, I construct the following hypotheses:

1. If bargaining capacity in the labor movement and the political system is more centralized, and labor's allies are in office, then unions are more likely to develop and maintain long-term, multi-issue, high-trust exchange relationships with top-level elected officeholders.
2. To the extent that such *centralized pluralism* develops, the legislative agenda of organized labor is likely to be broader, unions are more likely to help coalesce and aggregate other interests, and labor-endorsed legislation is more likely to be enacted.
3. If bargaining capacity in the labor movement and the political system is more fragmented, then lower-level congressional players are more likely to be the main focus of union bargaining efforts, resulting in more narrowly focused, one-shot deals between individual unions and individual members of Congress.
4. To the extent that such *fragmented pluralism* prevails, unions will experience less success on broad issues of social reform, will downplay their more visionary aspirations, and will find it more difficult to aggregate and coalesce other interests.

Of course, adequately measuring such concepts as "fragmentation" or "centralization" of bargaining capacity does present a challenge. There is no clear-cut, indisputable set of indicators on which all can agree. I include the following: the percentage of unions affiliated with the federation; the willingness of other national union leaders to follow the lead of the AFL-CIO president in electoral politics, lobbying, and collective bargaining; the extent to which national union lobbying efforts are coordinated by the federation; the extent to which the various state and local branches of the AFL-CIO obey the national federation headquarters; and the extent to which voting behavior and other local resources are mobilized in accordance with the preference of top union leaders. For the national political system, the concentration of bargaining capacity is measured by a president's ability to deliver legislative outcomes in Congress or by a congressional leader's capacity to do the same. "Cooperation" is indicated when the union leadership and national politicians alter their electoral activity, legislative agenda, and lobbying strategy in response to each other's preferences and in pursuit of a common end. Evidence of cooperation can be gleaned through examination of meetings, letters, memos, stated policy goals, lobbying activities, and so forth. I make judgments about these issues based on my own reading of the primary evidence, quantitative data, and the standard secondary literature.

The chapters that follow will test the above model by providing an analytical history of unions in national politics from the mid-1960s to the mid-1990s. This period supplies many examples of wide variation in the level of cooperation between union leaders and top Democratic officeholders. We will find striking cases of genuine partnership, as well as notorious episodes of distrust and bitterness. There is much to explain.

Part Two

UNIONS IN THE WASHINGTON POWER GAME

3 *Labor and the Johnson Administration: The Limits of Cooperation*

In late December of 1967, as the presidency of Lyndon Johnson increasingly came under siege from both disillusioned liberals and resurgent conservatives, AFL-CIO President George Meany wrote President Johnson a lengthy letter that outlined a program not for retrenching but for deepening the social and economic commitments of the Great Society. Although Meany contended that "nothing is more important than the war in Viet Nam," he rejected what he called the "false cry of 'guns or butter.'" There was no unavoidable trade-off, he argued, between fighting a war against Communism in Southeast Asia and pursuing a simultaneous attack on poverty and social inequality at home. A program of domestic reform could still be sustained if the federal government moved in the direction of "genuine economic planning," which would include a massive expansion of spending to address urban poverty, housing shortages, inadequate education, and lingering unemployment. Meany also called for the strengthening of the federal government's role in protecting consumers, preserving the environment, and defending the rights of racial minorities. While others were advocating a pause in the grand agenda of postwar liberalism, George Meany insisted that the project of social reform had just begun.

It was perhaps for this reason that the federation leader concluded his missive on a spirited note, predicting that although Johnson would be "attacked from the left and the right, both for this program and on the issue of the war in Viet Nam," he could continue to count on the strong support of the labor movement. The president's opponents, Meany averred, were extremists. Right-wingers, "undeterred by defeat at the polls, tirelessly prosecute their fanatical campaign against enlightenment and progress," while at the other extreme, leftists infiltrate peace organizations and the ghettos, "converting debate into disorder and mindless defiance of law" and "transforming the rightful quest for the redress of ancient grievances into violent civil disorders." Meany offered the president his reassurance: "They are your enemies, Mr. President, and they are ours. And, we know, as you do, that they will not prevail."[1] A few months later, on March 12, 1968, the same day as the New Hampshire primary, United Auto Workers President Walter P. Reuther was equally strident in his support of President Johnson. Reuther insisted at a news conference that "at the moment, no one on the horizon is remotely more entitled to my vote than he is. He has made a tremendous contribution on domestic programs, and I intend to support him in 1968. . . . I think that the vote that Eugene McCarthy gets is going to have no influence on the attitude of American labor."[2]

These endorsements reflected the remarkable unity of organized labor, despite its own internal conflicts, in support of the reelection of Lyndon Johnson. Even as the president entered the last embattled months prior to his withdrawal from the race for renomination, the labor leadership remained steadfast in its call for a second term. In the eyes of union leaders, Johnson had delivered on most of his promises to the labor movement. Their task, therefore, was to prove their loyalty by providing those political and economic resources that could help Johnson secure reelection and achieve his policymaking goals. In short, union leaders felt that their bargain with the president was a very good one, and they worked hard to perpetuate the conditions for its existence.

Crucial among these conditions was a distinct set of institutional arrangements that came into being in national politics during the mid-1960s. With bargaining capacity relatively concentrated in both the labor movement *and* the national political system, the stage was set for a relationship of productive cooperation between the president and top union leaders. In national politics, decision making was confined among a relatively small number of individuals within Congress, the executive branch, and the major interest groups (most notably, business and labor).[3] The internal rules governing Congress and the presidential nominating process reinforced the power of political brokers who interacted regularly, with little need to accommodate a more diverse and fluid range of interests. Interest group leaders, such as union presidents and lobbyists, could negotiate deals with presidents and congressional leaders and know with some reliability when—or if—the goods would be delivered. This cozy system of insider-oriented bargaining could be sustained with relative ease in an environment in which the number of influential interest groups was small, the issue agenda was predictable and controlled by elite actors, and there was little likelihood of a quick and sustained mobilization on the part of excluded or unrepresented groups.

During this same period, the nation's union leaders successfully forged a higher degree of centralized control over the economic resources generated by their organizations.[4] In the aftermath of World War II, a mature system of industrial relations emerged in the core sectors of the economy (such as steel, auto, trucking, airlines, rubber, and electronics). Most employers in these industries came to accept the legitimacy of union representation and collective bargaining, although only after a protracted process of conflict and accommodation. Likewise, most union leaders eventually accepted as legitimate the right of an employer to make the basic management decisions regarding the future of the enterprise. As this system of industrial relations became more stable and predictable, it also became more bureaucratic, professionalized, and legalistic. Collective bargaining was now carried out on a national basis, and the unions' own organizational hierarchy came to reflect the size and complexity of the corporations with which they bargained. Moreover, the influence of a small number of union leaders was enhanced by the growth of pattern bargaining, whereby all collective bargaining contracts generally followed the pattern set in negotiations by the strongest unions. This development meant that a relatively small number of pattern-setting contracts had major ramifications elsewhere in the economy.

The bargaining capacity of union leaders also grew more centralized with respect to control over the unions' distinctly political resources. Internal opposition to the political strategy of the union leadership lessened during the postwar period as members of the Communist Party were expelled or otherwise defeated, and as the alliance with the Democratic Party was consolidated. As the staff organization of unions became larger and more complex, and rank-and-file participation declined, the political activity of unions also grew substantially more hierarchical and professionalized. Political resources that were previously constrained by the changeable and uncontrolled attitudes of the rank and file could now be called forth in a more regularized fashion on the basis of standard operating procedures. Union money, organizational support, and, to a lesser degree, the votes of the membership could all be delivered to candidates at the behest of a semicentralized political operation using the latest techniques of modern campaigning. Thus, union political programs increasingly took on the character of "machines" that could be wielded autonomously by those at the top without having to engage in a systematic canvassing of membership preferences.[5]

Meanwhile, AFL-CIO President George Meany succeeded in establishing himself as the most powerful head of a national union federation in the history of the American labor movement. The 1955 merger of the American Federation of Labor and the Congress of Industrial Organizations occurred mainly on the terms of the much larger AFL, led by Meany after the death of President William Green in 1952. At the time of the merger, UAW President Walter Reuther was president of the rival CIO, but his position within that federation was fairly weak, especially in comparison to Meany's entrenched position within the AFL.[6] Reuther had barely won the CIO presidency in 1952 with only 52 percent of the vote, and he faced steady criticism from David McDonald, president of the Steelworkers, who opposed Reuther's left-wing political leanings. Meany skillfully took advantage of Reuther's and the CIO's weakness, effectively protecting AFL interests during the merger negotiations and laying the groundwork for his own leadership of the new unified federation. It was no surprise, therefore, that Meany captured the presidency of the AFL-CIO and soon even secured the loyalty of many leaders from the CIO. By the early 1960s Reuther was increasingly marginalized within the AFL-CIO Executive Council, and it seemed less and less likely that he would ever displace Meany. Meany was thus left in a good position to speak confidently for a united labor movement that recognized him as its preeminent voice.

The political and economic environment of the mid-1960s thus seems to have closely approximated the ideal-type of centralized pluralism as sketched in the previous chapter. As we will see, however, this regime was still far from completely centralized, and the bargaining capacity of key figures remained in important respects quite limited. On the side of organized labor, the relatively decentralized structure of the federation and the fragmented nature of collective bargaining kept it difficult for union leaders (and George Meany in particular) to deliver wage restraint and to coordinate union political activity. On the side of the administration, the continued weakness of party ties, the persistence of multiple veto-points in Congress, and the vitality of the "conservative coalition" made it hard for President Johnson to deliver the key legislative results he had hoped to provide the labor movement. The unions would, therefore, still confront many obstacles taxing their strategies and resources.

Organized Labor and Presidential Politics

The day after the assassination of President John F. Kennedy, Lyndon Johnson phoned both Walter Reuther and George Meany, soliciting their support and pledging to carry on in the best tradition of his predecessor. A week later, the president met personally with Meany, assuring him (as Meany later recalled) that he was "very anxious to go along with a list of things that we were for: federal aid to education, certainly the civil rights business."[7] The new president made similar comments when he met with the AFL-CIO Executive Council as a whole on December 5, 1963. Johnson stressed his commitment to jobs ("number one in priority today and tomorrow"), a tax cut, civil rights, and an "adequate medicare program." Johnson told the assembled labor leaders: "You represent the people. I need you and I believe that you should be standing by my side in this fight as you are today." After fifty minutes of discussion, the labor contingent left feeling inspired, and Johnson assured them: "I want you to know that the doors to this house will always be open to you for your ideas and problems. And the doors of the Cabinet officers, too." One labor leader concluded, "I think most of us felt he really meant it. We are very much encouraged."[8] Although Johnson also met the same day with the leadership of the business community, the union presidents clearly believed that the new administration would bring many possibilities for labor influence.[9]

Why did Johnson, who had previously maintained an uneasy relationship with organized labor, so diligently pursue the union constituency? Much of the answer can be found in the role that labor played in the Democratic Party's presidential nominating process. Union involvement in this system was profoundly influenced by the rules adopted at the state level regulating the selection of delegates to the Democratic national convention.[10] In most states, delegates were chosen at caucuses or conventions that were effectively dominated by "regular" party leaders. Delegates were selected on the basis of their commitment and service to the party, not because they supported a particular candidate—indeed, the delegates were often designated long before any candidates for the nomination had actually entered the race.[11] Logically enough, delegates selected in this manner were beholden to those party leaders who had chosen them, not to any of the individual candidates in the race for the nomination or to a larger body of Democratic voters. For candidates, therefore, the task was to accumulate a delegate majority at the convention by meticulously cultivating the support of the small group of powerful party leaders (often an influential governor or mayor in each state) who could reliably deliver the votes of their state's delegation. As described by journalist Theodore White, the convention was "a universe in itself, a nucleus of thirty or forty tough-minded power brokers, making decisions behind closed doors."[12]

The way in which unions maneuvered in this system has been described well by former AFL-CIO president Lane Kirkland. He argues that there was a "tacit, invisible but real arrangement" in which "the party leaders knew that, in the general election, they needed labor to draw some of the water and hew some of the wood. The leaders of the party wanted to win. They wouldn't nominate anyone who was too offensive to the trade union movement."[13] Kirkland claims that "it was a collective bargaining relationship, in effect: the key people involved in the process would discuss with us the acceptability of various candidates. . . . A relative handful of people exercised a profound influence on the process."[14] Although union leaders could not necessarily ensure the nomination of their first choice, they knew that party leaders would listen to their concerns, anticipate their reactions, and avoid choosing a candidate they actively disliked. And in those few states where primaries were used to select delegates, union leaders could mobilize their local membership to vote for the favorite candidate of the union.

In this context, the first order of business for someone with the moderate—even conservative—background of Lyndon Johnson was to consolidate the support of the left flank of the party coalition. Accordingly, Johnson provided union leaders with regular access to the White House and made promises to pursue a liberal program. More than this, he played a crucial role in securing passage of the 1964 Civil Rights Act and a major tax cut supported by labor leaders—all within his first year in office. The president also announced his support for an extensive "War on Poverty" and worked closely with union leaders in promoting the labor movement's ambitious proposal for Medicare. From the perspective of union leaders, the Johnson administration was providing real benefits, and there was the enticing prospect of much more to come.

For these reasons, union leaders made intensive efforts to support Johnson's election, assisting him in a variety of ways during both the Democratic nominating process and the general election. Although Johnson did not face any serious rivals for the nomination itself, he did have to maintain the unity of the fractious Democratic coalition. For this task, he sought the help of organized labor. His desire for that help was most clearly demonstrated in the events surrounding the efforts of the Mississippi Freedom Democratic Party (MFDP) to gain representation at the 1964 Democratic National Convention.[15] The MFDP was a group of black and white Mississippi Democrats, organized by the Student Nonviolent Coordinating Committee, who hoped to oust the "regular" Mississippi delegation to the 1964 convention. They contended that the all-white, segregationist delegation was neither representative of Mississippi Democrats nor in compliance with the national party's position on civil rights and other issues. The Freedom Democrats sought to be recognized on equal terms with the regular delegation as representatives of Mississippi—a move that could easily have prompted the regular delegation to bolt the convention altogether.

Johnson found the plans of the MFDP quite troubling. He feared the electoral consequences of an affront to the South, especially when there were already ominous indications of disaffection among white voters in that region. Thus, he sought to defuse the situation by enlisting Minnesota Senator Hubert Humphrey and Walter Reuther, both of whom had liberal credentials and ongoing ties with the civil rights movement, to hammer out a compromise. Although initially hesitant, Reuther worked closely with Humphrey, producing a compromise package that seemed to resolve the conflict quietly by allowing partial representation for the MFDP. The Freedom Democrats ultimately chose, however, to reject the package and publicly denounce the party for failing to adhere to its principles. Despite that failure, the UAW leader had demonstrated his loyalty to the president and a willingness to put the interests of the national party ahead of his immediate ties to the civil rights movement. The cost, however, was high: a crucial cadre of young black leaders would be alienated, later coming to see even Reuther as part of an insensitive and hypocritical white establishment that had concentrated its hold on power and was unwilling to incorporate newly active social movements into the political system.

Union leaders also manipulated their economic resources on behalf of the president's election campaign. Their actions reflected the interest of Johnson and his advisors in avoiding politically damaging strikes prior to the election. In August 1964 Supreme Court Justice Arthur Goldberg, the former secretary of labor in the Kennedy administration, wrote President Johnson, urging him to take measures "similar to those which the Labor Party in Britain has taken, to minimize serious strikes during the campaign."[16] Goldberg recommended that LBJ speak with Meany and Reuther, in particular, to avoid unseemly labor disputes. Secretary of Labor Willard Wirtz also wrote the president in September 1964, noting that Walter Reuther was "presently making strike plans. But he knows (and I have emphasized with him) that a strike now would make him look very bad—and would hurt us."[17] Reuther acknowledged to the UAW's executive board: "We are under great pressure in Washington."[18] Cognizant of the increased responsibilities inherent in the alliance with Johnson, Reuther sought to limit the disruption posed by his union's collective bargaining activity by encouraging a quick resolution of any strikes by UAW locals. Similarly, George Meany intervened when the New York building trades union planned a strike (opposing the use of nonunion workers on federal construction projects) on the very same day that Johnson was scheduled to visit the city for a "Salute to the President" rally.[19]

In this manner the labor leaders became committed to the political strategy of the administration, and deployed their political and economic resources accordingly. The question that remains, though, is whether the unions received something of value in exchange for their services. Was the exchange relationship a fair and equal one, from which the unions acquired tangible benefits? Or was it an example of labor leaders deluding themselves into thinking that the Democratic party had a serious interest in their concerns? The answers would depend not only on the actions of the Johnson administration but also on the behavior of members of Congress, who faced their own distinct set of political incentives.

The Limits and Possibilities of Congress

The election of 1964 seemed to provide a superb opportunity for the enactment of the main items on organized labor's legislative agenda. Not only had a Democratic president been elected by a landslide margin, but a huge Democratic congressional majority had been swept into office as well. Democrats now controlled the House, 295 Democrats to 140 Republicans, and the Senate by 68 to 32. These mammoth majorities were viewed as both ideal and necessary by labor strategists long familiar with the ability of congressional conservatives to block liberal legislation, even when Democrats nominally were controlling both chambers and the presidency. Under the conditions of the New Deal party system, liberal measures typically failed when southern Democrats aligned with Republicans in opposition to nonsouthern Democrats. This "conservative coalition" was also nearly always the main force behind the passage of the legislation that unions despised most. The Taft-Hartley Act, which placed new restrictions on union organizing and bargaining, was enacted with the support of the conservative coalition and over the veto of President Harry Truman in 1947. Similarly, in the early 1960s the unions and their liberal allies watched in frustration as the Kennedy administration was almost immobilized on domestic issues by the intransigence of conservative southern committee chairs.[20] The dramatic electoral outcomes of 1964 now promised to loosen this congressional logjam for the first time in decades.

But the arrival of a more liberal Congress by no means ensured the passage of the liberal agenda. While both the Senate and House now contained more liberal Democrats than ever before, congressional rules and procedures still presented impressive opportunities for delay.[21] These rules granted exceptional power to one group in particular: the chairs of standing committees. Selected on the basis of committee seniority, these chairs could act with considerable autonomy and could disregard the wishes of the majority of their own party, the congressional leadership, and even the members of their own committee. Chairs had the power to schedule hearings (or avoid them altogether), to create or dissolve subcommittees, and to fire or hire committee staff, and they aggressively used these powers to block or advance legislation. In the House, the Rules Committee was particularly notorious for obstruction, as its conservative chairman, Representative Howard Smith of Virginia, used the unique scheduling and procedural powers of the committee to block liberal legislation. Although committees were generally less crucial in the Senate, where there was no equivalent of the House Rules Committee and power was more widely distributed, other methods for blocking liberal initiatives were available; there was an "inner club" of senators, mainly conservative southerners, who were quite willing to use the filibuster.[22]

At the same time, the central party organs that might have challenged the power of committee chairs remained weak. Assertive leadership was made difficult by the heterogeneous membership of the congressional Democratic party, which ranged from southern conservatives, often openly racist and anti-labor, to northern liberals strongly committed to racial equality and the protection of unions. Centralizing reforms, such as an expansion of the powers of the Speaker of the House or the Senate majority leader, were likely to be blocked by southern Democrats. As Kenneth Shepsle has noted, because of this heterogeneity, "party leaders were agents for, rather than superiors to, committee leaders and members of the inner club."[23] The Speaker of the House and the Senate majority leader could sometimes influence legislative outcomes, but only because of their close personal relationships with committee heads, not because of any formal power to compel these chairs to comply with the majority will of the congressional party.

While this structure of power posed a real problem for the advancement of liberal causes, it had mixed effects on the ability of a president to influence Congress. On the one hand, the confinement of bargaining capacity among a relatively small number of committee chairs made it easier to negotiate reliable deals with key individuals. As one member of the House of Representatives noted during the mid-1960s, "There are only about forty out of the 435 members who call the shots."[24] A president at least knew with whom he had to bargain. On the other hand, because of their unconstrained power committee chairs could easily block presidential ambitions if they wished. In the final analysis, power was concentrated in committee fiefdoms, not top leaders, and this made it extremely difficult for the president and congressional leaders to deliver legislative outcomes of their own choosing.

As a seasoned veteran of earlier battles over liberal proposals (and, indeed, as a politician with experience on both sides of the liberal/conservative divide), Lyndon Johnson was keenly aware of the obstructive potential remaining within Congress. He knew that to enact his ambitious program of social reform he would have to concentrate power in the legislative process in his own hands and prevent its dispersion to committee bailiwicks. It was precisely this goal that encouraged Johnson to take advantage of the lobbying assistance and political clout of organized labor. As George Meany would later observe, Johnson was "quite aware of the fact that on some of these liberal measures where a few votes were needed to finally enact the legislation, our influence . . . could pick up votes that even he couldn't pick up as President." As a result, Johnson maintained regular contact with the federation president. Meany noted: "Every week there would be two or three telephone calls and visits. I was in the White House sometimes two and three times a week."[25] One biographer of George Meany simply concluded: "Johnson courted Meany more fervently than had any President."[26] Simultaneously, Johnson pursued the support and friendship of Walter Reuther, seeking the political and legislative assistance that the UAW, more than any other single union, could provide. Historian Nelson Lichtenstein has described well the intensity of Reuther's incorporation into national politics: "Never before had Reuther been on such close, continuous, and informal terms with an American president. Throughout 1964 and 1965 there were phone calls almost every week, dinner invitations to the White House, and the kind of open political collaboration that Reuther craved."[27] Reuther would write to LBJ that he considered himself "a devoted member of your working crew."[28]

Working closely with both Johnson and liberals in Congress, labor lobbyists thus came to function as a "bridge" between the executive and legislative branches, much like the political parties had traditionally done. Some observers even accused labor of going so far as to sacrifice its own interests in order to promote the administration's program. Arthur H. Raskin, the labor reporter for the *New York Times*, wrote that labor had "become a White House political appendage, rather than a vigorous initiator of independent policy."[29] But for most labor leaders such a role was entirely satisfactory, for they had few disagreements with the administration's legislative proposals.

In support of the president's program, the unions worked especially closely with the liberal Democrats in Congress—a group that was infuriated with the obstructionist tactics of committee chairs and the weak direction provided by the formal party leadership.[30] Lacking their own effective party apparatus with which to pressure wavering members, collect political intelligence, and coordinate legislative strategy, liberal members turned to organized labor as an entity that could help fulfill these functions. In his study of labor's role in Congress during this period, J. David Greenstone concludes that "the labor movement . . . provided coordination for pro–welfare state Democrats that the formal party leaders and organizations were too inhibited by geographical, institutional, and factional barriers to provide."[31] These included such specific tasks as providing accurate counts of where members stood on a bill, mobilizing the support of other liberal interest groups and providing them with financial assistance, generating pressure at the district level, serving as a neutral broker when liberal legislators disagreed, and producing substantive analyses and arguments in support of key legislation. In Greenstone's depiction, labor served as a vanguard for the liberal forces in Congress, constantly pushing and prodding where self-interested politicians would prefer to hold back. The community of Washington labor lobbyists was guided in these tasks by the AFL-CIO legislative director, Andrew Biemiller, a former member of Congress who possessed an astute knowledge of the inner workings of the House and Senate. Biemiller's contacts and experience made him particularly effective at the kind of insider bargaining that was still the most common form of congressional lobbying.

The labor/Democrat alliance soon emerged as a major factor in the impressive legislative outputs of the Johnson presidency. In the 1965 AFL-CIO legislative report, George Meany declared: "The first session of the 89th Congress enacted a tremendous volume of long-overdue social welfare legislation. It was the most productive congressional session ever held."[32] *Congressional Quarterly* came to a similar judgment: "The lawmakers' action in the fields of civil rights, anti-poverty, education, and other social welfare areas under Mr. Johnson's energetic and experienced leadership generally followed the unions' longstanding stance on social legislation."[33] Andrew Biemiller observed that "a radical change had come over Congress in the early months of 1965 as the President's legislative program moved swiftly through committees onto the floor of Congress, was debated and passed in record time. . . . Congress was once again functioning efficiently after years of foot dragging which had led many observers to voice the belief that the machinery of Congress was too weak to meet modern needs."[34] Suddenly, it seemed that Congress was indeed working again, and union leaders and lobbyists happily took their share of the credit for its success. Biemiller wrote to a friend, "I somewhat immodestly say I have had as large a role in legislative matters in the last four years as anyone," observing elsewhere that "there wasn't any question that our relations with Lyndon were so good as to be almost incredible."[35] *Congressional Quarterly* concluded simply: "The forces of organized labor comprised a major bulwark in the coalition which produced what was sometimes termed the legislative and political 'consensus' of the early Johnson years."[36]

Indeed, some of the most exciting accomplishments of the Johnson presidency revealed the hidden hand of union lobbying. For example, the AFL-CIO strongly supported President Johnson's civil rights agenda, hoping that his program would bring a transformation of the South's anti-union political tradition. Biemiller noted at the time, "The 1964 Civil Rights Act and 1965 Voting Rights bill will greatly increase the voting strength of Negroes in some of the previously uncontested, conservative districts in the South, bringing new forces into play in this long dormant area."[37] By forcing conservative southern whites out of the Democratic Party, the civil rights movement could align the region's politics more closely with national patterns. Biemiller reasoned: "We would have no objection to seeing a strong Republican party appear in the South. It might turn Southern Democrats into a more liberal group."[38] Thus, union leaders and lobbyists brought the political resources of the labor movement squarely behind the administration's civil rights agenda. Most notably, the AFL-CIO and the UAW helped to initiate and fund the Leadership Conference on Civil Rights, which united the leaders of some eighty organizations committed to the passage of reform legislation. Greenstone observes: "Labor representatives participated fully in the intricate tactical decisions involving the amendment of the administration's civil rights proposals. Most important, the unions supplied resources unavailable to church groups, including money, office space, and mimeographing and other clerical services, on which the conference's communication and coordination efforts depended."[39] Representative Richard Bolling, a key congressional supporter of the 1964 Civil Rights Act, stated: "We never would have passed the Civil Rights Act without labor. They had the muscle; the other civil rights groups did not."[40]

Labor played a similar role in facilitating passage of the Medicare program in 1965. The Social Security Department of the AFL-CIO, under the direction of Nelson H. Cruikshank, had worked assiduously during the 1950s and early 1960s to promote the idea of national health insurance for the aged.[41] The AFL-CIO also funded and staffed a separate organization, the National Council of Senior Citizens (NCSC), which became one of the most prominent of the organizations building support for the program. Union lobbyists and the NCSC mobilized local grassroots supporters, helped coordinate the activity of allied interest groups, and worked closely with the administration in lobbying Congress.[42] As James Sundquist observed, Medicare was "carried by the AFL-CIO all the way to the bill-drafting stage, and for the first few months, at least, it had only nominal sponsorship by a congressmen who had doubts about it and did little to promote it."[43] Union leaders and lobbyists worked to ensure that the bill was not trapped within congressional committees, stymied by other parliamentary maneuvers, or blocked by the aggressive opposition of the American Medical Association.[44]

The administration's "War on Poverty" provided another opportunity for union leaders to help originate new policy ideas and lobby for their enactment. The UAW, especially, sought a greater federal commitment to address the persistence of poverty in the midst of an increasingly affluent society. In January 1964 Walter Reuther and his top aides wrote President Johnson, calling for "a massive national effort to provide a better life for America's submerged third" through new spending on vocational training, unemployment insurance, federal aid to cities and disadvantaged areas, public housing and health care, and federal aid to education. Shortly thereafter Johnson announced his "unconditional war on poverty" and pledged the administration to a massive new effort to help Americans "escape from squalor and misery and unemployment rolls."[45] The UAW supported this effort by organizing and funding the Citizen's Crusade Against Poverty, a coalition of 125 liberal, labor, civil rights, and church organizations that was intended to play a galvanizing role similar to that of the Leadership Conference on Civil Rights. Reuther also was instrumental in the initiation of the Model Cities program for urban redevelopment, presenting an influential proposal for the program to Lyndon Johnson in a 1965 meeting.[46]

Thus, by the end of the 89th Congress, union leaders were deeply satisfied with and even astounded by the remarkable policy changes that had been wrought since 1963. George Meany summarized the beneficial accomplishments from the viewpoint of the AFL-CIO:

> Medicare and other sweeping social security improvements, aid to education at every level, federal protection of voting rights, a stepped-up war on poverty and a broad new regionally-based public works program, a new Department of Housing and Urban Development, a better and stronger housing program, a sweeping new attack on health problems, highway beautification, immigration reform—these are only highlights in a list too long to enumerate.[47]

In the area of social reform, the union movement had both benefited from and worked to maintain the legislative power of the Johnson administration. In this way, union leaders had encouraged a centralization of power in the administration in place of the diffusion of power to congressional committee chairs and filibustering senators antagonistic to the new federal role in domestic policy. Much as the model of centralized pluralism would predict, the agenda of the unions was broadened by their alliance with a strong Democratic president, and the unions themselves were increasingly led into the role of aggregating the diverse interests of the Democratic Party. Yet despite these historic successes, the labor movement was also acquiring a reputation as an ineffectual force when it came to legislation more directly concerned with unions as institutions. By the mid-1960s it was clear that organized labor could help enact a program of social reform. But could it also advance the legal changes needed to protect collective bargaining and unions in the workplace?

The Quest for Labor Law Reform

Ultimately, the grand sweep of liberal accomplishment during the Johnson presidency would bypass a long-standing goal of the labor movement: to repeal section 14(b) of the Labor-Management Relations Act. Known after its congressional sponsors (Senator Robert Taft of Ohio and Congressman Fred Hartley of New Jersey) as the Taft-Hartley Act, the law was originally enacted by a Republican-dominated Congress in 1947 over President Truman's veto. As we have noted, the most objectionable provision was section 14(b), which allowed the states to pass so-called right-to-work laws forbidding union shops, where employees were required to join the union (or at least pay dues) if they wished to remain employed. Many southern states adopted such "right-to-work" statutes, seeing in them a spur to the region's economic development that fit well with the South's traditions of states' rights and rigid anti-unionism.[48] The unions, of course, viewed such measures as a direct threat to their organizational status, undermining the institutional mechanisms they deemed necessary to overcome the "free-rider" problem inherent in any form of labor unionism. Repeal of section 14(b) would not only eliminate this threat but would reduce the need for expensive and time-consuming battles over union-security legislation at the state level.

Therefore, shortly after the 1964 presidential election the AFL-CIO began negotiating with the administration over a strategy for 14(b) repeal. Conflict soon emerged over the question of timing, with administration officials seeking to delay the controversial repeal effort until *after* the ambitious social welfare proposals had been enacted. Despite considerable disagreement within the AFL-CIO Executive Council, key figures in the labor leadership agreed to delay the launch of the repeal campaign until Johnson gave his approval.[49] Although Johnson expressed support for their efforts in his January 1965 State of the Union message, he did not give his official go-ahead for the repeal drive until May 1965. By late July the bill had moved through the House Labor Committee with full administration support, and was approved in the full House by a vote of 221 to 203. Northern and western Democrats voted overwhelmingly in favor of repeal, while southern Democrats were almost uniform in their opposition. With the Democratic Party so divided, the support of Republicans from northern industrial states was crucial in the final House victory.

The outcome in the Senate, however, would be far less fortunate for labor. Consideration of the bill was again delayed, as the administration worked on other items on its agenda and Senate Majority Leader Mike Mansfield postponed the scheduling of floor debate. By the time the bill arrived on the floor for consideration in fall of 1965, a major lobbying effort by the employer-backed National Right-to-Work Committee had stimulated hundreds of antirepeal newspaper editorials around the country and new grassroots pressure on wavering senators. Sensing the possibility of blocking repeal altogether, Senate Minority Leader Everett Dirksen chose to lead a filibuster. With Mansfield unwilling to schedule the around-the-clock sessions needed to help bring the filibuster to an end, a cloture vote in October 1965 garnered the support of only 45 senators, far short of the two-thirds margin needed to end debate. In February 1966 the labor movement and its Senate supporters again sought to achieve passage of the repeal legislation, but were defeated once more by a filibuster led by Dirksen and supported by Republicans and conservative Democrats. The labor movement did secure a pro-cloture majority, but the final tally was still only 50 to 49. Any hope of improvement in labor's situation was further undermined by the backlash against a two-week strike of public transportation workers in New York City in January 1966. Secretary Wirtz observed, "It left a very bad taste in people's mouths about organized labor."[50] Thus ended the battle for repeal in the 89th Congress; with major Republican gains in the 1966 congressional elections, labor's hope for reform had been decisively blocked for the foreseeable future.

To what degree was the Johnson administration responsible for this outcome? A common refrain is that the administration failed to exert sufficient pressure in favor of repeal and that this failure reveals the dependent and weak position of organized labor within the Democratic Party.[51] There is certainly evidence for such an interpretation in the significant political choices that made repeal less likely. Johnson and his aides delayed consideration of the bill until other, less controversial, measures had passed, which inevitably weakened the administration's bargaining power with Congress by the time repeal made it to the Senate floor. Johnson also seemed reluctant to use his famous powers of persuasion very forcefully. As Gilbert Gall has noted in the most comprehensive study of the repeal effort, Johnson apparently placed little pressure on Majority Leader Mansfield to take a more aggressive stance against the filibuster. Nor did Johnson push Minority Leader Dirksen and southern Democratic senators to drop the filibuster.[52]

Still, there is good reason to believe that labor's failure was also due to a number of tactical decisions on its own part, rather than any predictable betrayal by selfish allies. Union leaders chose, for example, to go along with the administration on the question of legislative timing, even though they were well aware that doing so would reduce the likelihood of passage. This willingness on the part of labor came after considerable internal conflict, and it is easy to imagine that a more militant leadership might have arrived at a different and more assertive strategy. As Secretary of Labor Wirtz noted in a memo to the president in December 1964, there was "unquestionably a sharp division on this within the AFL-CIO Council"; specifically, "there are some—particularly Keenan [president of the International Brotherhood of Electrical Workers] and Biemiller—who continue to insist that an Administration bill and message on this subject be sent to Congress very early in this session." But despite internal disagreement, the AFL-CIO chose to accept Wirtz's contention that "the timing of any Administration action regarding Section 14(b) should and must be left entirely a matter of Presidential determination." Wirtz informed the president that "this position has been accepted and meaningfully supported by Meany and [UAW President Walter] Reuther."[53] Neither Meany nor Reuther felt comfortable about hindering the enactment of Johnson's liberal agenda simply to promote 14(b) repeal, which many in Washington viewed as a parochial, special-interest proposal. In a February 1965 memo Wirtz told Johnson that Walter Reuther actually thought that AFL-CIO "pushing" of 14(b) repeal before other parts of the social-agenda were enacted would be "a serious mistake."[54]

Labor's unwillingness to compromise on its larger goals of social reform was further illustrated when Meany turned down a deal proposed by Senator Dirksen. The Republican minority leader offered to cease his opposition to 14(b) repeal if Meany would agree not to resist a constitutional amendment overturning the Supreme Court's recent ruling mandating reapportionment of state legislatures. The Court's decision was crucial for ensuring representation on the basis of one-person, one-vote in states where legislatures had traditionally been apportioned in favor of conservative rural areas. According to Meany, Dirksen made the following offer: "Give up your opposition to the reapportionment amendment and you can have 14(b) repeal." But Meany's response was a firm refusal: "As badly as I want 14(b) repealed, I do not want it that badly. And the Senate Minority Leader and all his anti-labor stooges can filibuster until hell freezes over before I will agree to sell the people short for that kind of a deal."[55]

Passage was also made difficult by the intensive grassroots campaign organized by the National Right-to-Work Committee, which flooded congressional offices with letters and helped invigorate the legislative opposition. The view of one senator who voted against repeal is particularly illuminating: "Repeal of Section 14(b) had no grass-roots appeal. Repeal was not important to the people who wanted repeal. But the opposition to repeal was impassioned. The people who wanted repeal were just a small number of union leaders."[56] While most of big business remained on the sidelines, small businesses inundated Congress with letters and telegrams opposing the legislation. Labor unions, meanwhile, apparently did a poor job of mobilizing their own membership in support of the repeal campaign.

Meany himself chose not to blame Johnson for the defeat, even in interviews conducted well after Johnson had left office. "He tried just as hard as he could, and he was quite helpful," Meany said in August 1969. "The 14(b) repeal was lost because of Dirksen's action in mounting the filibuster and Mansfield's refusal to use the full power of his position to break the filibuster."[57] Meany no doubt would have concurred with President Johnson's lament about Mansfield, as recorded by Joseph Califano: "On more than one occasion when some rough muscle was needed in the Senate, [Johnson] would sigh in exasperation: 'Why do I have to have a saint for Majority Leader? Why can't I have a politician?'"[58]

While it will always be arguable (and impossible to disprove) that Johnson might have made the difference if he had only worked harder, the deeper origins of labor's failure lay in problems that had dogged it for decades: its geographical concentration in a minority of states in the North and far West, its corresponding weakness in the South, its low standing in public opinion, and the existence of antimajoritarian features in the political system, most obviously the Senate filibuster. Labor's difficulty, in other words, was rooted more in adverse political alignments and long-standing institutional constraints than in any simple inability to compel aggressive presidential support. We can reinforce the point by comparing the 1965 defeat with the union effort to repeal section 14(b) in 1949, a mere two years after it was passed. In that instance, despite labor's major contribution to Truman's reelection and the return of a sizable Democratic majority to Congress, the repeal effort was turned back in the House by the conservative coalition. While most Democratic senators and representatives from northern, eastern, and blue-collar districts supported labor's position, their votes could not overcome the continued strength of the alignment of southern Democrats with a majority of Republicans. Labor's situation was made worse, as David Plotke has observed, by its geographic concentration: "More than two-thirds of union membership was concentrated in ten states: Because of single-member districts in the House and the allocation of Senate seats by state, any such concentrated force has great trouble gaining political representation proportionate to its weight in the national population."[59]

By the late 1940s, then, a pattern had been established in national politics: liberal legislation—especially that which improved conditions for African Americans or enhanced the power of labor unions—was blocked by southern Democrats and Republicans taking advantage of the peculiar institutional features of the American state. Selig Perlman's 1951 commentary on the political situation of organized labor was as apt as ever: "The American government with its states' rights, judicial review, and general checks and balances was a very limited instrument for labor's good and often a menace to be warded off."[60] Even when labor succeeded in securing the active support of a liberal president and a majority in both houses of Congress, the multiple veto-points and weak party discipline inherent in American political institutions presented sizable barriers. Moreover, the labor movement's own internal disagreements about priorities and strategy, as well as its incapacity to control the behavior of its constituent parts (as seen in the ill-timed New York subway strike), made it less able to effectively bargain with the president and to ruthlessly pursue its own interests. In this manner, the fragmentation of bargaining capacity conspired once again to obstruct labor's political potential.

Economic Policy

Political scientist Richard Neustadt has noted that issues of economic policymaking "underline a President's necessitous dependence on performance in the private sector, outside government as such. . . . Here is another set of separate institutions, indeed, another executive branch, walled off by the Bill of Rights, protected by the courts, in charge of decisions on investment, on production, prices, wages, and employment that can make or break Administration policy."[61] Among the private sector institutions that can "make or break" the economic plans of presidents are labor unions, which through their collective bargaining and strike activity can have a major impact on rates of inflation and economic growth. This was especially true in the postwar period, when because of the increased centralization of collective bargaining, as well as the consolidation of internal control by the national union leadership, unions were commonly recruited as allies in managing the economy. In particular, both the Kennedy and Johnson administrations sought union help as they attempted to achieve a high rate of economic growth while at the same time keeping inflation low or moderate.[62] This task required that unions restrain the inflationary wage demands of their members, in return for which they would be offered pro-union federal policies and privileged access to the executive branch—a trade-off that potentially offered union leaders an unprecedented level of integration into the economic policymaking process. But, as always, the attempt to construct a new role for both the labor movement and the state would ultimately reveal the continuing limits on centralized bargaining in the American polity.

The Johnson administration's efforts to engage unions had their origins in the economic policies initiated during John F. Kennedy's presidency. The Kennedy administration had pursued a strategy of "conservative" or "commercial" Keynesianism, emphasizing tax cuts and investment support, rather than increases in public spending, as the primary means to stimulate consumer demand.[63] Although the purpose of these tax cuts was to induce higher growth after the lackluster record of the late 1950s, its proponents were nevertheless quite anxious about the danger of also stimulating a rise in inflation. Therefore, the administration endorsed the use of voluntary wage and price guideposts—the core component of what would later be called an "incomes policy." Under this policy, the government approved figures that specified the appropriate rate of increase in wages and prices in order to achieve noninflationary economic growth. Business and union leaders who violated these norms, by increasing wages or prices beyond the appropriate level, would be subject to exhortation or, as it came to be known, "jawboning"—that is, political pressure from government officials to fall in line with "what was best for the country." The White House also used other measures at its disposal, such as the sale of government stockpiles, the disposition of federal contracts, and the threat of prosecution under antitrust laws, in order to convince business and labor of the virtues of "voluntary" restraint. To help implement the guidelines, the administration established the President's Advisory Committee on Labor-Management Policy, which served as a forum where both union and business leaders could discuss the mechanics of wage and price restraint with administration officials. The idea behind all these measures was that business and labor leaders could be convinced to alter their short-term behavior based on the long-term goal of economic stability, with the result being a superior balance between the employment level and price stability.

Most labor leaders were, however, deeply suspicious of guideposts, fearing that they would prove inequitable because wages could be restrained far more readily than prices. Wage increases could be easily monitored because they were codified in collective bargaining agreements, while price increases could not be checked so effectively. Many union leaders also disliked the guideposts because they contained no mechanism for ensuring that all unions sacrificed equally. The decentralized structure of American unionism, with nearly one hundred unions assembled in a weak federative structure, would make it difficult to avoid "free riders" in any agreements to hold back wage increases. Furthermore, the unspoken assumption behind the guideposts was that the prevailing distribution of income between management and labor was legitimate and fair, and should remain stable. The doubts of union leaders were, finally, exacerbated by their fears of a very negative reaction from the rank and file. As Johnson adviser Joseph Califano later observed, "Union leaders are elected by their members and the surest route to remain in office is a settlement big enough to discourage future opposition."[64]

But despite union anxieties, the liberal fiscal policies of the Johnson administration guaranteed that inflationary pressures would intensify and that policies such as wage and price guideposts would only grow in importance. The expansionary nature of the economic policy was most evident in the famous tax cut of 1964, which reduced individual income tax rates for all income levels, lowered the rate on corporate profits, and liberalized provisions for the depreciation of capital. By 1965 these tax reductions were expected to free up $14 billion, or nearly 2 percent of the GNP.[65] All these uncollected dollars would remain in the private sector, allowing both consumers and investors to spend more for the purchase of goods and services. The result would be higher economic growth, but always with the risk that excessive demand might unleash an inflationary wage-price spiral. With this in mind, the Johnson administration renewed its support for voluntary wage and price restraint.

Even as many labor leaders began to take the guideposts into account in their collective bargaining strategy, the official union position denied that such measures were necessary. As early as May 1964, the AFL-CIO questioned the entire rationale for guideposts, noting that "despite cries of alarm from some, inflation is not today's threat. Today's threat is idle men, idle plants, and idle machines." The AFL-CIO argued that "there can be no single national wage formula in a pluralistic economy, with thousands of diverse markets and industries. There must be determination by the employer and the union as to proper wage levels."[66] In a memo to President Johnson written shortly thereafter, Council of Economic Advisers Chair Walter Heller argued that the federation's public opposition was "pretty serious business so soon after you have told them you regard the guideposts as 'sensible and fair' and 'in the public interest.'"[67] Still, Meany and other labor leaders continued their criticism, which became even more pronounced as the evidence rolled in of increasing industry profits.

Regardless of the AFL-CIO's views, economic conditions soon made the need for stronger anti-inflation measures unmistakable. By the end of 1965 the economy had reached the Kennedy-Johnson target of 4 percent unemployment, and the real growth rate had risen to 5.9 percent per year. The boom was fueled by rising private investment, by growing federal spending on the administration's Great Society programs, and, increasingly, by military spending for the war in Vietnam. Administration economists, recognizing that this was a recipe for a dangerously overheated economy, concluded that deflationary measures (including a significant tax increase) were necessary.[68] On the basis of these concerns, in January 1966 the president approved an increase in personal tax withholding and an acceleration of corporate tax payments. But these small measures were far from sufficient, and many argued that a larger tax increase was required if a growing budget deficit and inflationary pressures were to be avoided.

At this juncture, Johnson clearly faced some unpalatable choices: he could simply accept a growth in inflation, with all of the accompanying political dangers; he could deflate the economy through budget cuts or new taxes; or he could intensify the use of "moral suasion" to convince business and labor to restrain themselves. All these options had their drawbacks. Continued inflation was, of course, likely to generate much public dissatisfaction. Yet a reduction in public spending was anathema to the liberal wing of the Democratic Party, to organized labor, and to Johnson himself. The AFL-CIO was one of the most vocal constituencies opposing the path of budgetary retrenchment. Joseph Califano, Johnson's special assistant for domestic affairs, describes the desire of the AFL-CIO leadership to avoid cuts in either domestic or military spending: "Andy Biemiller, organized labor's top lobbyist, sat in my office for an hour on December 25, 1965, delivering a stern message from the AFL-CIO president George Meany, who believed 'that the Great Society programs must not be gutted because of the war in Vietnam.' It wasn't that the labor movement questioned the President on the war; like LBJ himself; it wanted both to fight the communists in Southeast Asia and to fund an era of social progress."[69]

As Califano's comments imply, the growing unpopularity of the Vietnam War made the support of organized labor indispensable and guaranteed that the economic views of union leaders would be given even greater consideration. George Meany was a staunch supporter of the president's course of action in Vietnam, as were most other national union leaders. The union leadership's aggressive anticommunism stemmed from several sources: the personal experience of unionists who had fought against communists within the labor movement, the Catholic and Eastern European heritage of many of these leaders, and the patriotic (and sometimes highly nationalistic) strands of American working-class culture. Because of their anticommunist orientation, the AFL-CIO and many national unions actively cooperated with the State Department, the Central Intelligence Agency, and other agencies of the federal government charged with carrying out foreign policy. This collaboration reflected the ideological predilections of union leaders, but it also reinforced their organizational status by providing them with privileged access to policymakers as well as with government monies to use for internal patronage. In a time of decreasing public enthusiasm for the war, such loyalty on the part of the union leadership was crucial to President Johnson. Califano has observed that organized labor was "the most powerful soldier who remained with [Johnson] in the trenches, fighting both the war on poverty and the one in Southeast Asia."[70] But in making a commitment to retain union support, Johnson would find it even more difficult to make hard economic choices. Any domestic spending cutbacks that might slow inflation would also alienate one of the last groups in the liberal coalition that was still unreservedly behind the president's domestic and foreign policies.

A tax increase was the other logical alternative, but it also posed major political hazards. Here, too, Johnson would encounter opposition from union leaders, who viewed tax increases as deflationary measures that would reverse the considerable economic gains union members had only recently achieved. Moreover, a tax increase was unattractive because it would present the conservative coalition in Congress, revitalized after Democratic losses in the 1966 elections, with an ideal opportunity to launch new attacks on Johnson's treasured Great Society programs. Simultaneously, a call for increased taxes would give congressional opponents of the Vietnam War an opportunity to demand cuts in military spending. And, after all the ensuing controversy, it was entirely possible that Congress would ultimately choose to vote down such a politically unpopular request. Given these considerations, Johnson chose the safer course of avoiding any call for a significant tax increase for as long as possible. Instead, he endorsed a series of piecemeal tax and expenditure changes; but they were insufficient to offset the inflationary pressures.

Caught in this unenviable situation, the administration turned again to voluntary wage and price restraint as the means for cutting through the Gordian knot. Over the course of 1966 and 1967, Johnson and his advisors aggressively tried to influence wage and price developments in such pattern-setting industries as auto, steel, aluminum, and copper. Administration officials also sought to guide outcomes in less visible union settlements in other sectors of the economy (ranging from the cigarette industry to newspapers and construction). Though the results were mixed, there were sufficient victories for administration officials to claim that they had kept wages and prices in the most important settlements lower, thereby effectively moderating the aggregate rate of inflation.[71] Joseph Califano has commented that "it almost seemed as if LBJ could hold down prices and wages by the force of his presence and personality."[72]

The efforts at wage restraint were most successful, economist Arnold Weber later observed, when "union leaders were personally swayed by presidential blandishments or saw broader social goals in such cooperation."[73] Califano describes such factors at work in the relationship between President Johnson and I. W. Abel, president of the Steelworkers:

> the President privately called Abel over to his office. He said that, like the labor leader, he had run in tough elections and had made many promises during his campaigns. While the President understood that Abel had to go as far as possible in fulfilling the promises he had made to the steelworkers, the national interest must come first. Johnson said that if Abel put the national interest first here the President would put Abel's interests first when he had an opportunity to do so.[74]

The logic of exchange behind the wage guideposts was thus revealed. Although the precise terms of compromise were rarely explicit, union leaders were willing to moderate their use of economic power, but only when state policymakers in return provided benefits—ranging from executive branch appointments to regulatory implementation and contract procurement—that were under their control. In this sense, the guideposts partially resembled the centralized, high-trust exchange typical of neo-corporatist incomes policies in Western Europe, in which the leaders of well-disciplined labor federations would meet with their business counterparts and representatives of the state to hammer out comprehensive agreements on wage, prices, and public policy.[75]

But despite their attractions, the wage-price guideposts would not be politically or economically viable for more than a few years. Even by mid-1966, the temptation of high-wage settlements presented by increased corporate profits and tight labor markets became overwhelming for union leaders. Soon the administration found itself unable to secure union compliance. The deterioration was signaled by a contract achieved by the Machinists with the airlines industry. After a lengthy and bitter strike, the July 1966 final settlement called for a 4.9 percent annual increase in wages—well above the official guidepost figure of 3.2 percent. Economist Herbert Stein recalls the effect of this highly visible defeat: "A moment arrived in 1966 when the International Association of Machinists found themselves in confrontation with the President, tested his power, and found that nothing happened to them if they defied his wishes. After that the incomes policy was entirely ineffective as far as wages were concerned."[76]

Thus, it was clear that President Johnson was not willing to pay the political costs involved in applying greater pressure on union leaders for compliance. According to Califano, "Johnson's populist instincts tilted him toward the workingman's side, and Democratic party politics rendered unappetizing bare-knuckled scraps over wages with organized labor."[77] From late 1966 onward, the guideposts were increasingly ignored and the unions achieved ever-higher settlements. White House economists considered putting forth a new, somewhat higher wage guidepost but abandoned the idea, largely because it seemed likely that any new efforts at wage or price restraint would only generate yet more opposition from labor and business.[78] Thus, the guideposts were dead and the administration's anti-inflation strategy was left in disarray, with severe long-run consequences for price stability.

Labor's role in this pitiable outcome clearly revealed the institutional limits on the capacity of union leaders to sustain the kind of bargaining necessary for a functional incomes policy. George Meany's ability to serve as a partner in economic policymaking was severely restricted. Notwithstanding his consolidation of considerable organizational power within the AFL-CIO, Meany lacked any formal authority over the collective bargaining settlements of the national unions. What influence he did possess was entirely indirect, and of questionable effectiveness. The failure of the guideposts also made apparent the constraints on the leaders of the individual national unions. Even when they were attracted to the access and legitimacy derived from their new role in economic management, they still had to consider the threat of a rebellion from below by members unwilling to sacrifice. In the final analysis, the unions were large and centralized enough to make a credible stab at wage restraint, but insufficiently centralized to maintain such restraint when under pressure.[79] At the same time, the administration's inability to deliver Taft-Hartley repeal and its increasing weakness in Congress after the 1966 elections made its own reliability as a bargaining partner suspect.

The failure of this effort had a major impact on the course of economic policy. First, the administration's late and unsteady efforts let the inflation genie out of the bottle, creating a major policy problem for many years to come. Second, since the guidelines had failed, and since full-fledged government wage and price controls were considered far too drastic, Johnson was left with little choice but to endorse a tax increase in mid-1967. It was not until June 1968, however, that Congress approved a 10 percent tax surcharge (estimated to bring in an extra $10 billion). To Johnson's dismay, Congress also approved $6 billion in cuts from future appropriations and current spending—nearly $2 billion more than the administration had originally sought. Southern Democrats, including House Ways and Means Chair Wilbur Mills, had aligned once again with conservative Republican to extract a larger reduction in spending.[80] Thus, much as Johnson had feared, the request for a tax increase had provided the conservative coalition in Congress with an ideal opportunity to undermine the program of a liberal Democratic president.

In retrospect, the unions played a major role in hindering or blocking those governmental policies that might have brought inflation under control more easily. The labor movement opposed cutbacks in domestic *and* military spending, opposed significant increases in taxes, and ultimately prevented the implementation of a rigorous and enforceable incomes policy. In a memo to President Johnson, CEA Chair Gardner Ackley described the policymaking dilemmas presented by this experience: "Every free industrialized country which tries to maintain full employment faces this problem: strong unions have the power to push wages up faster than productivity and thereby to inflate costs and prices; and semi-monopolistic industries have the power to push up prices even if costs are stable. No country has really solved it. Sooner or later we will have to come to grips with it."[81] The most corporatist countries in Western Europe would soon come to grips with this problem through the construction of more elaborate forms of centralized wage and price determination during the 1970s. But, as the Johnson administration discovered, the institutional prerequisites for an effective, stable, and centralized incomes policy were lacking in the American political and economic environment.

The Politics of Access and the Meany/Reuther Dispute

While we see in economic policymaking the impediments caused by fragmented power structures, other episodes in national politics show the extent to which centralized bargaining nevertheless did take place in the Washington community. The full costs and benefits of such centralization would be on display in the relationship between George Meany and President Johnson, which developed a symbiotic aspect: each leader tried to assist the other as they tried to consolidate control over their respective political environments. The utility of George Meany's support for the advancement of Johnson's political aims—whether in social reform, economic policy, or foreign policy—meant that Johnson had a distinct interest in helping Meany maintain his position relative to rivals within the labor movement. Likewise, Johnson's pro-labor stance and willingness to grant Meany privileged access to the executive branch gave Meany further reason to support Johnson against his congressional and party rivals. For those on the outside the charmed circle, though, these arrangements would prove less attractive.

One factor that would regularly impinge on Johnson's relationship with organized labor was the long-standing rivalry between Meany and Walter Reuther, which had deep historical and sociological origins but was also exacerbated by the very different personalities of these two men. Johnson's handling of this dispute was crucial in determining the character of the relationship between the AFL-CIO and the administration. The roots of the conflict lay in the historic split between the AFL and CIO, itself a product of competing models of union organization and alternative views of the purposes of union political activity. Although some of the antagonism between the craft and industrial models of union organization had declined with the merger of the AFL and CIO in 1955, jurisdictional clashes continued between the building trades and their industrial union rivals. Since one of the main functions of the AFL-CIO was to mediate such disputes, the distribution of power within the federation could have a direct effect on the growth and viability of individual unions. Thus the splits within the AFL-CIO between the remaining craft-oriented unions and their industrial and public-employee rivals were wholly predictable.

Furthermore, the union factions differed over political program and strategy, despite their general agreement to work within the Democratic Party. Reuther and his few allies among the national labor leaders stressed the vital importance of a broad program of social reform based on alliances with other groups in the liberal coalition (such as the civil rights movement and progressive intellectuals). Reuther articulated with a Calvinist intensity a social democratic vision of the labor movement as the central vehicle for change in society, acting in the interests of the poor and unemployed as well as directly for the union membership. He argued that it was the role of labor to organize new "crusades"—as seen, for example, in UAW funding of the aptly named "Citizens' Crusade Against Poverty" and in support for various grassroots organizing campaigns among the urban poor. This vision also entailed an obligation to organize new workers into unions and to maintain at least rudimentary norms of internal union democracy. It mandated that union leaders live in relative frugality, spurning the huge salaries and luxurious expense accounts that could isolate them from the concerns of ordinary workers.

While Meany did not oppose in principle the notion of a broad role for the labor movement, he distrusted any commitments that associated labor with a "radical" program of social change or that threatened to undermine the insider, broker-oriented approach to political bargaining at which he excelled. Meany's own background was in the building trades (he was a second-generation member of the Plumbers Union), and this part of the labor movement remained a crucial source of his support within the Executive Council. Because of their exclusionary control of local labor markets, the conservative building trades unions often had minimal interest in organizing new workers. Likewise, they saw little value in the ambitious crusades for social reform and expanded federal action that so clearly animated Reuther. Instead, the construction unions concentrated their political activity at the local level, where they specialized in making deals with the leaders of urban machines who provided job patronage and backed the large construction projects that provided union members with well-paid employment. George Meany, as a product of this milieu, was far more comfortable with inside dealing and bargaining at the elite level than he was with mass mobilizations of the poor or racial minorities. In his view, the latter groups did indeed deserve their share, but only when they had gone through the proper channels of a boss-oriented political system. A leader such as Martin Luther King, Jr., was acceptable only insofar as he operated within the confines of traditional interest group politics. Mass mobilizations for civil rights, in contrast, were dangerous, unpredictable, and potentially counterproductive. It was precisely these considerations that led Meany to refuse to endorse the 1963 March on Washington for Civil Rights, to which Reuther gave his enthusiastic political and financial backing.

The friction between Reuther and Meany was also heightened by the inevitable rivalry between the two men for the top leadership position within the federation. Convinced that Reuther hoped to displace him as AFL-CIO president, Meany was determined to isolate and marginalize Reuther within the Executive Council. This was one reason for his vehemence in insisting to Presidents Kennedy and Johnson that he remain the primary conduit for communications between the labor movement and the White House. A "sensitivity to protocol," as one Meany biographer described it, was crucial to Meany's maintenance of internal power, and it played a large part in his assessment of presidential behavior.[82] As Nelson Lichtenstein has observed, Meany's dislike of Reuther was partly driven by his resentment of the latter's "fame and his independent access to so many politicians, diplomats, and leaders of the international labor movement."[83]

Given these concerns, Meany insisted that Johnson respect his demands about following set procedures for access, and Johnson was generally happy to do so. Meany later recalled that President Johnson "did all his business through the proper channels. In other words, if he had something of a general nature, he would call me; and if he had something that affected one union, he would call the head of that union."[84] Johnson told his biographer Doris Kearns that he realized that Meany "liked the visible signs of consultation, the formal appointments to commissions and boards and delegations, the invitations to White House functions, the pictures of the two of us together."[85] Johnson almost always accepted Meany's recommendations for appointments to government offices, spurning the suggestions of Reuther and other Meany rivals.[86] Johnson also made himself available to meet with Meany on a regular basis and consulted with the union leader about the major policy issues of concern to the AFL-CIO. As their relationship developed, the status of Walter Reuther and all other national union presidents would remain subordinate. Although Johnson remained on good terms with Reuther during most of his administration, there was never any doubt that Meany—comfortably ensconced at the AFL-CIO headquarters just a block from the White House—had the closer relationship with the president.

One reason for the ease of that relationship was the basic similarity between the two leader's notions of appropriate political leadership. Kearns's description of Johnson's approach to the Senate while majority leader characterizes equally well Meany's own approach to the AFL-CIO Executive Council:

> the possibilities of his leadership were confined by the same traits, experiences, and values that made his mediation so successful: his insistence on face-to-face relations, his secrecy, and his pragmatism. As a result of his preference for private negotiations and his penchant, even need, for concealment, he virtually abolished debate in an institution where debate, although frequently frivolous and often ignored, had also served to publicly expose problems and warn of errors.[87]

For both Johnson and Meany, however, this leadership style would ultimately prove self-destructive, as each proved incapable of adjusting his policies to reflect a fluid, rapidly changing environment.

Within the union movement, these problems became increasingly evident during the late 1960s. By 1966 Walter Reuther was publicly criticizing the means by which Meany had dominated the federation and achieved control over its political strategy. In Reuther's view, the concentration of bargaining capacity into Meany's hands had become exclusionary and undemocratic. He complained that Meany had undermined the institutional procedures for collective decision making that had been agreed on during the 1955 merger, replacing them with closed processes that misrepresented or ignored the views of Reuther and other dissident union leaders. Rather than reaching a consensus through deliberation in regularly scheduled meetings, Meany relied on backroom deals among key supporters—deals that increasingly excluded Reuther from the AFL-CIO's decision-making process. Reuther argued that these limits on internal debate had allowed Meany to shift the federation in a more conservative direction and to avoid the internal criticism that was necessary for the labor movement to retain its vitality and organizational efficiency.

Reuther's complaints about the violation of internal procedural norms were only deepened by his growing dissatisfaction with the substantive policies endorsed by Meany. The UAW leader claimed that Meany had squandered the opportunities for greater economic and political power presented by the unification of the AFL and CIO in 1955. Rather than overseeing an aggressive, federation-sponsored campaign to organize the unorganized, Meany had allowed organizing efforts to languish. Moreover, Reuther charged that Meany had, through rash and imprudent public statements, alienated many of the labor movement's natural allies among the young, intellectuals and academics, and racial minorities. Finally, the AFL-CIO's uncompromising support of the Vietnam War and of rigidly anticommunist cold war policies became less acceptable to Reuther, who grew more skeptical of the war and who also faced angry antiwar sentiment within the UAW.

As it became clear that Meany's position in the AFL-CIO was so well protected as to be virtually impregnable, Reuther began a prolonged process of disengagement from the federation. In February 1967 he resigned from the AFL-CIO Executive Council, and the UAW officially withdrew from the AFL-CIO in July 1968. As he left the federation, Reuther attacked the AFL-CIO leadership for becoming "an extension of the business community" and for abjectly accepting the status quo in American politics and society.[88] Although Meany clearly benefited from Reuther's exit—reinforcing as it did his dominance within the AFL-CIO—the UAW's departure was not without costs, including the loss of the union's large per capita fee payments to the national headquarters. More crucially, the departure foreshadowed the kinds of internal conflicts to which Meany's autocratic style of internal governance and his capricious control over the labor movement's political strategy would increasingly give rise.

For the time being, though, the efforts of both Meany and Johnson to please the rest of the labor leadership were successful, resulting in an exceptionally high level of union support for the president's reelection campaign. This support was all the more crucial as Johnson's political situation had grown even more precarious. The expansion of federal spending, new regulatory efforts, and the rise of inflation had alienated segments of the business community, and the administration's commitments on civil rights had undermined support among white southerners.[89] More important, the pursuit of the war in Vietnam generated virulent criticism—on radically different grounds—from both "hawks" and "doves," weakening the president's credibility as a competent and effective leader. Facing such adverse circumstances, union leaders did all they could to help Johnson avoid political embarrassment and retain the support of the liberal community and other elements within the Democratic Party. Both the UAW and AFL-CIO representatives in the liberal Americans for Democratic Action (ADA) opposed the organization's February 1968 decision to endorse Senator Eugene McCarthy's campaign for the party nomination. At Johnson's urging, the presidents of the Steelworkers, Communication Workers, and the International Ladies' Garment Workers Union all resigned from the ADA in protest (Walter Reuther, despite his support for Johnson, chose to remain within the organization, which he had helped found in the 1950s).

Union leaders also sought to maintain labor support for the president in the face of growing discontent among the secondary leadership and rank and file. In a memo to Johnson, presidential aide Marvin Watson recounted a meeting Meany had held with union political directors: "Meany read the riot act to the labor officials, saying those who attacked the president today will have it come back in their face in November. Meany also urged the labor officials to talk to the dissident Democrats . . . and tell them to either run with the president or that labor will find primary opposition to them."[90] Political operatives from the AFL-CIO Committee on Political Education, the Steelworkers, and other national unions were deployed in New Hampshire to work on the president's campaign.

Ultimately, most union leaders saw little to be gained in a defection to the candidacies of Robert Kennedy or Eugene McCarthy as long as Johnson, or his chosen successor, remained in the race. Their attitude to some extent reflected the distrust that Meany and other hawkish union leaders felt for any presidential candidate who actively opposed the Vietnam War; but more crucial was their determination to prevent the White House from being occupied by a president hostile to the labor movement. For the union leadership it seemed likely that the attacks on Johnson would primarily benefit the Republicans in their efforts to gain back the presidency. Such an outcome was to be avoided at all costs, for the immediate interests of the labor movement were deeply affected by executive branch decisions. The Vietnam War, even for those labor leaders who had doubts about its wisdom, simply was not important enough to justify the risks involved in defecting from the Johnson wing of the party—especially when rank-and-file support for the war still remained relatively strong. When Johnson finally did withdraw, most union leaders quickly moved behind the candidacy of Vice President Hubert Humphrey, for many of the same reasons that had led them to support the president. That intervention would, however, have an unintended consequence: it would deeply alienate other factions within the Democratic Party, including the newly insurgent forces of youths, minorities, women, and the opponents of the Vietnam War. The divisions unleashed would soon come to haunt the unions, as they contributed to institutional reforms that would make it more difficult, at least in the short term, to maintain labor's special role in presidential and congressional politics.

In important ways, the relationship between the unions and the Democrats in the mid-1960s approximated the model of centralized pluralism, with bargaining capacity relatively concentrated in both the labor movement and the political system. One result was that the relationship between the top labor leadership, especially George Meany, and the Johnson White House was both cooperative and productive: cooperative in the sense that common legislative and political goals were identified, and appropriate strategies and tactics coordinated; productive in the sense that many of these common goals were actually achieved, to the benefit of both the labor movement and the Democratic administration. When the unions and the administration could work together to overcome the fragmentation of power inherent in the separated institutions of the American constitutional structure, major legislative accomplishments ensued. And when unions possessed the institutional wherewithal to effectively coordinate wage demands, they also found themselves in a better position to secure privileged access and favorable policies from the executive branch.

Yet the limits on cooperation were also profound, in large part reflecting the extent to which centralized pluralism in the American context was always a pallid affair. The institutional fragmentation of power continued to stand in the way of labor advancement. Indeed, many of labor's most notable failures, especially the defeat on labor law reform, were rooted in adverse political alignments (the conservative coalition) whose effects were magnified by antimajoritarian political rules (such as the Senate filibuster). Likewise, a relatively decentralized structure for collective bargaining undermined efforts at union wage restraint, leaving unions open to the criticism that they were irresponsible and selfish in the face of rising inflation. Together, these multiple failures ensured that neither labor nor the party would be well prepared to confront the crises—both economic and political—that would grip the political system in the decade ahead.

4 *Crises of Representation, 1968–1976*

President Johnson—ever the master strategist of Washington politics—once proclaimed during a meeting with a key aide that there were only "30 key people in the entire Goddamn government—just 30 key people."[1] His focus on a small number of elite bargainers in the Washington community was a reflection of the partial centralization of bargaining capacity in the national political system achieved during the mid-1960s. But how capable were these "30 key people" of providing satisfactory representation for an increasingly mobilized and diverse community of political actors?

The course of events soon made the answer clear: not very capable at all. The mode of representation characteristic of national politics during the mid-1960s would fail, in spectacular fashion, when confronted with the need to incorporate quickly and flexibly the various new interests that emerged by the end of the decade. Within Congress, the presidential nominating process, and the labor movement itself, a concentration of power among a small number of actors hampered the speedy inclusion of new political forces. Much as the model of centralized pluralism would predict, this stimulated a series of interrelated crises of representation in which excluded actors mobilized to change the rules of the game. Such changes included a set of procedural reforms that distributed bargaining capacity among a much larger number of political actors than had been the case previously. They took effect not only in Congress and the Democratic Party but in the labor movement as well, where a series of internal conflicts reduced the power of the federation and dispersed bargaining capacity to individual national union leaders.

The crises of representation within American political institutions and the labor movement were neither entirely disconnected nor reflective of a single "global" crisis of the political system or society as a whole. Rather, they were responses to distinct norms, rules, and procedures within particular institutions that were triggered by the same phenomena: the rise of a set of constituencies that challenged the legitimacy of, as political scientist James Ceaser has put it, "those aspects of our political institutions that involved quiet group accommodations within traditional representative processes."[2] Arthur Schlesinger, Jr., perhaps captured the essence of the situation when he observed: "The Old Politics of the mediating institutions is now giving way to the New Politics of instantaneous mass participation."[3] The brokered politics of the post–New Deal era, which relied on large hierarchical organizations bargaining on behalf of relatively docile constituencies, proved to be remarkably unstable in the face of demands for greater participation.

The most important link among the diverse constituencies seeking to reform American institutions was their common opposition to the Vietnam War, which was viewed as the all-too-typical end result of undemocratic decision making by isolated elites. The unrepresentative consequences of this system became increasingly evident to antiwar activists as they encountered procedural obstacles within institutions, such as Congress and the party system, that were intended to channel societal demands to national policymakers. In response, the antiwar movement endorsed political reforms intended to "open up" national political institutions. These demands came to overlap with pressures for change arising from other sources. The goals of emerging activist groups concerned with women's liberation, racial empowerment, the rights of the young, environmentalism, and gay rights all fit well with the agenda of reformist liberals seeking to transform the rules of the political game. The resulting wave of reform diffused power both in national politics and within the labor movement, with lasting consequences for the nature of union political involvement.

The Origins of Crisis in the Presidential Nominating Process

The most important and visible of the crises of representation during the late 1960s and early 1970s occurred within the presidential nominating process of the Democratic Party. Its magnitude was displayed physically in the violence in the streets of Chicago in 1968 and procedurally in a set of major changes in party rules. These changes disrupted and eventually undermined the power broker role that union leaders had developed in the postwar period. The post-1968 reforms also shifted power away from the AFL-CIO leadership and its more conservative building trades allies, and toward the more liberal and activist unions that maintained the political machinery needed to take advantage of the new rules of the presidential nominating system. Thus changes in institutions external to the labor movement effectively empowered some unions while weakening others, thereby altering the nature of labor's overall impact within the American political system.

To understand the origins and consequences of the crisis in the presidential nominating process, we should begin by examining the role of labor in the nomination of John F. Kennedy in 1960—the last truly competitive nominating contest prior to the blowup at the 1968 convention. Despite a large number of attractive candidates, union leaders reached an early consensus that Senator Kennedy was the best candidate: that is, both friendly to labor and capable of winning the general election. Though Senator Hubert Humphrey, with his staunch brand of traditional liberalism, retained the support of a large segment of the labor movement, many labor leaders questioned his capacity to win in the general election. AFL-CIO President George Meany later observed: "By the time 1960 rolled around, I could say quite safely that [Kennedy] was practically the unanimous choice of our people. . . . I would say that he had tremendous support in the labor movement."[4] Meany himself remained neutral until the eve of the convention, but the leaders of several of the national unions were quite active (if still officially "neutral") in assisting the Kennedy campaign in several important primaries and in the ongoing process of rounding up support within each state delegation.

The involvement of David McDonald, president of the United Steelworkers of America, in promoting Kennedy's candidacy is particularly instructive. McDonald was approached in October 1959 by Joseph Kennedy, who sought the union leader's support for his son's campaign. As McDonald described the process, "Ambassador Joe asked me if I would work in behalf of Jack so that he would get the nomination for the presidency of the United States. I said I would. I said, 'I will have to do this my own way. If it's all right with you, Mr. Ambassador, I would like to do it quietly and under cover.' So I began to work immediately, under cover, to develop in the steelworkers and other AFL-CIO unions, political action groups, behind his campaign for the nomination and the presidency."[5] Although McDonald did ask Steelworker locals to mobilize the membership on behalf of Kennedy in the crucial primaries in Wisconsin and West Virginia, much of his energy was focused on placing what he called "heavy pressure" on the leaders of uncommitted state delegations (such as Pennsylvania Governor David Lawrence and Governor Robert Meyner of New Jersey). In his memoirs, McDonald emphasizes the almost clandestine nature of his involvement in the campaign: "I made no political speeches because it would have been the end of Kennedy to put a tag on him as a labor candidate at that juncture."[6] Deeply aware that highly visible union support was as likely to hurt Kennedy as to help him, McDonald concentrated on mobilizing support within the union's own membership and among other party elites.

At the Los Angeles convention, McDonald continued this elite-oriented approach: "I chivvied and bullied and pleaded and traded and threatened and maneuvered on the convention floor to get him votes. While Bobby [Kennedy] was riding herd on the delegate strength he had painfully put together, I delivered the hundred Steelworker votes, prodded the Pennsylvania delegation (headed by a Catholic who thought a Catholic couldn't win) into voting as a bloc for Kennedy, and perhaps convinced a scattering of others from the depths of my own conviction."[7] McDonald also maintained an operating office at the Biltmore Hotel, from which he could supervise a network of political operatives deployed on the convention floor and in the adjacent meeting rooms and hotel suites where crucial deals were often made. UAW President Walter Reuther, George Meany, and other union leaders operated in much the same fashion at the convention, covertly rallying support for Kennedy among party leaders, even while publicly denying that they were playing any role in the party's nominating process.[8] Reuther even proclaimed that "the UAW has not—nor will we—endorse a candidate for the presidential nomination of any party. This is properly the responsibility of the delegates who make up the conventions of both parties."[9]

Shielded by assertions of nonpartisanship, union leaders enjoyed a high degree of autonomy in this system, insulated both from their own membership and from other leaders in the union organization. In fact, a strong union president could endorse a candidate without undertaking any serious process of internal consultation and then could promote that candidate behind the scenes, protected by a facade of neutrality. This informal and unpublicized means of exercising influence almost never required the mobilization of the rank and file prior to the general election, nor did it draw significantly on union financial and organizational resources. The only exception was found in those few states where primaries were held; there, national unions might seek to mobilize their members to vote for the leadership's favorite candidate. In general, though, it was entirely possible for a labor leader to accomplish much for a candidate simply by bargaining with and persuading delegates and party elites prior to and at the convention itself.

The freedom of union leaders to act regardless of preferences was reinforced by these leaders' steady adherence to what Michael Rogin has usefully called the "myth of nonpartisanship."[10] Rogin argues that in the first half of the twentieth century, AFL leaders used claims of "nonpartisanship" to increase their autonomy vis-à-vis internal and external critics, and to obscure the real, and often self-serving, ties that union leaders forged with local machine politicians. In the 1960s the ritualistic denial by the AFL-CIO leadership and other union leaders of their real activities in the Democratic nominating process served an analogous function. Meany boasted, for example, that the AFL-CIO was "the only trade union movement in the world that is truly independent—politically and every other way. . . . We maintain an arm's-length arrangement with the political parties." Similarly, he declared: "The Gompers philosophy basically was that labor should not tie itself to a political party in any way at all. This is still our policy."[11] In insisting that they were not involved in the presidential nominating process—indeed, that they were not even committed to one of the two parties—union leaders obscured the extent of their actual involvement in presidential politics. One result was that they were able to shield their role in nominating politics from the intrusion of any procedures, such as polls or membership forums and discussions, that would make them directly accountable to the rank and file. Much as it had done in earlier decades, the idea of nonpartisanship "served to disguise political strategies, not to describe them."[12]

In such a system, there might be a serious disjuncture between the preferences of union leaders and those of their members. But this possibility would remain of little consequence as long as the nominating process remained free of intense conflict over crucial issues on the national agenda. By the late 1960s, however, the passions engulfing the country as a result of the Vietnam War meant that the nominating process was no longer a relatively cordial and low-key affair. It became instead the center of a maelstrom of fervid and occasionally violent conflicts over foreign and domestic policy and, more broadly, the future of the Democratic Party. As these conflicts deepened, both the party and the labor movement would become more sharply divided, and previously static and hierarchical relationships would be shattered.

These new pressures came at the very moment that the AFL-CIO leadership (as distinct from that of the national unions) emerged as the dominant power broker for organized labor in the Democratic nominating process.[13] In 1968, unlike some earlier nominating contests, the AFL-CIO leadership abandoned any pretense of neutrality—in practice, if not in rhetoric. In the months prior to Johnson's withdrawal, George Meany pledged his complete support for the president's renomination. When Johnson chose not to seek it, Meany moved quickly to encourage Vice President Humphrey, later taking credit for his candidacy: "Lane [Kirkland] and I went over to see Hubert Humphrey and got him to agree he would run."[14] Meany also issued an AFL-CIO press release: "We . . . strongly urge that Vice-President Hubert Humphrey declare himself now as a candidate for the presidency. In no other way can the American people be assured of an effective spokesman and advocate for the programs needed to continue the social and economic progress of the past eight years and to unite the American people behind the defense of freedom and democracy in the world."[15]

Although his use of "we" implied an official organizational commitment, Meany's intervention followed no formal procedures or deliberation within the federation.[16] Meany chose to endorse Humphrey, and to actively oppose the candidacies of Senators Robert Kennedy and Eugene McCarthy, well before the candidates' electability or appeal to union members had been tested in caucuses or primaries. Meany justified this intervention by reference to Humphrey's pro-labor record in the Senate and his support as vice president for President Johnson's Great Society. But Meany's opponents within the labor movement had a different explanation: they noted that both Kennedy and McCarthy potentially threatened the existing pattern of union access and involvement in national politics—a pattern that clearly benefited Meany over rival union leaders. It was conceivable, for example, that should Robert Kennedy succeed in his quest for the presidency, he would favor the exiled UAW and its leader, Walter Reuther.[17] Indeed, the senator had evinced a considerable respect for Reuther (a genuinely "tough" liberal, by Kennedy's way of thinking) since the days of congressional hearings on union corruption in the late 1950s.[18] Any alliances the UAW leader might cement with a new Democratic president were particularly troublesome to the AFL-CIO leadership because Reuther was, by July 1968, in the midst of forming an alliance with the Teamsters Union that threatened to become the prototype for a new federation to compete with the AFL-CIO. Privileged access to a new president in the White House would no doubt help such a rival federation in drawing affiliates away from the AFL-CIO.[19]

Thus organizational imperatives, ideological predilections, and genuine policy commitments conveniently overlapped, and all strongly reinforced the determination of the AFL-CIO leadership to deliver the Democratic nomination to Humphrey. Lane Kirkland, who was AFL-CIO secretary-treasurer during this period, later recalled the ensuing role of the federation: "I was involved with others in putting together a committee—a labor committee—for Hubert Humphrey. It was an informal operation, but I assure you it had the blessings of George Meany or I wouldn't have been doing it. . . . Labor was instrumental in rounding up the delegate votes to get him nominated. We didn't do that by participating in primary elections. I think Hubert only entered one or two elections. But in the non-primary states, we rounded up most of the votes."[20] In his analysis of the 1968 nominating campaign, Theodore White likewise noted that "Humphrey had entered no primaries, which he later regretted; but the AFL-CIO structures had delivered to him almost all of Pennsylvania, Maryland, Michigan, and Ohio."[21] In this sense, the AFL-CIO clearly acted in the old power broker role: elite networks and traditional party contacts were tapped in order to help pull together a delegate majority in favor of Humphrey. Any preferences for Kennedy or McCarthy that might have existed among the membership had no impact whatsoever on the activities of the AFL-CIO and of most national union leaders concerned with the presidential nomination process.[22]

One of the few unions that operated differently in 1968 was the UAW, where the union's long-standing democratic traditions made it impossible to project an image of total unity behind either Johnson or Humphrey. The leadership of the union was deeply split over the Vietnam War and the related question of whom to support for the Democratic nomination. Even before Johnson withdrew from the race, important leaders within the union had endorsed Robert Kennedy and were actively working on his behalf in primary states and among state delegations. After the president's withdrawal, Reuther chose to maintain a studied neutrality, deeply torn between long-standing allegiances to both the vice president and to Senator

Kennedy.[23] Meanwhile, the rest of the UAW leadership divided in their support, with Paul Schrade, West Coast regional director, playing a crucial role in the Kennedy campaign in California. After Kennedy's June 5 assassination (during which Schrade himself was grazed in the head by a stray bullet), most UAW leaders accepted the need to support Humphrey, but with little enthusiasm.

While the UAW was rendered less effective by its own internal divisions, Meany positioned the federation, as an organization separate and distinct from the affiliated national unions, as the principal representative of organized labor in the nomination contest. David Broder observed that "never before has the national labor federation become so openly involved at so early a stage in the fight for the Democratic presidential nomination."[24] The enhanced status of AFL-CIO was particularly evident at the Democratic convention itself. The *Wall Street Journal* concluded: "Mr. Humphrey has no more important ally at this convention than labor. With his Southern supporters showing signs of restiveness over Humphrey-backed rule changes, Northern liberals expressing uncertainty over his 'electability' because of Vietnam, and political powerhouse Mayor Richard Daley of Chicago still fence-sitting, the unions are the Vice President's bedrock of support."[25] While the AFL-CIO had only about 200 delegates out of a total of 3,084, it claimed to influence three times as many, including numerous state and local officeholders who were indebted to labor for campaign support. Spread among forty-four delegations, the labor delegates provided useful intelligence to AFL-CIO Committee on Political Education (COPE) Director Alexander Barkan, who coordinated and directed the activities of these delegates and other union leaders in order to promote Humphrey's candidacy.

In the general election, the federation further expanded its activities, attempting to take up the slack left by Humphrey's poorly run campaign, the deterioration of most of the big-city machines, and the near collapse of the national Democratic Party structure.[26] By all accounts, the AFL-CIO went to extraordinary lengths to assist Humphrey's campaign—indeed, in some respects, it became the campaign. Lane Kirkland, Meany's executive assistant at this time, was blunt: "We had to do what we did because the party was bankrupt intellectually and financially. I reached the point where I said I'd never go into Democratic headquarters. I'd go in feeling good and come out feeling terrible. The only useful thing they did was television, in the last couple of weeks, and beyond that they didn't do a goddamned thing except cry."[27] White enumerated the details of the AFL-CIO's help:

> The dimension of the AFL-CIO effort, unprecedented in American history, can be caught only by its final summary figures: the ultimate registration, by labor's efforts, of 4.6 million voters; the printing and distribution of 55 million pamphlets and leaflets out of Washington and 60 million more from local unions; telephone banks in 638 localities, using 8,055 telephones, manned

by 24,611 union men and women and their families; some 72,225 house-to-house canvassers; and, on election day, 94,457 volunteer serving as car-poolers, materials-distributors, baby-sitters, poll-watchers, telephoners.[28]

Although AFL-CIO leaders were obviously disappointed when Richard Nixon achieved a narrow victory over Vice President Humphrey, they deemed their own involvement in presidential politics a quite impressive success. It was, however, precisely the nature of that success that would generate a counterattack from the very forces who had been vanquished at the Democratic National Convention. Humphrey's nomination had been attained the "old-fashioned way"—through the traditional methods of political brokerage. He had not entered a single primary. In contrast, Kennedy and McCarthy, who had prevailed in several primaries, appeared to have been directly endorsed by rank-and-file Democrats. Thus, from the perspective of many of Humphrey's opponents, the nomination was basically illegitimate and unrepresentative of the true preferences of Democratic voters.

The perception of unfairness was reinforced by an unsavory record of procedural irregularities in the process of delegate selection. In some states the winner of the primary did not receive the majority of the state's delegates, who were still chosen by regular party leaders. In Pennsylvania, for example, McCarthy was the only candidate on the primary ballot, and he received 428,259 votes; Hubert Humphrey gained only 73,263 write-in votes. Nevertheless, under the state's system of delegate selection, McCarthy was allotted 25 delegates, while Humphrey received 130. In other states the selection of delegates had taken place years in advance, and it therefore was impossible to choose delegates on the basis of their position on the Vietnam War. Such procedures contributed to the belief that the nominating system had been rigged. At a time of fierce conflict, these serious doubts about the fairness of the process generated a crisis of representation: those groups that felt excluded now banded together to demand serious consideration of the reform agenda. It was in this context that dissident elements were finally able to secure agreement to establish a reform commission that would evaluate party rules and determine the appropriate changes.

Party Reform and the Growth of Labor Disunity

As an immense academic literature has shown, the series of reforms approved by the Democratic Party's Commission on Party Structure and Delegate Selection, later known as the McGovern-Fraser Commission, transformed the dynamics of political bargaining.[29] First, the commission voted to require affirmative action for blacks, women, and young people—groups that had been underrepresented among delegates at previous conventions. Second, and more important, the commission specified that starting in 1972, delegates would have to be selected either through primary elections—used in only sixteen states in 1968—or in caucuses or conventions open to all party members. In response to the commission's new guidelines, most states chose to employ primaries. The commission thus succeeded to a greater degree than most had expected in forcing a major change in the nominating system.

The old nominating system, in which state party leaders were able to choose as delegates loyal party servants under their control, was now no longer viable. Under the new rules, delegates would be pledged to candidates much earlier in the process, and as a result of the decisions of large bodies of Democratic voters. Labor leaders could thus no longer sustain their traditional role as power brokers, bargaining with a discrete set of elite actors. If they hoped to exercise influence within the reformed system, they would have to ensure that their members actually participated in crucial primaries or caucuses. While the deployment of union financial and organizational resources could still be helpful, candidates in the new system had a more fundamental need—the support of groups that could bring out their members to vote in a predictable fashion. Should the union membership be significantly divided or even opposed to the leadership's choice, their wishes would now have political consequences: the members could vote for a different candidate in primaries or caucuses. Moreover, candidates could, if they so chose, appeal directly to union members in their capacity as primary voters, thus bypassing those union leaders who would otherwise have presented themselves as brokers for the union's electoral and organizational resources.

These features of the new system suggest why the AFL-CIO quickly became strongly opposed to the reform process. The AFL-CIO's (or more precisely, President George Meany's) satisfaction with how the federation had functioned in 1968 gave the leadership little incentive to endorse a process that would threaten that brokering role. As far as Meany and COPE Director Barkan were concerned, the old system had done a fine job of selecting electable and competent presidential nominees; there was no need to change it. It is hardly surprising, therefore, that federation officials sought to undermine the McGovern-Fraser Commission's initiatives. Their first strategy was to urge I. W. Abel, president of the Steelworkers, who had been appointed as a union representative on the commission, to boycott the commission's meetings. They argued that the commission was far too biased in favor of reform to give Abel's opposition much credence and that his presence would only further legitimate the commission's proposals. The AFL-CIO believed that the reforms could instead be stopped at a later stage, either in the Democratic National Committee or at the state level. This tactic backfired, however, when the commission's proposals were quickly approved by the national party and state legislatures. In this early encounter with the forces of the so-called New Politics, Meany and Barkan had demonstrated an ineptitude that would mark much of their interaction with the Democratic Party during the 1970s.

Despite the views of the AFL-CIO establishment, several important unions actually supported the reform efforts. William Dodds, the UAW's political director, served on the McGovern-Fraser Commission, and local UAW members testified in favor of reform at commission hearings around the country. The UAW also provided important funding for the commission at a time when it was threatened with a considerable budgetary shortfall.[30] Several unions still affiliated with the AFL-CIO also supported reform, including the Communications Workers of America (CWA), the International Association of Machinists (IAM), and the American Federation of State, County, and Municipal Employees (AFSCME). As Stephen Schlesinger notes, these unions "sent their officials to testify in favor of the guidelines at the McGovern Commission hearings; they proselytized for the changes at union meetings; they alerted their local chapters to the delegate elections; and they applied heavy pressure on state parties to comply with the commission's recommendations."[31]

The degree of union support for party reform seems anomalous to those who view the campaign for party reform as little more than an effort by "white-collar elites" to take power away from unions and other working-class constituencies.[32] But the puzzle is resolved if we consider how the emerging political strategy of the UAW and other liberal unions differed from that of Meany and his conservative allies. The UAW and its allies supported party reform in the hopes of forging a lasting alliance with the activists who had surged into the party in the late 1960s. Walter Reuther's willingness to consider fundamental change was shared by other union leaders who had grown dissatisfied with Meany's stewardship of the federation and his management of labor's role in the Democratic Party. These leaders, mainly from unions composed of either industrial workers (CWA, IAM) or the growing ranks of service and public sector employees (AFSCME), were strongly committed to advancing policies at the national level that ranged from the protection of union organizing rights to the expansion of the welfare state. The more liberal Democratic Party that reform might bring about was likely to fulfill these national policies. The liberal unions were also led by men who possessed a broader, sometimes even social democratic, conception of the purposes of the labor movement. Because of their ideological commitments, they supported a more programmatic, policy-oriented party system—a goal that the liberal reformers also claimed as their own.

This strategy differed profoundly from that pursued by Meany and his allies in the AFL-CIO hierarchy and the building trades. The conservative bloc of craft unions sought to deepen an alliance with city machines, traditional party leaders, and sometimes even southern conservatives on behalf of the procedural status quo and the existing distribution of power within the national party. The building trades unions who formed Meany's base of support were usually more concerned with local politics than with national policy outcomes. Their favored strategy was to ally with machine politicians in the big cities who could fulfill union demands at the local level—in other words, to enter as junior partners into the locally dominant "growth coalition."[33] The success of this approach only reinforced the determination of the craft unions to oppose a party reform effort that seemed likely to strengthen its intraparty opponents, such as the New Politics insurgents, upstart minorities, and the more liberal industrial and public employee unions.

Given the thoroughly partisan commitments of the craft unions and the AFL-CIO establishment, it is all the more noteworthy that Meany still publicly defended a nonpartisan mode of political action. When Senator Edward Muskie appeared before the AFL-CIO Executive Council in March 1969, Meany disingenuously commented that Muskie "talked about some of the problems the party faces which are quite interesting but, of course, hardly our business."[34] Paul Schrade of the UAW blasted Meany's posturing: "This is strange coming from the President of the AFL-CIO who sits in his hotel room at Democratic conventions trying to dictate on candidates, platform and credentials. He also ran the heaviest-handed floor operation at the Chicago convention, which was loaded with 'heavies.' This negative attitude on party reform is very disturbing because less than 1% of the delegates to the Democratic Party Conventions are from unions. . . . That's why the charge of bossism is so valid, and why reform is so necessary."[35] For unions such as AFSCME and the UAW, Meany's repeated insistence on his noninvolvement in the party was little more than a subterfuge designed to deflect attention from his own quite substantial role in discouraging reform efforts contrary to his interests.

The complaints of the liberal unions reveal a major weakness in much of the academic commentary on party reform. For those who have opposed reform—both academics and politicians—identifying the AFL-CIO hierarchy as the representative voice of the American labor movement, and indeed of the working class as a whole, has served an ideological function. By disregarding the internal conflicts within the labor movement, and therefore the degree to which the interests of the AFL-CIO leadership depart from those of the rank and file, they can claim that the AFL-CIO was, in opposing reform, simply defending the political power of workers. Byron Shafer, for example, presents AFL-CIO COPE as the unquestioned and fully legitimate voice of the nation's labor unions: "The AFL-CIO was the numerically preponderant unit within organized labor. COPE was the official spokesman for the 16 million members of the AFL-CIO. The largest independent union for which it could not speak, the Teamsters, had been written out of reform politics from the beginning. As a result, when COPE broke with the Party Structure Commission, it created a break between organized labor and the new reform enterprise."[36] This description overlooks three important facts: The UAW (not just the Teamsters) also was no longer in the AFL-CIO, several national unions with very large memberships supported reform, and COPE is not the "official" spokesman for 16 million union members, but only the spokesman for a *federation* of union organizations. In the AFL-CIO, unlike the national unions, not a single official has been elected to office by rank-and-file union members; the degree to which COPE really represents the views of ordinary union members is certainly arguable.

The larger point is that AFL-CIO opposition did not simply reflect a struggle between the "blue collars" and the "white collars," as Shafer and others would have it. The real issue was that the preservation of the old system would have been more likely to empower one segment of the labor movement (the AFL-CIO leadership) while weakening another (liberal industrial unions). When the AFL-CIO opposed party reform, then, it was not acting simply or purely out of a regard for the effects of reform on the power of the labor movement as a whole (although, to be fair, this may have been one concern); it also had a strong institutional interest in forestalling the alternative strategy of the UAW and the more liberal unions.

Why Not McGovern?

The conflict between the two loose blocs of liberal and conservative unions climaxed during the 1972 nominating process and the ensuing debate over whether the federation should endorse a presidential candidate in the general election. When Meany succeeded in convincing the AFL-CIO Executive Council to endorse (by a vote 27 to 3) an official policy of neutrality in the race between Richard Nixon and Senator George McGovern, he precipitated independent political action by those national unions still favoring the Democratic nominee. The resulting divisions within organized labor produced a corresponding fragmentation in the labor movement's bargaining capacity in national politics.

Given its momentous consequences, Meany's motive for insisting on AFL-CIO neutrality in 1972 has caused some puzzlement, especially in the context of Richard Nixon's long-standing anti-union record (indeed, in 1968 Meany had asserted that "the election of Nixon would be a disaster for the ordinary people of this country").[37] Meany pointed to substantive aspects of McGovern's record, noting McGovern's "wrong" vote during the effort to repeal section 14(b) of the Taft-Hartley Act in 1965, his support for grain sales to the Soviets, and his opposition to the Vietnam War. Meany also castigated McGovern because he had "repeatedly denounced 'big labor,' 'labor bosses,' and 'union power brokers."[38] These justifications were not entirely convincing, however, because Nixon's labor record was clearly much worse, and as late as February 1969 Meany had publicly stated that "McGovern's record as a Senator, with very, very few exceptions, has been very favorable to the things that we are interested in."[39]

Some authors therefore relate AFL-CIO opposition to the cultural aspects of the liberal-conservative divide, drawing attention to Meany's and Barkan's lurid pronouncements about homosexuals and hippies taking over the Democratic Party. Meany issued some notorious invective. In the aftermath of the 1972 convention, he declared: "We listened for three days to the speakers who were approved to speak by the powers-that-be at that convention. We listened to the gay-lib people—you know, the people who want to legalize marriage between boys and boys and legalize marriage between girls and girls. . . . We heard from the abortionists, and we heard from the people who look like Jacks, acted like Jills, and had the odor of johns about them."[40] Thus, J. David Greenstone concludes that the AFL-CIO's nonendorsement was primarily due to cultural conflicts. He believes that the AFL-CIO "refused to endorse the Democrat because . . . its cultural ideology ascribed such great importance to differences on foreign policy, and to such cultural issues as permissiveness, the work ethic, and social and sexual deviance."[41] To be sure, McGovern was an unattractive candidate to Meany on these grounds, and many other labor leaders questioned McGovern's ideology and personal reliability. But these factors fail to fully explain the extent of Meany's opposition. The fact remained that McGovern's labor record was vastly superior to that of Nixon. Furthermore, many national unions within the federation were relatively comfortable with McGovern and quite dissatisfied with Meany's hostility toward the Democratic nominee. As sociologist William Form has recently noted, "In terms of rational choice theory, the stand of the AFL-CIO's top leaders seems inexplicable unless one assumes that they thought foreign policy more important than union goals and party influence."[42]

There is, however, another kind of "rational" explanation that we should consider: the claim that the behavior of AFL-CIO leaders grew largely, if not exclusively, out of their desire to maintain the power broker role to which they had grown accustomed, and which buttressed their organizational status. The cause of reform, now embodied in McGovern's insurgent candidacy, threatened this traditional role, and for this reason it would not be surprising if both McGovern and the reform process itself were vehemently opposed. From this perspective, the principal "irrationality" of Barkan and Meany lies only in their failure to appreciate the extent to which the conditions for power broker politics had already decayed beyond repair and to adjust to the participatory logic of the new system.

The extent to which Meany and Barkan had failed to come to grips with the magnitude of the changes in party politics became clear in the federation's misguided strategy during the 1972 nominating process. Barkan's original plan was to field slates of uncommitted delegates, composed of local union officials, in each state's primaries or caucuses. Supposedly, voters and caucus attendees would elect these uncommitted union delegates, who would then be under the influence of the AFL-CIO at the convention. The AFL-CIO would thus be able to maintain and perhaps even enhance its own role as a power broker at the convention. The problem with this approach, however, was that Democratic voters saw little reason to endorse a neutral AFL-CIO slate when they could vote directly for a slate of delegates committed to a candidate of their choice. The federation plan would have worked only if candidates had not run their own slates of delegates and had chosen instead to defer to the federation's uncommitted slate. Unsurprisingly, candidates did not regard such deference as in their own interest and, as a result, the AFL-CIO strategy was a complete flop.

It was in this context that the federation leadership came to consider whether to endorse George McGovern. Meany was adamant that the thirty-five-member Executive Council should unanimously refuse an endorsement. The pressure he applied on wavering union presidents was so intense that two members voted to support federation neutrality even though they subsequently approved their own unions' separate endorsement of McGovern's candidacy.[43] The final vote in the council was 27 to 3 in support of neutrality, with 5 abstentions. The three union leaders who voted for a McGovern endorsement were Jerry Wurf of AFSCME, Paul Jennings of the International Union of Electricians, and Al Grosspiron of the International Union of Oil, Chemical, and Atomic Workers.

The intensity of Meany's opposition to Senator McGovern was closely related to McGovern's unique route to the nomination. AFSCME President Jerry Wurf noted in 1972:

> The Executive Council vote had more to do with how McGovern won the nomination than with his record before or during the campaign. . . . The 14(b) vote, the wheat business, the McGovern stand against the war—all of these were secondary in the AFL-CIO leadership's mounting opposition to McGovern. The real concern was participation and access, the AFL-CIO's vested interests which ignored the rich opportunities for workers and their unions in the more open, "new" party.[44]

This motivation was hardly a secret. A McGovern operative remarked, "The one thing the AFL-CIO can't forgive McGovern for is the one thing he can't do anything about: if he's nominated, he won't owe them anything."[45] Not only would McGovern not owe the AFL-CIO anything, but a President McGovern (like a President Robert Kennedy) would be likely to align with the new forces of insurgency within the unions, particularly with those liberal unions critical of Meany.

The vote for neutrality was also intended to teach the Democratic Party a lesson for not having properly consulted the labor leadership. Meany and Barkan apparently believed that after a defeat in 1972, party leaders would be forced to roll back the reforms and treat the AFL-CIO leadership with a new and more appropriate respect. As Al Barkan reportedly told a party leader who had supported McGovern: "You so-called responsible leaders of this party seem to think the kids and the kooks and the Bella Abzugs can win you some elections. Well, we're going to let them try to do it for you this year."[46] But this tactic was certain to fail under the new system, because there were no reliable elites left to receive the lesson and act on its implications. Meany and Barkan were unable to recognize that party regulars simply no longer had the power to undo the reforms in order to placate the labor movement. Wilson Carey McWilliams was not exaggerating much when he concluded toward the end of 1972, "It has been a year of stupefying ineffectiveness for a man who calls himself a 'realist,' a performance of blunder and bobble which has reduced Meany to a position of embittered impotence."[47]

The most important long-term consequence of the AFL-CIO's intransigence was, therefore, not a rollback of reform but an exacerbation of internal conflict within the labor movement. Meany's insistence on neutrality in 1972 spawned an unprecedented development: a separate campaign on McGovern's behalf by over forty national unions, which represented nearly half the union members in the federation. The coalition eventually formed in support of McGovern included such important unions as AFSCME, the CWA, the IAM, the Oil, Chemical, and Atomic Workers, the International Union of Electricians, the Retail Clerks, and the Graphic Arts International Union. These unions, which had been among the most politically active in the federation, traditionally provided campaigns with large amounts of money and impressive numbers of volunteers. They were joined in their pro-McGovern efforts by two large unions outside the AFL-CIO: the UAW and the National Education Association.

Despite the lopsided vote in the AFL-CIO Executive Council favoring neutrality, the maverick unions had little hesitation about working on McGovern's behalf. The leaders' anger at Meany's mishandling of the reform process and his maladroit involvement in the 1972 nominating campaign helped justify their move toward a more independent role. AFSCME's Jerry Wurf made the point clearly: "COPE took positions in the nineteen seventy-two primaries for Humphrey and Jackson or uncommitted slates without consulting us despite the fact that they were using our funds. Then at Miami, I was distressed that COPE was croaking McGovern unilaterally after he had fairly won the Democratic nomination. I thought we should let all the AFL-CIO unions decide for themselves on the presidential endorsement."[48] Several unions, including the CWA, IAM, and AFSCME, went so far as to cut off their financial support to AFL-CIO COPE in protest of the neutrality decision. Joseph Beirne, president of the CWA and previously considered a Meany and Barkan loyalist, had no second thoughts about his decision:

> I withdrew from COPE because it was out of touch with what was happening in the political process—with the reforms which I think were a natural evolution in the Democratic Party, and with McGovern who was the candidate who had done the most for the working man. COPE must be changed. We who contribute to it have no control over it or participation in its policy decisions. The COPE leaders live in the dreams of the past, where they wheeled and dealed in politics. The Executive Council of the AFL-CIO should be reformed, too. All we do there is endorse candidates and nothing else. Our union now feels we can make our own political decisions and spend our money more fruitfully by going it alone.[49]

The 1972 election thus proved to be a turning point for many unions: no longer would they be willing to let the AFL-CIO bureaucracy serve as their main vehicle for influencing presidential politics. They developed their own political machinery and the capacity to follow a path independent of COPE and federation headquarters.

Meany's campaign to restore the old politics of brokerage also stimulated new organizing activity among African Americans and women in the labor movement. In 1972 the Coalition of Black Trade Unionists (CBTU), an organization of black union leaders and rank-and-file members, was formed, in the words of one of its organizers, "out of the frustration that came from the Executive Council of the AFL-CIO assuming a neutrality position on the question of McGovern vs. Nixon, which was absolutely in opposition to the desires of black workers and the black community."[50] To the dismay of Meany and his allies, the CBTU strongly supported affirmative action, both in the workplace and in the delegate selection process of the Democratic Party. Likewise, the formation of the Coalition of Labor Union Women in March 1974 was prompted in part by a thoroughgoing dissatisfaction with the AFL-CIO's shenanigans in presidential politics, as well as by the desire to strengthen the voice of women within the labor movement. Both of these developments were clearly related to the larger crisis of representation that now engulfed both the party and the labor movement itself. These developments further belied claims that the AFL-CIO hierarchy provided an unbiased expression of the preferences of its members in presidential politics.

The trends toward fragmentation were evident once again in Kansas City in December 1974, when the Democratic Party held a midterm "mini" convention, as mandated under the McGovern-Fraser reforms. The AFL-CIO contingent of delegates, following as always the lead of Al Barkan, again made a clumsy attempt to roll back the McGovern-Fraser reforms virtually in their entirety, with special emphasis on the rules that required de facto racial quotas in each state delegation. In response to the concerns of the AFL-CIO and others, the convention did approve, with the strong support of the reform-oriented unions (including such huge unions as AFSCME, the CWA, the UAW, and the IAM), a compromise proposal that explicitly prohibited racial quotas. Nevertheless, Barkan and other AFL-CIO leaders argued that the compromise was inadequate because it contained "implied quotas." The AFL-CIO's efforts to secure further changes foundered when the reform unions decided to ally with regular party elements and with the now-tamed "New Politics" insurgents of previous conventions in support of the compromise measures.[51] At the end of the convention, the *New York Times* concluded that "Alexander E. Barkan, a presence in Democratic politics since the Depression, had all but officially been dethroned as the broker of labor power inside the Democratic Party."[52]

The final impact of Meany's effort to maintain a system of hierarchical brokerage was a backlash within the labor movement that left bargaining capacity dispersed among a larger number of union leaders. This outcome constituted the de facto solution to the crisis of representation that had emerged full-blown during the 1972 election season. As one observer noted, "Shutting out McGovern's New Politics opened the way for New Politics in the federation."[53] *New York Times* labor reporter A. H. Raskin was surely prescient when he wrote in the fall of 1972:

> For the first time since Meany scored a monumental personal triumph in 1955 by ending two decades of warfare between the AFL and CIO, unions are running their own political action drives, free from the Meany yoke. That heady experience almost surely will wind up in a resolve to go it alone in future campaigns and thus deprive the parent federation of its main reason for being. The great unifier may wind up in labor history as the great disintegrator.[54]

This fracturing, and the ensuing weakness of Meany and his allies, meant that the future involvement of labor unions in national politics would be far more diverse and decentralized than it had been previously.

Furthermore, party reform also undermined the capacity of individual national union leaders to serve as power brokers in their own right, except to the extent that they could convince their own members to support a particular candidate. This was, of course, a considerably more arduous and time-consuming task than meeting behind closed doors for a few days at a party convention. As a result, union leaders often found it more difficult to maximize their bargaining leverage in the postreform environment. As both George McGovern and, later, Jimmy Carter were to demonstrate, candidates could now bypass the union leaders and seek the direct support of voters—both union members and others—in the caucuses or primaries. No longer would union leaders be needed to "chivvy and bully and plead and trade and threaten and maneuver" on the convention floor, as Steelworkers President David McDonald had done in 1960.[55]

The Crisis of Representation in Congress

The presidential nominating process was not the only national political institution to pass through crisis and reform in the early 1970s. The U.S. Congress, and especially the House of Representatives, experienced comparable change, with similarly fragmenting effects on the distribution of power. There, however, the motivating concern was not so much an excessive centralization of power but the degree to which bargaining capacity was neither fully concentrated in top party leaders nor doled out equally to every member. Rather, power was concentrated in a relatively small number of committee chairs, usually conservative southern Democrats with decades of seniority, who were not held accountable to congressional majorities. In the opinion of liberal members of Congress, therefore, the rules of the House and Senate gave disproportionate power to conservatives. As the liberal forces gained strength, their dissatisfaction with the rules grew. These tensions would not be alleviated until the movement for reform finally triumphed in the early 1970s, bringing with it a transformation in the structure of congressional power.[56]

The success of the reform forces within Congress marked the culmination of many years of liberal agitation for a power structure more representative of the policy preferences of the Democratic majority. The growing role of African Americans in the South and the activation of new liberal constituencies—such as suburban reformers, the women's movement, and the antiwar movement—helped strengthen reform sentiment among congressional Democrats. These efforts were, in turn, strongly backed by the labor movement. The AFL-CIO provided financial help to the House Democratic Study Group (DSG), an organization of members of Congress seeking to promote both liberal policies and institutional reform, giving $20,000 to the organization in 1965 and $25,000 in 1966.[57] AFL-CIO Legislative Director Andrew Biemiller also specifically endorsed the reform proposals enunciated by Rep. Richard Bolling (D-Mo.), a leading figure in the DSG.[58] This support reflected long-standing commitments. As early as the 1950s, AFL-CIO President George Meany attempted unsuccessfully to convince House Speaker Sam Rayburn that the Democratic Party should pledge to abandon the seniority system. Meany said that Rayburn's subsequent refusal meant that even if the Democrats won the election, "we will have the same anti-labor groups controlling the committees as we have today, if they happen to live."[59] In the early 1960s, Andrew Biemiller predicted that there would be "one Hell of a drive made during the next year through COPE and every other mechanism we've got to try to get people lined up to not only change the rules of the Senate and House of Representatives, but also the Democratic Caucus in the House." Biemiller, perhaps recalling his own years in Congress, noted the desperate need to "strengthen the hand of the liberals in the Democratic Caucus" and concluded, "The AFL-CIO is clearly on record . . . that there is a need for a thorough overhauling of the procedures of both houses of Congress."[60]

The House reforms that were finally enacted in the early 1970s directly addressed the concerns of liberals and their union allies. Kenneth Shepsle's summary is apt: "The decade of the 1970s was truly an age of legislative reform. It witnessed a representational revolt against a system that dramatically skewed rewards towards the old and senior who were often out of step with fellow partisans."[61] First, the autocratic powers of committee chairs were drastically reduced, and the power of committee majorities and subcommittees was correspondingly increased. Second, measures were taken to strengthen the House Democratic Party leadership, especially the power of the Speaker to refer bills to different committees and to control appointments to the House Rules Committee. Third, the new power invested in the House leadership was placed under the collective control of the Democratic caucus rather than in the hands of an unaccountable, autonomous Speaker. As David Rohde notes: "The leadership (like the chairmen) was to be responsible to the members, *not* the other way around."[62] These changes were intended to enhance party coherence by reducing the capacity of committee or subcommittee chairs to deviate from the views of the majority of Democrats in the House.

Similar, if less dramatic, reforms in the Senate were also approved, with the same goal of redistributing power more broadly and in more representative fashion. In particular, liberal senators led by longtime labor ally Senator Walter Mondale of Minnesota succeeded in changing the rules regulating filibusters. The number of senators needed to reach cloture was dropped to sixty—a small but helpful reduction from the two-thirds vote previously required. Given the historical role of conservative-led filibusters in obstructing 14(b) repeal and other union endorsed measures, the AFL-CIO was delighted with this move and strongly supported Mondale's efforts.

Union leaders and lobbyists initially greeted the reforms warmly. The AFL-CIO's annual legislative report congratulated the House Democratic Caucuses in the 93rd and 94th Congresses for their enactment of "labor backed reforms affecting the structure and procedures of committees."[63] The AFL-CIO endorsed almost the entire panoply of House and Senate reforms. The UAW's legislative director also noted that the union was "pleased with the progressive steps taken at the start of the 93rd Congress—actions which have had the effect of helping to open up the process and make the House more accountable." The UAW urged "further actions to improve the operation of the House and make it a more responsive legislative body."[64]

Notwithstanding these statements of support, by the early 1970s tension emerged between the AFL-CIO leadership and House reformers; the sequence of events was all too reminiscent of the conflicts over party reform. The AFL-CIO leadership became distrustful of many reformers, who were often vocally opposed to the Vietnam War and allied with the new social movements that most labor leaders disliked. Union lobbyists grew concerned that the new breed of congressional Democrats elected in the early 1970s—and especially the members of the famous "Class of '74"—were less reliable than other northern liberals on traditional economic policy issues. Kenneth Young, a prominent AFL-CIO lobbyist, observed in 1975: "The freshman Democrat today is likely to be an upper-income type, and that causes some problems with economic issues. It's not that they don't vote what they perceive to be working class concerns, but I think a lot of them are more concerned with inflation than with unemployment. They aren't emotionally involved with unemployment."[65] Such "new class" Democrats, often elected in suburban districts that had previously voted Republican, prided themselves on their independence and evinced little loyalty either to party leaders or to traditional interest group barons. Although never antilabor in the sense that southern Democrats often were, the unpredictability of these new members made them potential obstructions to union political strategies.

This latent conflict came to a head almost immediately; in 1974 the AFL-CIO opposed a House reorganization proposal drawn up by a select committee chaired by Representative Bolling, a longtime labor ally and leader of House reform efforts. The federation chose to oppose Bolling's reform program because it required the division of the House Education and Labor Committee into two separate committees. According to news reports, federation leaders feared that a "separate Labor Committee would become painfully polarized between pro-labor Democrats and anti-labor Republicans." Moreover, the Bolling reforms also required the elimination of the Merchant Marines and Fisheries Committee, which had long protected the particular interests of the maritime unions (and which would finally be killed off by a Republican-controlled House in 1995). With their close ties to George Meany and the more conservative bloc of craft unionists, the maritime unions bolstered the AFL-CIO's hostility to Bolling's plan. Ultimately, it was defeated in the House Democratic caucus by 16 votes. An angry Bolling blamed the AFL-CIO, telling *Congressional Quarterly*: "We could have beaten everybody else, but labor put the muscle in that beat us. They support so many Democrats for re-election that it was very destructive in the caucus."[66]

Despite this episode, the overall record of AFL-CIO support for congressional reform was sustained into the 1970s. Its continuation—in notable contrast to the AFL-CIO's persistent opposition to the presidential nominating reforms—was due to three factors. First, unlike party reform, congressional reform had been supported by all wings of the labor movement throughout the postwar period. Second, congressional reform was neither as immediately nor as obviously threatening to the power of the AFL-CIO vis-à-vis the other national unions as was party reform, which had at once shifted power to the UAW and other maverick unions. Third, the AFL-CIO's Andrew Biemiller was, as chief lobbyist, considerably more flexible than COPE Director Al Barkan, who delighted in fulminating in colorful language against his opponents. Biemiller, more accustomed to legislative give-and-take, was willing to work with doves and the exponents of the New Politics as they gained influence among congressional Democrats. Moreover, Biemiller no doubt recognized that while the AFL-CIO might be willing to bear the cost of alienating a presidential candidate (especially one likely to lose in any case), it could scarcely afford to antagonize its limited base of congressional support, which remained the crucial rampart against anti-union legislative initiatives.

In the long run, though, the congressional reforms did undermine many of the power relationships forged by the AFL-CIO, and the mechanisms were not dissimilar to those that dissolved the AFL-CIO's brokering role in the presidential nominating process. The prereform Congress had relied on modes of elite political brokerage highly compatible with the boss rule and insider bargaining characteristic of the AFL-CIO leadership. Members of the prereform Congress "had been trained to be deferential," having come up through a machine-based "political apprenticeship in which leadership and hierarchy were normal and accepted."[67] The typical union leader found a politician of this type easy to work with, as the union leaders too had risen through the ranks in a long apprenticeship in which loyalty, deference, and the acceptance of hierarchy were cardinal virtues. Thus, the interaction between union leaders and Democratic members of the old Congress was in many respects a relationship between old-time pols with fundamentally similar conceptions of the rules of the political game.

This affinity in political styles and identities facilitated the customary practices of AFL-CIO lobbying. William Lunch's description of the workings of the prereform Congress is particularly noteworthy: "The old Congress was a secretive place. Committee deliberations were nearly always behind closed doors, and no records were kept of committee votes, except for the result. Even votes on the floor were frequently shrouded in mystery. Behind the closed doors, bargains were easier to strike . . . and members who had to be implacable foes in public could work together."[68] This process was not too different from the insulated, closed-door negotiations between labor and management that was the union leader's stock-in-trade in collective bargaining. It was, moreover, not very different from the elite brokerage that the AFL-CIO had systematically practiced and defended in the presidential nominating process. The common thread in these activities was a commitment to insulated bargaining by elite actors unconstrained by any mobilized constituency that might hold the leadership democratically accountable.

This traditional mode of interest group lobbying grew increasingly obsolete as congressional reform consolidated and deepened. The most crucial change was that bargaining capacity—which had previously been concentrated among several dozen committee leaders—was now dispersed much more widely. The latent centralizing potential of the House reforms, to be eventually tapped in the late 1980s by House Speaker Jim Wright, remained dormant in the 1970s. The immediate effect was instead a chaotic fragmentation of power that seemed to encourage only gridlock, not partisan coherence. The new rules thus made Congress look even more like the ideal-type of fragmented pluralism than it had before, and made it that much harder for the unions to grasp the reins of power. As one commentator noted wryly, "The autocracy of the chair broken, Congress was transformed from an institution in which power was closely held by a few to an institution in which almost everyone had just enough strength to toss a monkey wrench."[69] While more members had a share of power, fewer individual members had the capacity to make credible, wide-ranging, or long-lasting bargains with other members, the president, or interest group leaders. Deals worked out behind closed doors with a small group of members were no longer the most reliable means for affecting congressional outcomes, and the traditional skills of a lobbyist such as Andrew Biemiller were rendered anachronistic.

The new environment of atomized decentralization also created incentives for interest groups both to expand the number of their lobbyists in Washington and also to engage in more lobbying at the district level by local members (so-called grassroots lobbying). The new opportunities for grassroots lobbying and the greater number of access points encouraged individual national unions to augment their lobbying staffs and pursue their own legislative initiatives. Unions that had taken on a new role in the nominating process, such as AFSCME, the NEA, the IAM, the AFT, and many others, also rapidly expanded their own Washington offices. As these unions enhanced their political expertise, they grew less willing to subordinate their activity to any unilateral demands emerging from federation headquarters.

In this way the reforms and their attendant effects significantly undermined the centrality of the AFL-CIO as the primary voice of organized labor on Capitol Hill. Just as the model of fragmented pluralism predicted, congressional lobbying would no longer consist of a small number of members of Congress making deals with Andrew Biemiller; it would now take on a more diffuse form, with greater numbers of union lobbyists interacting with greater numbers of individual members of the House and Senate. As this process unfolded, James Sundquist's description of the dynamics within the House also came to fit the power relations within the union federation: "Junior members [or national union leaders] will accept leadership only on their own terms, and subject to their continuous control. They insist on the right to decide day by day and case by case, without coercion, when they will be followers and when they will assert their right of independence."[70]

Thus, the fragmented Congress of the 1970s met an increasingly fragmented labor movement, one in which the national unions possessed the will and the capacity to go their own way regardless of the AFL-CIO leadership's preferences. "Bossism" as a mode of internal governance and decision making had been decisively superseded, in Congress and to some degree even in the labor movement, by a new politics of direct participation and policy-based disagreement. By 1976 the old politics of the Johnson years, although less than a decade past, seemed light-years away, well beyond any hope of successful restoration. Clearly, the age of secretive, inside deals among elite actors—Lyndon Johnson's "30 key people"—had come to a close. The ensuing decentralization of power made the relationship between national policymakers and labor leaders increasingly unmanageable and prone to conflict, and close cooperation became all the more difficult to arrange. The preconditions for centralized pluralism, which had already been reachable only with great effort, now seemed even less likely to be achieved. The age of a truly fragmented pluralism had begun, and with it would also come many new challenges for the labor leadership.

5 *Labor and the Carter Administration: The Origins of Conflict*

Shortly after Jimmy Carter had finished his first year in the White House, George Meany was asked by a reporter to give the president a grade for his performance thus far. Meany promptly replied that Carter deserved no better than a "C minus." A few months earlier, Meany had commented: "I think the President is a conservative. . . . He seems to have some idea that his greatest accomplishment would be balancing the budget by 1981." In late 1978 Meany complained that President Carter's biggest problem was his political weakness—his inability to deliver legislative results: "If he were a stronger President—stronger in relation to Congress—I think he might have been helpful to us." [1]

As Meany's comments suggest, the labor movement's relationship with Carter, while not without its moments of cooperation, was marked by much disappointment, and eventually by a high and protracted level of conflict. Very early in the administration, labor leaders came to criticize the president for abandoning treasured parts of the Democratic agenda and for neglecting the needs of important Democratic constituencies, including organized labor itself. By late 1978 the administration's relations with the AFL-CIO plummeted to such a low point that President Carter and George Meany were briefly not even on speaking terms. By the end of Carter's presidency, most union leaders were despondent—some desperately betting that a new and different Democratic nominee could do better than Carter, others forlornly hoping that the renominated president could somehow effect his own reelection. Either way, union leaders saw little hope for a major revival of labor's political fortunes.

This outcome raises an important question: What had changed since the mid-1960s so that cooperation had been replaced with conflict? The answer proposed here emphasizes how the fragmentation of bargaining capacity—both within the national political system *and* within the labor movement—

affected the possibilities for sustained cooperation. The Carter administration, to be sure, faced economic policy dilemmas of a greater magnitude than those confronting the Democratic administrations of the 1960s. But dealing with them was made all the more difficult by the increased diffusion of power in the Washington community. The scattered and even chaotic nature of political bargaining between unions and Democratic Party officeholders in the postreform environment exacerbated suspicions and sapped trust. Even when President Carter sincerely wished to deliver on his promises to organized labor, he had little capacity to do so. Similarly, diminished unity within the labor movement hampered both national union leaders and federation officials as they attempted to keep their commitments to the administration. In a word, fragmentation undermined cooperation, and the cohesion of the Democratic Party suffered accordingly.

The Nomination and Election of Jimmy Carter

A top aide to President Carter once commented, "Certainly Jimmy Carter could not have been elected President twenty or even ten years ago. Only because of the fragmentation that's taken place in the Democratic Party was it possible for him to be elected President."[2] This fragmentation was, of course, largely rooted in the crisis of representation that had erupted in the presidential nominating process in the late 1960s. Taking advantage of the newly reformed system, Carter ran a campaign that emphasized direct communication with party voters through the mass media, without the interposition of the usual party or union organizations. Contrary to some accounts, however, Carter did not gain the nomination against the wishes of a labor movement united in opposition to his candidacy, nor did he ever deliberately spurn labor support. In fact, faced with an increasingly splintered labor movement, Carter was rather successful in securing the support of those unions that were genuinely open to persuasion.

The tendency of national unions to act with increasing independence from the political tutelage of the AFL-CIO, first evidenced in 1972, grew even more pronounced during the 1976 presidential nominating season. Those unions that had spurned the AFL-CIO's demand for neutrality in 1972 concluded that the labor movement needed to be directly involved in the caucuses and primaries that were now the chief means for delegate selection. Thus, a coalition of nine unions formed in order to coordinate their involvement in the nominating process. Dubbed the "Labor Coalition Clearinghouse," it included the Communication Workers of America; the United Auto Workers; the International Association of Machinists; Graphic Arts International Union; the American Federation of State, County, and Municipal Employees; the International Union of Electrical, Radio, and Machine Workers; the Oil, Chemical, and Atomic Workers; the United Mine Workers; and the National Education Association. All but the UAW, UMW, and NEA were AFL-CIO affiliates.

In deciding whom to endorse in the primaries, the coalition unions faced an unusually large field of candidates, including Senator Birch Bayh of Indiana, Senator Henry "Scoop" Jackson of Washington, former Georgia governor Jimmy Carter, Representative Morris Udall of Arizona, former governor Terry Sanford of North Carolina, former senator Fred Harris of Oklahoma, Pennsylvania Governor Milton Shapp, former vice presidential nominee R. Sargent Shriver, California Governor Jerry Brown, Senator Frank Church of Idaho, Texas Senator Lloyd Bentsen, and Alabama Governor George Wallace. Confronted with such a large field, which included many candidates who could legitimately claim to have a strong pro-labor record, an endorsement of a single candidate by the coalition seemed impossible. Thus, the coalition unions agreed to work separately for the candidates of their choice. Although this decision reduced the potential for conflict within the labor movement, it also diluted the unions' political influence.

Power was even more fragmented when, in many cases, state and local leaders of the national unions were allowed to decide whom to endorse in their state's primaries or caucuses. As Alan Ehrenhalt of *Congressional Quarterly* noted, "Many of these labor moves [to endorse] are local, the product of decisions made as far down as the shop steward or business agent level in the different states."[3] One result of this uncoordinated involvement was that activists within the same union could end up supporting different candidates from state to state. Local UAW leaders supported Mo Udall in Wisconsin, for example, while UAW activists in Florida and Michigan supported Jimmy Carter. With such a structure in place, it was not uncommon for the national union leaders to be reduced to doing little more than lobbying their own local officials and rank-and-file members on behalf of their favorite candidate.

Nevertheless, some national union presidents did play a very important role in delivering the political support of their union. This was particularly true of Leonard Woodcock, who was elected to the presidency of the UAW after the death of Walter Reuther in a plane crash in 1970. Woodcock knew Carter personally from their mutual attendance at meetings of the Trilateral Commission (Woodcock was one of several labor members), and they had developed a friendly relationship.[4] Woodcock saw Carter as a candidate capable both of winning the South for the Democrats and of effectively blocking the presidential aspirations of Alabama Governor George Wallace. His support was crucial in the Iowa caucuses, where he helped to secure an endorsement of Carter by the state's influential UAW leadership. Autoworker activists and members showed up in large numbers at the caucuses, helping Carter win an important early victory. In the Florida primary, Woodcock personally campaigned for Carter and strongly urged the state's large community of UAW retirees as well as the Florida Community Action Program (the UAW's version of the Committee on Political Education) to endorse Carter's bid for the nomination.

It is not surprising, therefore, that when Carter chose to deliver a prominent speech on national health insurance later in the campaign, he consulted closely with the UAW. Stuart Eizenstat, then head of the campaign issues staff, recalls: "The UAW . . . was a key element in any Democratic coalition, organizationally, financially, and intellectually. Its big issue was national health insurance. . . . The UAW insisted on knowing what our position was. And we negotiated with them for a quite lengthy period in terms of exact language and there were certain buzz words, 'comprehensive,' 'all-inclusive,' and so forth that they had to have in order to be enthusiasts in the campaign."[5] As a result, UAW leaders were very satisfied with Carter's position, which endorsed a national health insurance system funded through employer and payroll taxes as well as general revenues.[6]

The relationship between the AFSCME union and the Carter campaign also revealed the extent to which Carter reached out to traditional party constituencies. After Carter visited AFSCME President Jerry Wurf in April 1975, Wurf agreed to endorse Carter and to organize members on his behalf. According to one of Wurf's top aides, in return for his union's support "Wurf got Carter to make some fairly significant commitments: revenue sharing, counter-cyclical spending, collective bargaining for public employees."[7] Wurf carried through on his commitment by mobilizing AFSCME members to volunteer for Carter in the crucial Florida primary. Along with the other coalition unions that joined the pro-Carter effort in Florida, AFSCME was widely credited with helping Carter to an early breakthrough victory.[8]

At the same time, the AFL-CIO leadership announced that the federation would be neutral, in keeping with an executive council policy renouncing involvement in the Democrats' affairs until after the party had selected a nominee. COPE's Al Barkan gave the official rationale: "The biggest reason for staying out of the primaries is that you're forced to pick and choose among your many friends if you don't [stay out]."[9] But despite such comments, which were very much in the traditional "nonpartisan" vein, the AFL-CIO leadership and the building trades unions were actually making a major effort to help their own favored candidate, Washington Senator Scoop Jackson. Jackson was appealing because of his virulent anticommunism, his strong support for New Deal social programs and economic policies, and, not least, his outspoken opposition to the party's reform wing. As Elizabeth Drew surmised, the support for Jackson by the "old labor crowd leaders" was "motivated in part by the fact that they like his politics and in part by their rivalry with the more liberal labor unions."[10] In Massachusetts, Pennsylvania, and New York, AFL-CIO leaders and the more conservative craft unions worked intensively on behalf of Jackson's campaign.[11] When Jackson's star faded after several successive defeats in crucial primaries, the AFL-

CIO leadership tried, much as it had in 1968, to encourage former vice president Hubert Humphrey to enter the race. This "draft Humphrey" effort went nowhere, though, because Humphrey was not interested in running as a spoiler and, more important, because the new nominating system made a late entry by *any* candidate far less feasible.

By the time of the convention, then, the liberal unions had consolidated their ties with Carter, while the AFL-CIO remained distant. In this regard, the dynamics of the reformed system had strengthened the left-liberal unions, to the detriment of the more conservative sections of the labor movement. As political analyst Alan Baron noted: "The whole situation puts the unions more and more to the left in the Democratic Party. The politically active unions are the liberal ones. I've been to a lot of political meetings, and I don't see pipefitters or plumbers."[12] Al Barkan meanwhile denigrated the unions in the Labor Coalition Clearinghouse as not in the "mainstream" of the labor movement and argued that there were "more important things" for organized labor to do than to become involved in the primaries.[13]

Notwithstanding the AFL-CIO's early opposition to his candidacy, Carter made a considerable effort to secure the federation's support once he had gained the nomination. After all, the AFL-CIO still controlled impressive resources for use in the general election. As Al Barkan emphasized in his discussions with Carter aide Hamilton Jordan, the AFL-CIO had computerized phone lists for millions of voters, the majority of whom were concentrated in sixteen states that could produce 41 percent of the popular vote. Barkan also told Jordan that what labor could spend on getting out the vote would be worth $20 million to the Carter campaign, and that the federation would be able to reach millions of union voters and distribute 90 million pieces of campaign literature.[14] With the ultimate disposition of such resources no doubt in mind, officials in the Carter campaign negotiated an adequate working relationship with the AFL-CIO for the duration of the general election campaign.

Clearly, many important unions did have a long and close involvement with the Carter campaign prior to his nomination. This finding, it should be noted, contradicts that of many interpreters. According to Nelson Polsby, for example, "Nothing in Mr. Carter's prior experience of the nomination process led him to the view that he needed to come to terms with the rest of the Democratic Party."[15] Such claims take the AFL-CIO and many of the more conservative unions, who indeed had little meaningful contact with the Carter nominating campaign, for all of organized labor. Other powerful unions, mainly in the liberal or reform wing of the labor movement, had early and congenial links with Governor Carter, and these ties ensured that Carter had considerable experience in "coming to terms" with at least part of the labor movement. However, Carter arrived in the White House with better ties to individual union leaders than with the AFL-CIO itself, and this fact would eventually have significant consequences.

The Politics of Access and the Emergence of Conflict

The AFL-CIO leadership's anxieties about Carter's ties to the liberal unions grew deeper when Carter appointed University of Texas economist Ray Marshall as secretary of labor. George Meany had made it clear to Carter during the transition period that his favorite for the post was former Ford administration labor secretary John Dunlop, with whom the AFL-CIO had worked closely in the past.[16] Meany expected, on the basis of his past experience, that he would be closely consulted regarding this and other appointments of concern to the labor movement, and that a strong preference on his part would probably be honored. Thus, Carter's choice was quite troubling, even though Marshall was a liberal labor economist whose views generally accorded with those of the AFL-CIO.

The politics surrounding the appointment were particularly unsettling for the AFL-CIO leadership because they suggested a latent alliance between reform elements in the Democratic Party, dissident labor leaders, and the newly elected administration. Dunlop had been most strongly opposed by those groups that had crossed swords with the AFL-CIO leadership in the protracted battles over the procedures and direction of the Democratic Party. Rumors of Dunlop's possible appointment prompted protests by women and minority activists who claimed that Dunlop had demonstrated a lack of commitment to affirmative action in prior government service and in administrative posts at Harvard University. Equally important was the opposition of Jerry Wurf, president of AFSCME. Wurf, who considered John Dunlop a captive of Meany and the conservative building trades unions, urged the Carter administration to appoint someone more acceptable to the liberal wing of the labor movement. Wurf would later comment, "I didn't get much out of Carter, but one thing I did get is that Dunlop did not become Secretary of Labor."[17] In this context, the AFL-CIO saw the Marshall appointment as a capitulation to the demands of the liberal reformers and union rivals with whom Meany had been feuding for years.

Especially disturbing was its implicit threat to the principle that the AFL-CIO should control communication between the White House and the labor movement. This issue was always crucial for Meany, for it directly affected his ability to maintain his own leadership position. Were administration officials to communicate directly and regularly with individual union presidents (as their attention to Wurf suggested they might), the functional importance of the federation as the locus for political activity would be diminished. Furthermore, bypassing the AFL-CIO would simultaneously strengthen the administration's ability to manipulate divisions within the labor movement and weaken the AFL-CIO's ability to coordinate the diverse demands of its constituent unions. Although the Marshall appointment was the first decision to raise suspicions among Meany and his associates about the administration's commitment to "properly" consult labor, concerns with the appropriate method of consultation would repeatedly emerge throughout the Carter years.

Jimmy Carter's governing philosophy contributed to the frequency of such conflicts.[18] He had developed a political worldview that stressed the need for virtuous leaders to promote the public interest against the parochial demands of self-seeking interest groups and legislators interested in little more than their own material aggrandizement and reelection. The dominant model of interest representation in Washington, typified by bargaining among special interests with inside access to decision makers, was anathema to Carter. While he saw cultivating political support as a necessary part of the legislative process, it could wait until after the policy proposal had been perfected.

It is hard to imagine a conception of representation and governance that could be more alien to that of America's labor leaders. For the union leaders, their organizations were not "special interest groups" undermining the public good but legitimate representative bodies that deserved to be consulted—not merely out of politeness or political expediency, but exactly because of their genuinely representative character. Rather than being corruption, this was the essence of a political system based on bargaining and compromise. The president's approach, in contrast, seemed disconnected from the realities of governance; it appeared all too likely to bypass the views of labor in favor of those who claimed to be closer to the "grassroots" but who were in reality only detached political "amateurs."

Although it offended the union leadership, Carter's vision of governing was popular in a country still recovering from the turmoil of the previous decade. With his critique of politics-as-usual and of interest group liberalism, Carter spoke to a public that no longer trusted the representational capacity of the national political system. It is thus no accident that a man with Carter's philosophy should have risen to the presidency when he did. The fragmentation of power and the ideological disarray produced by the earlier crises of representation were prerequisites for his own success, opening avenues to power that were entirely new or had become newly effective. The question soon to be faced, however, was whether the same factors would prevent the new president from developing his own capacity to bargain effectively in national politics.

Economic and Social Policy

As unease over issues of access and appointments simmered, early conflicts were also emerging over the shape of the economic stimulus package that the new administration would present to Congress. These were the first signals of clashes over economic policy that were to grow in intensity as the administration confronted the danger of inflation. The administration's desire to control inflation inevitably conflicted with the AFL-CIO's interest in tight labor markets and high employment. Thus, although the AFL-CIO and the administration agreed that some form of economic stimulus was needed, they would soon disagree over the details.

In early January 1977 the administration presented a stimulus plan with four main components: a fifty-dollar rebate to every taxpayer, increased public works spending, additional public service employment and job training, and a small, permanent reduction in taxes for individuals and corporations. The AFL-CIO quickly attacked the plan as underemphasizing public job creation and overemphasizing tax cuts, which they considered a slow and inegalitarian means of stimulating the economy. Thus, while the administration sought $31.2 billion in tax cuts and job creation spread over two years, the AFL-CIO proposed a program of at least $30 billion spent in only one year and solely devoted to job creation efforts: "We believe the two-year package is too small, takes too long and is too ill-advised to give the economy the stimulus it needs. We consider this a retreat from the goals which we understood President-elect Carter to have set during last year's campaign."[19] Most of the package was eventually approved by Congress, with the exception of the proposed tax rebate, which Carter eventually withdrew from consideration on the grounds that it was no longer necessary and was potentially inflationary.

A more acrimonious dispute soon followed over the appropriate size of a minimum wage increase. In April 1977 the administration proposed an increase of only twenty cents, from $2.30 to $2.50 an hour, while the AFL-CIO had been publicly urging Congress to increase the rate to $3.00 an hour. Meany castigated Carter, stating that the small increase was a "bitter disappointment to everyone who looked to this administration for economic justice for the poor."[20] AFL-CIO Secretary-Treasurer Lane Kirkland meanwhile complained that the AFL-CIO had read about Carter's decision in the newspapers rather than being notified directly. By July a final compromise between labor and the administration was struck around the sum of $2.65 an hour, including indexing to increase the wage in the future (the indexing proposal was ultimately rejected by Congress). Despite such efforts, the administration's apparent reluctance to begin bargaining, along with the inadequacy of the consultation that finally occurred, left AFL-CIO leaders dissatisfied. For its part, White House officials felt that the AFL-CIO had formulated its demands with little respect for the administration's need to balance competing goals.[21]

The same pattern of conflict was repeated in the area of health care reform. The AFL-CIO and, more important, the UAW had called for the establishment of a comprehensive system of national health insurance financed through payroll taxes, a tax on unearned income, and general revenues. Although Carter had endorsed a program generally along these lines during the primaries, officials in his administration, as well as the president himself, soon became worried about the potential budgetary and inflationary consequences.[22] The debate quickly became entangled with the presidential aspirations of Senator Edward Kennedy, who was the foremost congressional proponent of a comprehensive plan that would reduce the role of private insurers. A tug-of-war emerged between Kennedy and Carter over the support of the UAW, with Kennedy berating the administration for betraying its promises to support a federally funded national health insurance plan and Carter attempting to placate labor with various half-measures. Eventually, the Carter administration presented a plan of its own, but it was decidedly less than both the unions and Kennedy had been demanding; it was never approved by Congress. Moreover, the final proposal did little to keep the UAW and other unions from gravitating closer to Kennedy as he became increasingly critical of the president.

Carter would experience greater program success when he committed the administration to creating a separate Department of Education. But ironically the resulting improvement in relations with the National Education Association came only at the cost of increased conflict with the American Federation of Teachers, the NEA's rival union, which was part of the AFL-CIO.[23] Both the AFT and the AFL-CIO opposed a separate department, which they considered unnecessary, politically divisive, and prone to capture by the larger and nonaffiliated NEA. After some deliberation, Carter chose to fulfill his 1976 campaign promise to the NEA and support a new department, which was approved by Congress in late 1979. But because this achievement benefited only one union, and a nonfederation union at that, the political payoff was quite limited.

The passage of the Humphrey-Hawkins bill (formally known as the Full Employment and Balanced Growth Act) in October 1978 also should have improved relations with organized labor, but the benefits to the Carter administration were again meager.[24] Sponsored by Sen. Hubert Humphrey (D-Minn.) and Rep. Gus Hawkins (D-Calif.) with strong labor support, the bill was originally intended as an part of ambitious effort to commit the executive branch to an expansionary program of economic growth and lowered unemployment. The version passed, however, required only that the president set five-year goals, left nonbinding and unenforceable, for employment, production, and real income. President Carter had initiated a major White House lobbying effort on behalf of the bill, but among labor leaders and other liberal constituencies he received relatively little credit for his support.[25]

The Agony of Labor Law Reform

Although the initial disputes over economic and social policy troubled labor leaders, more disturbing still was the outcome when they again pursued a reform of the nation's labor laws. By the late 1970s the signs of a decline in union density had become undeniable, and the unions were eager to make statutory changes that would improve their position in collective bargaining and enhance their capacity to organize new workers. They would soon find, however, that despite congressional reforms and an apparent weakening of the conservative coalition, the old patterns that had traditionally stymied labor's agenda were still very much in force.

The first labor law proposal heralded by the unions was a bill to legalize a practice known as "common situs" picketing. The legislation would have allowed construction unions in a dispute with one subcontractor at a building site to picket other contractors and subcontractors at the same site, thereby enabling strikes to be more effective. Such "common site" picketing was rendered illegal by a 1951 Supreme Court decision. Legislation overturning the decision had passed Congress in 1975, only to be vetoed by President Ford. A new bill now had the support of President Carter, and Secretary of Labor Ray Marshall testified in its favor on Capitol Hill. The lobbyists of the AFL-CIO, and especially of its Building and Construction Trades Department, fully expected that the common situs bill would again move through Congress just as it had two years before.

The union lobbyists were, therefore, shocked and embarrassed when the bill was narrowly defeated by a vote of 217 to 205 in the House of Representatives in March 1977. As the lobbyists would later admit, they had unwisely taken for granted a repeat of the earlier congressional vote.[26] AFL-CIO lobbyist Ken Young remarked: "We had a new Congress; we had a Democratic President; and we just assumed that the people who had voted with us in the previous Congress that had passed situs picketing . . . would still vote with us. And instead of making sure those people were going to remain consistent, we started talking to newly elected Members and our opposition went to work on a lot of the older Members and turned them around."[27] Crucial factors in the defeat were the defection of northern Republicans and the increased opposition among southern Democrats. Indeed, every Democrat from Arkansas, Alabama, Georgia, Mississippi, and North Carolina voted against the bill, while a large majority of northern Democrats supported it.

An important role was also played by grassroots lobbying by business groups—especially those in the construction industry. Rep. William D. Ford (D-Mich.), a key supporter of the reform, called the business campaign "the best-organized, best-financed effort to create the impression that you have grass-roots support for your position that I've ever seen. They used all the new developments in fund-raising and targeting. They targeted the vulnerable members. They blanketed newspaper ads and direct mail, and they picked members' districts where they thought they could create the most heat." Rep. Frank Thompson (D-N.J.), chair of the House Education and Labor Subcommittee on Labor-Management Relations, similarly concluded,

"The Associated General Contractors in particular launched a fantastic mail drive. They even sent employers packets of postcards for employees to send in to members of Congress. I think the business groups surprised themselves by coalescing so successfully and defeating situs picketing."[28]

But the outcome on common situs only foreshadowed worse to come for the labor movement. A far more bitter defeat would occur on the Labor Law Reform Bill of 1978. This bill was advanced after union leaders chose not to pursue repeal of section 14(b) of the Taft-Hartley Act. Their decision rested on several considerations, the most important of which was the likelihood that such an effort would again meet defeat in the Senate—just as it had in 1965. Instead, the AFL-CIO focused on legislation implementing an interrelated set of reforms in the nation's labor laws, designed in large part to ameliorate some of the causes of union decline.[29] As introduced in the House in July 1977, with White House support, the labor law reform bill contained provisions to (1) expand the National Labor Relations Board from five to seven members in order to expedite the processing of unfair-labor-practice cases, (2) mandate representation elections within thirty days after a union presented membership cards signed by a majority of employees, (3) grant back pay of up to 150 percent to workers illegally fired for union activity, (4) allow union organizers equal time to address any workers forced by management to attend anti-union meetings, (5) deny federal contracts to companies found guilty of violating labor laws, and (6) award workers back pay if the NLRB found that a company refused to negotiate in "good faith" with a newly certified union.

President Carter played a significant role in preparing the legislation, claiming that he had "personally helped to draft every single paragraph."[30] Although he had insisted on some revisions as a condition for his support, the AFL-CIO's early negotiations with the White House ensured the president's unqualified endorsement of the final bill. Thus, labor law reform easily passed in the House of Representatives in October 1977 by a vote of 257 to 163, with 36 Republicans voting in favor. A total of 59 Democrats, all but 6 of whom were from the South, voted against the bill, leaving 221 Democrats (and 29 southern Democrats) in the majority. This margin of victory was sufficiently large to ensure that the legislation would have been passed even without a single Republican vote. The degree of success among southern Democrats was especially impressive, and the AFL-CIO attributed it to the "line of communication to the southerners from Speaker Thomas P. O'Neill and Majority Leader Jim Wright of Texas, and the regional whips," as well as to the reservoir of support among southern Democrats for President Carter.[31]

Despite its strong victory in the House, the reform bill encountered major difficulties in the Senate. An initial problem was the decision by President Carter and Senate Majority Leader Robert Byrd to delay a vote on the bill until after ratification of the Panama Canal Treaty. The decision to delay meant, first, that the bill's opponents would have more time to mobilize and second, that it would come to the floor only after much of the administration's political capital had already been depleted on a prior "liberal" vote. Moreover, the decision of the United Mine Workers to begin a controversial 110-day strike (from December 1977 to March 1978) created, as had the similarly ill-timed New York transit workers' strike in 1966, a public relations disaster for labor.[32] Thus, debate on the measure opened in May 1978 to an intense barrage of opposition. A large portion of the early protest came from small business owners who barraged the Senate with letters and phone calls.[33] They were soon joined by organizations representing large corporations, including the National Association of Manufacturers and the Business Roundtable. The strong resistance to the bill encouraged Sens. Orrin Hatch (R-Utah) and Richard Lugar (R-Ind.) to lead a filibuster. After several roll calls failed to achieve the sixty votes needed to invoke cloture, a compromise proposal was put forth by Sens. Harrison Williams (D-N.J.) and Jacob Javitz (D-N.Y.). Although this significantly more moderate proposal was greeted with a mixed reaction by organized labor, it gained only a few more votes for reform; the final effort on June 15, 1978, to invoke cloture fell two votes short. Labor law reform had once again been defeated, despite labor's best efforts and Democratic control of Congress and the presidency.

A noteworthy change in this Senate battle was in the role of the Democratic Party leadership. In 1965, after the failed effort to repeal section 14(b), union leaders complained about the laxness of the party leadership when it came to pressuring senators to vote for cloture. But in the fight for labor law reform, Majority Leader Robert Byrd of Virginia tried strenuously to obtain the sixty votes needed.[34] In this respect, the party leadership and organized labor were acting together—albeit unsuccessfully—to enhance party cohesion on a bill that had the clear support of President Carter.

Perhaps because the support of the congressional Democratic leadership was clearly strong, many have chosen to blame President Carter for the outcome, arguing that the administration did little to help the bill. Thomas Ferguson and Joel Rogers, for example, wrote in 1979 that the fate of the bill showed "the inability of trade union leaders . . . to exact major support from an Administration they helped place in power."[35] Archival sources show, however, that administration lobbyists, and the president himself, devoted considerable energy to promoting the bill, despite some initial reluctance. In the midst of the battle for cloture in the Senate, Stuart Eizenstat, head of the White House Domestic Policy Staff, wrote to President Carter that "everything that we have heard indicates labor is very satisfied with our efforts thus far. The Administration has done, we believe, a good job in working with the Congressional leadership and with labor on the bill." Eizenstat continued: "Your standing with the AFL-CIO and other unions would be greatly enhanced if, at this critical juncture, you publicly become more involved in the effort to get cloture. . . . I do not think there is much political downside to a more visible presence in this effort by you: the business groups already know of your position on the bill, and they are unlikely to regard us any more highly if you stay away from more public involvement."[36] In response to this memo, Carter phoned two of the three southern senators whom Eizenstat had identified as crucial to the legislative outcome.[37] Another Carter aide remarked, "We busted our ass on that labor law reform, and it cost us politically."[38] Thomas Donahue, a top assistant to George Meany, later concluded flatly: "The Carter administration could not have done more than it did on labor law reform."[39]

But there is also good reason to believe that President Carter could have taken on a more forceful role in promoting the legislation, both by attempting to shift public opinion and by taking more time to persuade recalcitrant senators. Carter rarely commented publicly on the bill, and when he did his comments seemed defensive and guarded.[40] Moreover, research by historian Martin Halpern shows that during the crucial days and hours when the effort to overcome the Senate filibuster was in full swing, Carter apparently did not make it a top priority. The president's official diary indicates that on the days leading up to the final vote he did not meet personally with any senators and spent no more than twenty minutes on the phone promoting the bill. In stark contrast, Carter made eighty-seven phone calls to senators prior to the vote on the Panama Canal Treaty. As Halpern concludes, on labor law reform "there was no inclination to wheel and deal to get the bill passed."[41]

Still, one can question how much difference a forceful presidential effort could have made. The one thing we know for certain is that the capacity of the conservative coalition in the Senate to block pro-union legislation was unimpeded. Out of eighteen southern Democrats voting in the Senate, fifteen opposed the key cloture motion and thereby contributed decisively to labor's defeat. And of the three southern Democrats who voted for cloture, two of them, Wendell H. Ford and Walter Huddleston, were from Kentucky, a border state. The third Democratic senator, Jim Sasser of Tennessee, voted with labor but, according to *Congressional Quarterly*, only at "considerable political cost to himself."[42] At the same time, only two nonsouthern Democrats voted consistently against the cloture votes. Finally, there was unanimous support for cloture by the members of *both* parties from the Northeast. The solid southern opposition, grounded in generations of regional antipathy to unionism, was therefore a major cause of the bill's defeat.

Crucial to this exercise of southern power was the filibuster. The UAW's chief Washington lobbyist, Howard Paster, commented: "The biggest thing working against us was an undemocratic system."[43] The AFL-CIO concluded that "In the end, the bill failed because majority rule and compromise were not allowed to work."[44] It seems likely, then, that the United States long ago would have experienced labor law reform, as well as the repeal of section 14(b) of Taft-Hartley, if the Senate had not maintained this antimajoritarian institution.[45]

In addition, the conservative coalition was reinforced by business interests, which were more engaged in politics during the late 1970s.[46] The AFL-CIO's Andrew Biemiller observed, "A major reason for the negativism of the 95th Congress was increased activity on the part of business lobbyists. Their principal tactic was back-home contacts. For years the labor movement relied on this tactic as well, just as we did in the current Congress. The cold fact is, however, that business did it more often, with more people and with a zeal orchestrated by highly paid public relations consultants who made each fight appear to be a holy war that commanded the all-out support of businessmen from around the country."[47] As the battle over common situs picketing had shown, business organizations such as the Business Roundtable, the National Federation of Independent Business, and the U.S. Chamber of Commerce had learned how to effectively flood Capitol Hill with letters, mailgrams, and phone calls from members' local constituents. Another major factor in business lobbying efforts was a remarkable increase in campaign contributions. The number of business-oriented political action committees expanded sixfold in the years leading up to the labor law reform vote. From 1972 to 1978, the total expenditure of corporate and trade association PACs grew from $8 million to $39 million, while union PAC expenditures grew only from $8.5 to $28.6 million.[48]

However, it is not clear that a sudden business mobilization was really a major cause of labor's failure to win labor law reform. Viewed in historical perspective, the political patterns and alignments revealed in this defeat in the 1970s share much with those in earlier periods. Labor's influence was actually constrained in the old-fashioned way—by the appearance of the regionally based conservative coalition, aided and abetted by the business community putting to use intensified, but hardly novel, techniques of grassroots and insider lobbying. The labor movement, for its part, responded by allying with a Democratic president and congressional liberals to wage common struggle against the forces of congressional obstruction. In this regard, at least, the way in which organized labor tried to maneuver through America's labyrinthine system of "separated institutions sharing powers" had not changed fundamentally: these were very old patterns, dating back to at least the New Deal era.

We must also question the more polemical assertions that labor's interests were betrayed by the Democratic Party as a whole. Prominent labor historian David Montgomery, for example, concluded shortly after these defeats that "years of loyalty to the Democrats are now yielding the most paltry rewards for the labor movement." Likewise, Joel Rogers complains about "massive Democratic defections" on all labor law reform bills in the postwar era. Mike Davis even calls the 1978 defeat "the biggest debacle in the AFL-CIO's history."[49] In making such claims, neither Montgomery, Davis, nor Rogers engages in any detailed analysis of the course of the labor law reform battle, or in any explicit evaluation of competing explanations for reform's defeat. They overlook the key role of the conservative coalition acting in the Senate, miss the massive Democratic majority for reform in the House, and ignore the consistent support among the vast majority of Democrats in both bodies for labor's position.[50] In reality, there was no massive "betrayal" of labor interests by northern Democrats. *Instead, we find just the entirely predictable hostility to union demands on the part of southerners who did not have a labor constituency in the first place, and therefore owed labor no "loyalty."*

Nonetheless, the defeat of labor law reform produced much frustration among union leaders. Many had sincerely believed that the bill could pass, and they had hoped, perhaps naively, that chief executives in many unionized corporations would stay neutral in such a battle. When such business officials joined the opposition or acquiesced in the Business Roundtable's high-pressure campaign against reform, the labor leaders were especially incensed.[51] In the aftermath of the defeat, UAW President Douglas Fraser furiously accused business leaders not just of attacking organized labor but of waging a "class war": "I believe leaders of the business community, with few exceptions, have chosen to a wage a one-sided class war today in this country—a war against working people, the unemployed, the poor, the minorities, the very young and the very old, even many in the middle class of our society. The leaders of industry, commerce, and finance in the U.S. have broken and discarded the fragile, unwritten contract previously existing during a period of growth and progress."[52]

This frustration eventually came to be directed toward President Carter, notwithstanding his support for the bill. Thus, while Fraser privately wrote Carter to say that "no one can fault you, Secretary Marshall, or your staff for failure of will—we just couldn't make it," he publicly complained of "an ineffective Administration, unable to come to grips with the problems of the nation."[53] Presidential assistant and labor liaison Landon Butler told Carter in a memo that "most rank-and-file labor leaders blamed the labor law reform loss on the Administration, and the leadership did little to discourage that view." In that December 1980 review of the administration's relationship with organized labor, Butler concluded that the internal disunity of the labor movement made it all the more likely that union leaders would blame Carter for defeats that were not the president's fault: "I believed then, and I believe now, that the extra degree of bitterness that infused the labor movement's criticism of the Administration throughout late 1977 and 1978 stemmed from the severe institutional disarray that existed at that time within the labor movement itself."[54]

Labor's "institutional disarray," distinctly rooted in the labor movement's own earlier crisis of representation, kept union leaders from reliably delivering labor's political resources or effectively managing the growing discontent in the ranks. Such debilities came exactly at the time when Congress and the Democratic Party were manifesting institutional fragmentation and disintegration in their own ways. The combination of factors made the defeat of labor law reform more damaging to the labor/Democrat alliance than had defeats in the 1960s and before. The harm to that relationship was the most important result of the weakening of concentrated bargaining capacity: by hindering coordination and consultation, fragmentation ate away at trust and imperiled cooperation between labor leaders and the White House. Mutual scapegoating and "acting out" threatened to become the prevailing modes of action, as a sullen withdrawal of the two sides to a more comfortable arm's-length distance seemed unavoidable. It was while relations were in this delicate condition that conflicts over how to best manage inflation would take their toll.

Battles in the Great Inflation War

Like the Johnson administration before it, the Carter administration faced an inflation problem and tried to secure the help of the unions in managing it. As before, the cooperation of the unions in wage restraint was seen as essential if inflation was to be fought without turning to tight monetary policy or higher taxes. Moreover, the effort to obtain union cooperation had similarly contradictory results: it both pushed the White House and the labor movement toward closer collaboration and fostered greater hostility between them. The key difference between the two cases was that in the 1960s, Johnson chose to abandon a serious battle against inflation in order to retain labor's support, while in the 1970s Carter was ultimately forced to choose a recessionary solution that ensured the enmity of a large portion of the union leadership.

During the 1970s inflation emerged in all advanced industrial societies as a severe problem that seemed to threaten the stability of the social order as a whole. The reasons for this inflationary surge continue to be debated.[55] Some scholars have blamed the Johnson administration, which had been unable and unwilling to raise taxes sufficiently to cover the increased government outlays needed to pay for both the Vietnam War and the Great Society. Others have pointed to the effects of excessive wage settlements and declining worker productivity, an undervalued dollar in international currency markets, lax monetary policy by the Federal Reserve Board, rising food and energy prices on international markets, excessive government regulation, and the rise of self-fulfilling inflationary expectations among both consumers and producers. Whatever the merit of these various explanations, it was clear to the administration that a high inflation rate was a major political danger: President Carter was determined to take the steps necessary to slow or reverse it.

Administration economists believed that to bypass a deflationary economic downturn, some system of wage and price guidelines had to be adopted, requiring the cooperation of both labor and business. In June 1978 Jimmy Carter wrote to George Meany, "A joint effort by business, labor and government to achieve a deceleration of wage and price increases is . . . an essential ingredient of any strategy to bring down inflation without putting the economy through the wringer."[56] But the unions were skeptical of this idea for the same reasons as during the Johnson presidency: they doubted that the guidelines could be implemented fairly or effectively, and they feared the effects of wage restraint on internal union politics. In any case, the decentralized and localized character of much of American collective bargaining—not to mention the limited powers of the AFL-CIO over the individual national unions—raised serious questions about the feasibility of coordinated union wage restraint. As Labor Secretary Marshall noted in a letter to President Carter, George Meany was "unwilling to make a call for cooperation that would be repudiated by a large number of labor leaders. Specifically, he states clearly that he, *Meany, does not want to make a commitment that he cannot keep*. . . . He does not want to be put into the embarrassing position of being repudiated as the leader of the labor movement."[57]

Thus, the AFL-CIO and national union leaders resisted any form of incomes policy, proposing instead that inflation be lowered either through direct intervention against rising food and energy prices or through selective credit controls. But even as the AFL-CIO was complaining, the inflation rate crept upward, forcing administration officials to anxiously appraise their policy options. The result would be a televised speech to the nation on October 24, 1978, in which President Carter announced a regime of voluntary wage and price guidelines, along with a renewed commitment to reducing the budget deficit and scaling back unreasonable government regulations. The president called inflation "our most serious domestic problem" and declared: "We must face a time of national austerity."[58] Under the proposed guidelines, wages would be expected to rise no more than 7 percent a year, and prices would increase no more than 5 percent over their average level in the preceding 1976–77 period. Employers who violated these norms would be denied federal procurement contracts. In order to help implement the guidelines, the president appointed economist Alfred Kahn to serve as chair of the Council on Wage and Price Stability, a new White House body composed of key administration economic policymakers.

The AFL-CIO response to the initiative was not favorable. Meany lambasted the policy, with its array of positive and negative incentives for compliance: "Nobody knows how it is going to work. And I'm a little bit skeptical about something that is referred to as the 'carrot and stick' approach. . . . Now, the carrot and stick approach is used on a beast of burden, and it works quite well. You see, you get him a carrot and then beat him a little bit with the stick. But I never heard a horse say that he approved of the idea."[59] Furthermore, Meany called the whole program "inequitable and unfair," going so far as to suggest that even a program of mandatory wage and price controls would be superior. "The way to control inflation is to control it—not to throw cream puffs at it," Meany insisted.[60] White House officials, for their part, viewed these comments as hyperbole intended to deflect attention from the AFL-CIO's own lack of any coherent ideas about how to combat inflation.

Meany's public hostility to the program also reflected his irritation at the way in which the administration had gone about preparing the initiative. In fact, issues of access and consultation were soon to profoundly affect labor/Democrat ties. In September 1978 Meany had demanded a personal meeting with Carter before any new anti-inflation program was announced. Carter was, however, increasingly angry with Meany for his repeated public criticism of the president's performance. In August 1978 Meany had publicly attacked the administration for brokering a restrained wage settlement between the U.S. Postal Service and its unions—a settlement the administration considered crucial to its anti-inflation strategy.[61] And long before that Meany had given his notorious "C minus" grade to Carter for his first year in office. In light of this rhetoric, Carter was wary of giving Meany yet another public opportunity to vent his ire, and he declined any further meetings with the AFL-CIO leader during the fall of 1978.

From Meany's perspective, that decision constituted a major violation of the mode of personal consultation on which he had insisted as a condition for his support. The result was a profound rupture in the relations between Carter and Meany—and, more broadly, between the AFL-CIO and the administration—which lasted from late September 1978 to early January 1979. All discussion came to a halt, and Carter conspicuously refused to reappoint Meany to a position he held on the Communications Satellite Corporation board. AFL-CIO Secretary-Treasurer Lane Kirkland subsequently resigned in protest from his positions on the Advisory Committee of the Arms Control and Disarmament Agency and the National Advisory Committee for Women. Carter White House aides described Meany as a "senile old man," and Carter reportedly was "absolutely livid" with anger at the federation president.[62]

The breakdown in communication also threatened a key source of Meany's power over other union leaders, as Carter's top labor advisers (Landon Butler, Stuart Eizenstat, and Ray Marshall) noted in a memo to the president: "Since one of the AFL-CIO's most important political resources with their affiliated unions is access to the Administration, the decision not to meet has created a special problem for George Meany. This is compounded by growing criticism within the AFL-CIO Executive Council of the way Meany has handled his relationships with the Administration."[63] Indeed, by late 1978 discontented union leaders sought to establish new lines of communications with the administration, effectively bypassing Meany and undermining his role as federation president. Carter labor liaison Landon Butler described these developments:

> Although Mr. Meany kept up a constant barrage of public criticism during this period, a number of influential labor leaders (including Paul Hall of the Seafarers, who was regarded as one of Meany's most loyal allies) were telling me privately that many key labor officials believed that Mr. Meany had gone too far. Hall and others urged me privately to begin circumventing the AFL-CIO by establishing direct political ties with the Presidents of major unions. I followed their advice and, in October, I began working directly with the presidents of the forty or more individual AFL-CIO unions which were large enough to command the attention of the White House.[64]

In December, Glenn Watts, president of the Communications Workers of America, charged publicly that Meany's attacks on the Carter administration were "terrible" and that Meany had "done a tremendous disservice to the country and the labor movement" by allowing the "estrangement" from the administration to become so protracted. "Unfortunately, the chief spokesman for labor somehow has become estranged from the administration so no effective representation can be made" on any major issue by the union movement, Watts claimed.[65]

The breakdown in relations was equally disturbing to the political and economic advisers to the president. Stuart Eizenstat, along with Charles Schultze, chair of the Council of Economic Advisers, and anti-inflation czar Alfred Kahn wrote a joint memo to the president in early December 1978, stressing the importance of reconciling with Meany. They noted that "the present tense situation is, we think, highly unfortunate" and continued: "Whatever the validity of his assertions, it is unfortunate to have the leader of the country's largest labor federation feel, as he has indicated to several people, that the President has not fulfilled his one promise to him, namely, to be available to him whenever he asked."[66] The advisers also pointed out that the dispute made it all the more difficult to secure union cooperation with the wage and price guidelines.

As a result of these various pressures, a meeting was finally arranged on January 12, 1979, to forge a reconciliation. The gathering—President Carter and Vice President Mondale, several of their key advisers, and George Meany, Lane Kirkland, Thomas Donahue (a top aide to Meany), and six national union presidents—was widely viewed as a turning point in the AFL-CIO/White House relationship. According to Kirkland, the union leaders "expressed some dissatisfaction with the fact that we were frequently getting surprised by positions taken in areas of very direct concern to us, winding up in battles that could have been avoided with proper advance notice and consultation."[67] To address the problem, the principals agreed on a more structured mode of consultation, whereby AFL-CIO leaders as well as several national union presidents would meet on a regular (usually monthly) basis with Vice President Mondale (who was considered a labor ally within the administration), relevant cabinet secretaries, and the major economic policy advisers. The meeting also led to an agreement to broaden the representation of other union leaders in top level consultations, thereby to some degree alleviating the problem of long-standing personal conflicts between Carter and Meany.

The National Accord

While the new consultative format did not resolve fundamental policy conflicts, it did facilitate the development of one of the more interesting (and least remembered) political innovations of the Carter years: the so-called National Accord between the administration and organized labor. This arrangement grew out of the administration's efforts to obtain the cooperation of the labor movement with the voluntary wage standards announced in October 1978. During 1979 the high inflation rate persisted, alongside continued problems of low productivity and slow economic growth. From December 1978 to December 1979, the consumer price index rose by 13.3 percent. The record of union wage restraint over this time was at best mixed, and further efforts to secure union cooperation seemed to require deeper ties with labor.

The response of both the administration and labor was described in a memo by Landon Butler: "In April and May, 1979, Lane Kirkland told me privately that he was prepared to enter into a 'social contract' with the Carter Administration. Lane pointed out that the Callaghan government's social contract in England involved specific concessions on policy questions in return for the cooperation of the British trade unions in a voluntary wage guideline program."[68] In this spirit, Butler and Kirkland engaged in a series of meetings on the shape of an American version of a social contract. Butler stated that on behalf of the administration, he hoped to obtain labor's support for arms control agreements, the energy program, and continued wage guidelines. For his part, Kirkland wanted administration assurances on federal pay, on maritime issues, on enforcement of trade agreements, and on regular consultation between the administration and organized labor regarding major economic decisions.

These discussions, which often included Secretary of the Treasury William Miller and Labor Secretary Ray Marshall, finally resulted in a statement released on September 28, 1979, proclaiming an "accord" between the administration and the "American labor leadership."[69] The accord was based on the need declared by both parties "to assure that the austerity arising from battling inflation is fairly shared, while protecting those members of society who are least able to bear the burden." The AFL-CIO acknowledged that inflation "must be the top priority of government," while the administration recognized that fighting inflation through increased unemployment was "inconsistent with the equitable sharing of sacrifice." The administration hoped that the accord would create a more favorable setting for union wage restraint—in effect providing a cover for union leaders who resisted "excessive" wage increases in collective bargaining. The AFL-CIO, in its turn, expected more involvement in budgetary and economic decision making, as well as more thorough consideration of its views on a range of union-related issues. An important supplement to the accord was the establishment of a fifteen-member tripartite Pay Advisory Board that would assist in formulating voluntary wage guidelines and would monitor their success. John Dunlop, the former secretary of labor so well trusted by the AFL-CIO establishment, was tapped to head the new board, further helping to instill union confidence.

Like the Johnson-era efforts at union inclusion, the National Accord bore a resemblance to neo-corporatist developments in Western Europe. AFL-CIO spokesman Allen Zack told a reporter, "It is quite a historic document. It's about as far as you can go toward a social contract here in the U.S. without a parliamentary system. Never before has the legitimate role of the labor movement been recognized in such a way."[70] In reality, though, the accord suffered the same constraints that had undercut similar policies during the 1960s: namely, decentralized collective bargaining and the inability of White House officials (including the president) to really deliver budgetary and policy outcomes favorable to the labor movement. Likewise, the decentralized and fragmented nature of business organizations, and their complete lack of control over the pricing decisions of individual firms, meant that the third side of any genuinely "tripartite" arrangement was also deficient.

Whatever its limitations as an instrument of economic management, the accord did improve the relationship between the AFL-CIO and the Carter administration. The relationship was smoothed further by the decision by George Meany to step down as AFL-CIO president in November 1979 (at the venerable age of 85), allowing the accession of his designated successor, Lane Kirkland. Kirkland already had developed far better personal ties with Carter. Like the president, Kirkland was an intellectual and a southerner, and they shared a maritime background—Carter in the navy, and Kirkland as a former first mate in the merchant marines. They did not have to bridge the personal and cultural gulf that had separated the New York Irish plumber from the southern farmer/engineer in the White House. As Labor Secretary Ray Marshall later commented, "Lane Kirkland had a more accommodating style in approaching problems than George Meany. . . . Lane is less blunt, more flexible, more of a negotiator."[71]

The improvements in personal relationships and formalized modes of consultation would, however, do little to extinguish the conflicts between labor and the administration. The limitations of the accord became clear soon after January 1980, when the administration announced its fiscal year 1981 budget. The initial budget proposal seemed to have protected many of the interests of organized labor and other liberal constituencies. In his analysis of the agreement, Robert J. Flanagan declares that "as a result of the National Accord, the AFL-CIO was granted an unusually large amount of information and consultation concerning details of the Carter administration's 1981 budget proposal as that proposal was in the final stages of preparation in late 1979."[72] The AFL-CIO claimed to have been instrumental in pressing the administration to expand spending on youth unemployment programs and low-income housing and in discouraging the administration from proposing a balanced budget.[73] But these gains were soon threatened by increasing political and economic pressure on the administration, both from Congress and from Wall Street, to get the inflation rate under control. As demands for a balanced budget grew on Capitol Hill, the administration felt compelled to present a revised and more restrained budget. The new budget proposed in March contained $17 billion in cuts, including many reductions in programs (such as public works, public service employment, and the indexing of social security benefits) that the AFL-CIO had originally entered the accord to protect.

Meanwhile, Federal Reserve Board Chairman Paul Volcker was advancing his own agenda for fighting inflation—one that took even less heed of the interests of organized labor. President Carter had appointed Volcker in July 1979, in part with the aim of reassuring the financial world at a time when inflation was rising precipitously. Volcker and his monetarist allies at the Reserve Board believed that the only remedy for out-of-control inflationary expectations was a sharp tightening of the money supply. Under Volcker's leadership, the board quickly carried out such a policy, but in the first few months of 1980 the effects appeared to be very limited. In March 1980, therefore, President Carter invoked the Credit Control Act, asking the Federal Reserve Board to impose new controls on consumer credit, including credit card purchases. But when consumers complied with unexpected readiness to these new incentives and the president's calls for austerity, the result was an excessively large reduction in consumer borrowing and a steep decline in economic growth. Through the joint action of the Reserve Board and the administration, the economy had been inadvertently plunged into the kind of major recession that the White House had been trying to avoid. Unemployment quickly rose from 6.3 percent in March 1980 to 7.8 percent by July, and industrial production decreased by more than 8 percent. The economy would not regain prosperity for the remainder of President Carter's term in office, especially since the Reserve Board remained determined to quash any remaining inflationary impulses.[74]

By 1980 it was clear that Carter's efforts to manage inflation through a nonrecessionary strategy had failed. There were many reasons for that failure, not the least of which was the rise in oil prices engendered by the Iranian revolution and subsequent pricing decisions by the Organization of Petroleum Exporting Countries (OPEC). But it was also of some consequence that the AFL-CIO proved incapable of initiating and implementing a forward-looking and feasible set of alternative policies. Because of the deterioration of the economic resources of the labor movement and its own internal conflicts and inadequate leadership, the federation could hardly play the role sketched out for it under a broad reading of the National Accord. Meany's obstreperous attacks on Carter and facile demands for "mandatory controls on everything" were no substitutes for a program that could unite the labor movement around policies balancing the interests of society with those of unionized workers. Thus, the conclusion of Carter aide Landon Butler still stands: "To a distressing degree the institutional decisions which labor reached during this period were designed simply to mollify vocal minorities within the labor movement itself; and, more often than not, the easiest way to mollify the critics was to attack the Administration. Organized labor, as an institution, was unable to cope with its responsibilities when a Democratic Administration took office."[75] At the same time, the weakening of presidential bargaining capacity had prevented Carter from delivering on his share of the promises implied by the National Accord.

In the final analysis, the problems the administration faced were deeply rooted, reflecting adverse international economic developments as well as the fragmentation of bargaining capacity in the political and economic environment at home. As the simultaneous experience of the Callaghan government in Britain (like the later travails of the Mitterrand government in France) suggests, the exigencies of the international economy at this time invariably produced tensions and sometimes major confrontations between social democratic governments and their core constituencies.[76] In neither Britain nor the United States did incomes policies succeed. Given these constraints, it is hard to see how even the most talented of political leaders could have governed without confronting key elements of the Democratic coalition. Ultimately, it would take a Republican president willing to oversee the worst economic downturn since the Great Depression to finally arrest inflation.

Fragmentation Redux: The 1980 Nominating Process

"In January, 1979, there was the real possibility that organized labor would abandon *en masse* the Carter/Mondale ticket in 1980," recalled Landon Butler in a letter to the president during the waning days of the administration.[77] The loyalties of the unions weighed on the minds of administration strategists as they pondered the means to derail the campaign of Senator Edward Kennedy for the Democratic nomination. As one Carter aide observed in reference to the more liberal, activist unions: "They're probably the most important group in Democratic Party politics. No other group in the Democratic Party has the money. When you get into voter registration, that's who you go to. And these groups get involved in the primaries." [78]

Motivated by such concerns, the administration launched a concerted effort to shore up union support.[79] Key to the administration's strategy was the fulfillment of the specific needs of individual unions. The bargaining power of the national unions was enhanced by Kennedy's threat to the president's renomination, and union leaders took advantage of the opportunity to secure administration support for their particular demands. The White House helped the Steelworkers, for example, by imposing a "trigger price" on steel imports in order to prevent domestic steel from being undersold. For the apparel and textile unions, the administration tightened restrictions on imports and exempted many clothing and textile products from deep tariff reductions in the newly negotiated multilateral trade agreement. The maritime unions gained support for cargo preference legislation, and the building and construction trades benefited from continued administration support for the Davis-Bacon Act. The politically crucial UAW sought and received administration endorsement of the Chrysler loan guarantee, a proposal that also required congressional approval. Such relationships constituted, as Elizabeth Drew has noted, a "cat's cradle of arrangements between the White House and labor which it would be very difficult for many unions to pull out of." [80]

As it made these deals, the administration found itself increasingly dependent on the more conservative wing of the labor movement, dominated by the maritime unions and building trades. Thus, while in 1977 Hamilton Jordan had considered such progressive unions as the Machinists, UAW, and Communication Workers "our real base of support in labor," by the end of Carter's term those were the unions defecting to the Kennedy campaign.[81] The administration therefore found it more feasible to pursue narrow deals with conservative unions than to attempt to resuscitate the more liberal union coalition that had promoted Carter in 1976.

Meanwhile, Machinists President William Winpisinger was organizing union support for the Kennedy campaign. Kennedy's appeal to union leaders rested on his consistent record of support for labor's legislative aims, including national health care and labor law reform, and his opposition to the administration's budget cuts and its tacit approval of a restrictive monetary policy. In addition, many unions simply doubted that Carter could be reelected. Thus, such politically powerful unions as the Machinists, AFSCME, and the AFT all endorsed Kennedy and worked actively for his nomination. Nevertheless, Kennedy ultimately failed to secure the sweeping support within organized labor that some had predicted, and his campaign suffered from this loss. In the end, the efforts of the pro-Kennedy unions could not overcome the inherent liabilities of their candidate and the impressive strengths of an incumbent president.

After Carter finally secured renomination, and it was clear that Ronald

Reagan would be the GOP nominee, the unions united in active support of the Carter campaign.[82] Landon Butler recalled: "The labor movement was an integral part of our general election campaign. There were many states, such as Michigan, Ohio, and Pennsylvania, where labor was the backbone of our field effort; in these states and others, labor may well have had more paid staff working for the Democratic ticket than the Carter/Mondale campaign itself."[83] But these resources were not enough to revive the electoral prospects of the beleaguered Democratic nominee. As the election approached, both unemployment and inflation exceeded the levels that had existed when Carter beat Gerald Ford in 1976. Moreover, in response to continuing inflation, the Federal Reserve Board tightened reserves and raised interest rates further, only causing more damage to the president's tenuous reputation as an economic manager. Even though exit polls showed that union households gave Carter a plurality of 49 percent of their vote versus 41 percent for Ronald Reagan, the president lost by a lopsided margin.[84] After four years of splintering and fragmentation, the Democratic Party was out of power, and organized labor faced a new administration—one that felt little need to consult, much less to appease, the leadership of the labor movement.

There were certainly multiple causes of the level of conflict between the unions and the Democratic administration. Differences in ideology and personality between Meany and Carter played a role, as did issues of consultation and organizational privilege. Also, the defeat on labor law reform left labor leaders very disillusioned (although, in truth, it was hardly a novel outcome, and it was not fair to lay the blame at the president's door). But the most important single cause, the constant irritant that provoked both sides, was the rising rate of inflation, which created tremendous pressures to take steps that no one was institutionally or politically capable of carrying out. Much like the budget deficit in the 1980s and early 1990s, the need to slow inflation was an external condition that simultaneously constricted the liberal agenda and induced painful friction between Democratic policymakers and their interest group allies. Inflation drove the administration toward wage and price guidelines that the unions hated and, when those failed, toward tighter fiscal and monetary policies that the unions hated even more. But labor had no plausible alternatives of its own.

Managing these problems was complicated by the greater fragmentation of bargaining capacity in the Washington community. The levers of power in Congress and the Washington community that Carter might have manipulated in order to deliver on his promises were increasingly difficult to grasp. At the same time, the deep divisions within the labor movement and the weak bargaining capacity of George Meany made labor an unreliable partner for national Democratic officeholders. We can imagine a very different scenario: if Congress had been more cohesive, President Carter might have seen labor law reform and other liberal measures through to enactment, and that measure of success might have made the unions more willing to cooperate in other areas. Similarly, if the labor movement has been more unified, the initial conflicts with Carter over issues of access and appointments, which were mainly driven by union factionalism, could easily have been avoided (as, in fact, they were during the Clinton administration). If labor had controlled its own economic resources more effectively, it might have delivered effective wage restraint and thus averted the need for a recessionary downturn. And if labor had generated stronger central leadership, accepted as legitimate by the rest of the labor movement, the scapegoating and petty quarrels that erupted in labor's relationship with Carter might never have arisen.

Sadly, perhaps, the model of fragmented pluralism stands largely confirmed by this story of conflict. A fragmentation of bargaining capacity made trust and cooperation more difficult, and it precipitated a higher level of conflict and disillusionment when hard times arrived. Unions pursued social welfare legislation in Congress with less success than before and became preoccupied with the defense of earlier achievements. And as the house of labor fell into disarray, other interest groups increasingly found their own paths through national politics, becoming in the process less willing to let labor dominate the leadership of the Democratic coalition. Finally, there was even a partial descent into a new particularism, as unions struck separate deals with the administration for various union-specific benefits.

For union leaders, much that they had liked about national politics in the mid-1960s had now been destroyed or disrupted. If labor ever hoped to recreate the more cooperative relationships of the past, a major program of institutional reconstruction would be required. This program would have to encompass both the labor movement and the Democratic Party, and it would take many years of steady work to accomplish. The question for the decade ahead was whether the unions would be able to pursue such a program—and, if so, whether they could prevail over the centrifugal forces still so strong in the American polity.

6 *The Union Strategy to Regain the Presidency*

In the aftermath of a deeply troubled Democratic administration and the election of an unusually conservative Republican president, the political strategy of the labor movement was left a shambles. In reviewing the wreckage, union leaders became convinced that inadequacies within the Democratic Party's *structure*, especially its decision-making and nominating procedures, were the main reason that the party had suffered such alarming electoral defeat and been burdened with such unreliable or ineffectual officeholders, both in the White House and on Capitol Hill. The solution was an increase in union power, which would both make the Democrats more favorably disposed toward labor interests and also ensure that the Democrats nominated more electable and reliable candidates. As union leaders saw it, the party had lost its moorings, and Jimmy Carter had alienated key constituencies. If labor should become stronger, such constituencies (especially working-class white men) could be won back, and the old New Deal coalition would be revived. The leadership believed that the basic formula for Democratic electoral success and effective governance had been perfected in the campaigns and administrations of John Kennedy and Lyndon Johnson. To reclaim such successes, labor need only find the right candidates and secure their nomination by the Democratic Party. In pursuing this strategy, the unions saw themselves not just as interest groups seeking benefits from the party most predisposed toward their interests but also as *partisans* seeking to improve the overall health of the party as a competitor in national elections.

This view translated into a new labor effort to strengthen its bargaining position within the presidential nominating process. Achieving this goal required unions not only to augment their political resources (such as money and votes) but also to achieve a much greater degree of unity and coordination in deploying such resources. Greater coordination would, however, necessitate that power be concentrated in fewer hands—moving precisely in the opposite direction of the recent reforms. The crisis of representation in the nominating process in the late 1960s had dispersed power outward and downward to local union activists, to a multitude of campaign contributors, and to numerous primary voters and caucus participants. The incentives of this new system had also made labor union participation more fragmented and localized, and even national union leaders found it difficult to deliver the political resources nominally at their command. Thus, in the eyes of many union officials, as well as the federation leadership, this dispersal of power had gone too far. It was now time to restore the clout of the labor movement through a renewed coordination of union involvement in nominating politics. But any such effort would have to steer clear of the tendencies toward autocratic "bossism" that had destroyed the more hierarchical decision-making processes of the 1960s. Especially given the anxieties of the more liberal unions, the new version of interunion coordination could only gain general support if the AFL-CIO would play a reformed role, closer to a facilitating agent than a presumptive and unrepresentative broker for the entire labor movement.

The aspiration among unionists to enhance their power was, of course, greatly intensified by their profound dislike—even hatred—for the administration of Ronald Reagan. Although Reagan, who had led the Screen Actor's Guild in the 1940s, was the first union leader ever elected president, most labor leaders believed that his administration was engaged in a systematic effort to destroy the foundations of union economic and political power. To stop Reagan, the Democrats would have to maintain control of Congress and, ideally, elect a new president. In the next chapter, labor's strategy toward Congress will be explored. In this chapter, I describe how the AFL-CIO sought to gain more influence in the Democratic presidential nominating process, in some ways trying to resuscitate elements of the old power broker role that the shift toward primaries and caucuses had undone. To achieve this goal, the federation sought to reconcentrate bargaining power in the nominating process among a smaller number of top leaders, while avoiding the unacceptably exclusionary features of the earlier mode of elite brokerage. Although this effort would meet with only partial success, it did show the extent to which the new system created avenues for impressive new forms of union activism.

Labor's Renewed Commitment to the Democratic Party

The November 1981 AFL-CIO convention in Washington, D.C., initiated a series of important developments in the role of organized labor in the Democratic Party. Alexander Barkan finally stepped down as director of AFL-CIO COPE, replaced by his second-in-command, John Perkins—a former carpenter who had worked in the Washington headquarters of the Committee on Political Education since 1971. Within days of Barkan's retirement, Perkins met with AFL-CIO President Lane Kirkland (himself in the job for only two years) to discuss ways of improving the AFL-CIO's relationship with other constituencies within the Democratic Party, including the liberal "New Politics" faction that had become so alienated from the AFL-CIO during the previous decade.[1] Rather than continuing the Meany/Barkan policy of intransigent opposition to all forms of affirmative action and party reform, Perkins and Kirkland now seemed willing to accept the irreversibility of many (but not all) of the reforms of the 1970s. From now on, the federation leaders would pursue a policy of constructive engagement, encouraging union leaders and activists to publicly intervene in party deliberations and to exercise greater influence over the national party apparatus.

A key part of this strategy was the establishment of the Political Works Committee within the AFL-CIO Executive Council. Composed of sixteen union presidents representing the principal factions within the federation, the committee was charged with formulating and coordinating a long-term political strategy for the labor movement. One of the chief goals it endorsed was to strengthen union power within the Democratic National Committee (DNC). To achieve this end, union leaders soon gained 35 seats (out of 325) on the DNC, including 15 of the 25 at-large seats and 4 of the 35 seats on the party's executive committee. At the same time, labor unions increased their financial support for the DNC, providing $2.5 million of the total 1983 budget of $7 million.[2] Labor also played a crucial part in securing the selection of Charles T. Manatt as the DNC's new chairman, and Manatt in turn supported the incorporation of union leaders within the party machinery.

Under the supervision of COPE Director Perkins, the federation also turned in a limited way to the use of "outsider" tactics of political mobilization. In September 1981 the AFL-CIO sponsored a giant "Solidarity Day" demonstration in Washington, D.C., in an effort to show the continuing vitality of the labor movement's mass base; it drew at least 250,000 union members. The demonstration was a significant departure from the AFL-CIO's previous antagonism toward most forms of mass protest. Solidarity Day also helped strengthen the AFL-CIO's relationship with other parts of the liberal coalition (such as women, gays, blacks, consumer groups, middle-class liberals, etc.) with whom ties had grown strained during the 1970s. Indeed, by the summer of 1982 one journalist would comment that "it is a measure of how far the AFL-CIO has traveled that Al Barkan's successor, Mr. Perkins, was recently the guest of honor at a Washington dinner sponsored by a homosexual political-action group."[3]

Perkins also began to modernize COPE's technical capacities, including its use of computers, television, direct mail, and polling.[4] These enhanced capacities were made available to both state and local federations, as well as to the individual national unions. State labor organizations installed computer terminals in order to have direct access to COPE's data banks, which held economic indicators, public opinion polls, and the names and addresses of union members. The federation also approved in 1981 a special $2 million assessment to establish the Labor Institute for Public Affairs (LIPA). Utilizing an elaborate new television studio setup at the AFL-CIO's Washington headquarters, LIPA produced radio and television commercials, including the highly visible "Union, YES!" campaign, and other informational programs for use by affiliated unions and state federations. These new commitments were funded by dues increases throughout the 1980s, funneling more money to the AFL-CIO headquarters and to the programs of national unions.[5]

As part of the strategy to deepen its party ties, the AFL-CIO also sought to influence the activities of the new Commission on Presidential Nomination—yet another Democratic Party commission set up to evaluate party rules and the delegate selection process. Organized in 1981 under the leadership of former governor James B. Hunt of North Carolina, the commission was co-chaired by UAW President Douglas Fraser and included broad union representation. The commission proposed, and the DNC ultimately approved, a set of changes intended to protect the interests of party regulars and the AFL-CIO by facilitating the early nomination of a "mainstream" candidate. The rules changes included (1) creating a class of "superdelegates"—mainly party officials and elected officeholders—who would be likely to support a more electable, traditional Democrat; (2) raising to 20 percent the amount of the vote needed in a congressional district or state before a candidate received delegate representation; and (3) instituting a thirteen-week window within which all caucuses and primaries (except Iowa and New Hampshire) would be held. This window would reduce the length of the campaign season and, union leaders hoped, would increase the likelihood of an early victor, thus securing party unity well before the onset of the general election campaign.

In addition to promoting these rules changes, President Kirkland and the federation's Political Works Committee began to consider the possibility of an official AFL-CIO endorsement of a candidate for the Democratic nomination. Kirkland argued that since 1968 unions had fallen into "a pattern that . . . was damaging to the internal solidarity of the trade union movement. With a premium on early and active participation in support of a prospective candidate, different parts of the trade union movement went for various candidates without consultation among themselves. . . . So you had the development of factionalism, with unions competing and vilifying each other."[6] The obvious solution was for the federation to forge an agreement among the national unions to endorse either a single candidate in the primaries or none at all. A unified endorsement promised a considerable enhancement—and recentralization—of union bargaining power in the nominating process, and the idea was immediately attractive to both Kirkland and national union leaders. As Kirkland observed, "If we are not in it, if we wait until the convention is over, then we are stuck with other people's choices one more time. Why should we be stuck with other people's choices—particularly if it coughs up candidates who are not saleable?" Steelworkers President Lloyd McBride stressed the need for a mechanism to discourage a union free-for-all: "We need a harness—something to prevent someone from laying hands on a candidate early. We need to stay hitched, so no one stampedes."[7]

For these reasons, in 1982 the Executive Council approved a plan for a federation endorsement in the 1984 nominating campaign. The body designated to make the official endorsement decision was the AFL-CIO General Board, composed of the presidents of all ninety-nine of the affiliated unions (the Executive Council, in contrast, then consisted of only thirty-five). To compensate for the widely varying sizes of the national unions, the vote of the union presidents would be weighted according to the numbers of members in each union. Thus, the presidents of the largest unions would have the most influence on the final decision to endorse. In order to ensure a wide base of labor support, the federation also required that any endorsement be approved by a two-thirds majority of the weighted votes.

Conceivably, a consensus within the federation on a single candidate might have been difficult to reach. The wide-ranging field included former Florida governor Reuben Askew, California Senator Alan Cranston, Ohio Senator John Glenn, the Reverend Jesse Jackson, Colorado Senator Gary Hart, South Carolina Senator Ernest Hollings, former vice president Walter Mondale, and former South Dakota senator George McGovern. Many of these politicians had long and impressive records of support for traditional labor issues. Nevertheless, it was Walter Mondale who quickly emerged among union leaders as not only the most reliably pro-labor candidate in the field but also the most electable. On October 1, 1983, he was endorsed by an overwhelming majority of the AFL-CIO General Board. Shortly thereafter, the 1.7 million member National Education Association (unaffiliated with the AFL-CIO) also endorsed Mondale, as did the National Organization for Women. The AFL-CIO found itself once again internally unified and comfortably allied with several other major elements of the liberal coalition (including the majority of black elected officials, who had also endorsed Mondale).

Both union leaders and Mondale operatives were well aware, however, of the perils inherent in the federation's move. One risk was that Mondale would be publicly tagged as the "big labor" candidate and suffer corresponding electoral damage. But Mondale's advisers felt that since Mondale would be characterized as an errand boy for the unions even without their endorsement, it made sense to seek and accept the benefits of the AFL-CIO's official support. Paul Jensen, the Mondale campaign labor liaison in 1984, concluded that "the value of the endorsement far outweighs its liabilities. There is no question, it is worth fighting for."[8]

Another drawback was that once the endorsement was made, the nonendorsed candidates would have little reason to avoid criticizing or even directly attacking the AFL-CIO itself. Indeed, shortly after the selection of Mondale was announced the Reverend Jesse Jackson attacked the AFL-CIO endorsement as an undemocratic decision by union "bosses." Jackson also declared that candidates who represent blacks, Hispanic voters, or women "don't have a snowball's chance of being heard" by the federation's white, male leadership.[9] It was not long before Senators Hart and Glenn also condemned the union intervention as a form of special interest bossism that diminished the influence of average Democratic primary voters.

A third danger was that the AFL-CIO and its affiliated unions would not be able to produce the promised resources. As one union leader warned, "If we are, in fact, a paper tiger, we certainly are going to be making that clear."[10] The most difficult task was to deliver the votes of the membership, which was of crucial importance in a system where primary voters and caucus participants determined the allocation of most of the delegates. Obviously, the effectiveness of the AFL-CIO's intervention largely rested on its being able to succeed in this area. Yet too much internal mobilization could be dangerous. Internal union dynamics, which sustained the leadership in power, were often predicated on a quiescent membership that did not challenge the status quo.[11] A mobilized membership could make new demands on the established leaders, possibly threatening their incumbency. Thus, a delicate balance had to be maintained between mobilizing the membership and encouraging the unpredictable and disruptive entry into the union power structure of members made newly active.

The dilemmas of mobilization became clear when unions and state federations experimented with new methods for activating the membership. One effort was called the "Face-to-Face" program, which required that shop stewards meet individually with union members to discuss political issues and the upcoming campaign. This on-the-job interaction promised to take advantage of the unions' existing structure to mobilize the membership, rather than bypassing such institutions through direct mail to members' households. Jan Pierce, an assistant vice president in the Communication Workers of America, explained the attraction of the approach: "The shop steward is the person closest to the member, has the best rapport, and is absolutely the most effective at breaking down the notion that the leadership is directing the membership on how to vote."[12]

However, effective grassroots mobilization was often severely constrained by the nature of the incentive structure in which local union leaders functioned. Such leaders were primarily interested in ensuring their own reelection, a preoccupation that did not make them particularly interested in spending precious time and energy on political activities that distracted from collective bargaining duties. William Winpisinger, then-president of the Machinists union, identified the major problem: "The weak link was the business agent at the local level. He'd get the message loud and clear, but even if he was a supporter of the message, he often would goof off in terms of the ABCs of getting it done."[13] Elected business agents were often overworked, and they feared the possibility of creating new avenues for internal rivals to gain influence. As another AFL-CIO leader complained, "Nothing happens unless the business agents and shop stewards are frightened for their jobs. Only that will move them. Local leadership does not perceive politics as part of its job. There is even some resentment at having to do politics. They understand they have to dump Reagan, but there's this inability and unwillingness to do anything about it."[14]

Despite these real limitations, the labor movement did eventually provide most of the financial, organizational, and electoral resources that it had originally promised to the endorsed candidate. The scale of the AFL-CIO's involvement is captured well in COPE Director Perkins's description of the role of labor in the New York primary:

> We had coordinators in every major population area, working full time on our program, and we had liaison persons in most local unions of 200 members and higher. . . . We had thousands of members and their spouses—*volunteers*—staffing phone banks in dozens of locations, polling our members, canvassing, distributing materials, conducting the register-and-vote drives.
>
> We distributed to our members in personally addressed letters to their homes, and in the form of leaflets at the job site and union halls and in neighborhoods, more than two million messages urging their support of Mondale and providing information on the records and policies of the candidates.[15]

Such activities led campaign specialists Herbert Alexander and Brian Haggerty to conclude that "labor's endorsement of and activities on behalf of Mondale were an influential—and probably essential—factor in his nomination. Mondale won seven of the 10 states with the largest blocks of AFL-CIO affiliated unionists, including New York, Pennsylvania, Illinois, Michigan, and New Jersey."[16] Even in the South, where unions have historically been underrepresented, AFL-CIO support was important, especially in the Georgia and Alabama primaries. The increased role of African Americans and unionized public employees (especially schoolteachers) in Democratic primaries enhanced labor's power even where its density in the workforce remained quite low. It seemed clear to journalists Jack Germond and Jules Witcover "that without the backing of the AFL-CIO and the NEA, [Mondale] would never have been nominated at all. Labor rescued him in the Alabama and Georgia primaries on Super Tuesday, in the Michigan caucuses the following Saturday, and in Illinois, New York and Pennsylvania in succeeding weeks."[17]

Labor union financial support was an important part of these electoral successes, although determining the exact expenditures by the unions is difficult.[18] Officially, labor unions declared that they spent about $3.1 million to support Mondale during the nominating contest. But unofficial estimates placed the total monetary value of union activity at somewhere between $10 and $20 million.[19] Even the lower of these two figures would make union contributions equivalent to nearly half the $20 million officially spent by the Mondale campaign prior to the nomination. Labor unions also leased phone banks and office space to the Mondale workers, thus saving the campaign the costs of outfitting its own offices (and some critics charged that unions leased these facilities at prices that were considerably less than their full market value). In the general election, it has been estimated, unions spent another $20 million.[20] This figure included $1.4 million in reported expenditures on pro-Mondale internal communications, $500,000 contributed to state-level Democratic Party voter turnout drives, and $1 million spent on AFL-CIO-produced television ads on labor issues. In addition, a good deal of money was spent on organizing hundreds of telephone banks and producing and distributing masses of campaign literature. These activities were coordinated by AFL-CIO COPE, which used its computer programs to tailor direct-mail appeals to union members in different industries and unions.

The actual behavior of union voters in the general election has often been interpreted as indicating a serious failure in electoral mobilization. Indeed, it has become the conventional wisdom that voters from union households defected from the Democratic candidate to an unprecedented degree in 1984. Reagan's 43.2 percent share of these voters, compared to Mondale's 56.8 percent, seemed to represent sad proof that unions were ineffective in influencing union members and their families. However, a more detailed voting analysis, recently conducted by political scientist David Sousa, leads to different conclusions.[21] First, it is not true that the percentage of union members voting for the Democratic presidential candidate represented a new low. Mondale's 56.8 percent of the union vote was quite near Hubert Humphrey's 57.9 percent in 1968, and it exceeded Jimmy Carter's 55.3 percent in 1980 and George McGovern's dismal 43.1 percent in 1972. Second, a comparison of the percentage of unionists who voted for Mondale (56.8 percent) with the percentage of *nonunion* voters for Mondale (37.4 percent) shows that labor was able to maintain the cohesion of the union vote despite the landslide for Ronald Reagan. This 19.4 percent difference was the largest since the 1964 election. Third, when only union *members* are counted, rather than the members of union households, Mondale won by 61 to 39 percent.[22] These new figures, as well as other voting studies, show that unionized workers have been rather consistent in their partisan commitments, despite much evidence that blue-collar workers as a whole have grown more disaffected from both the Democratic Party and the political system as a whole.[23]

What the 1984 experience showed conclusively was that it was possible for organized labor to make effect use of primaries and caucuses, thus confirming the argument that the UAW, AFSCME, and other party reformers had made over a decade earlier but that had been so long resisted by the AFL-CIO establishment and its conservative allies. While many critics have since argued that the unified early endorsement was foolhardy because it made labor a lightning rod for the criticisms of the nonendorsed candidates, the endorsement was in many ways a successful intervention. Mondale did secure the nomination, and he was clearly in debt to the AFL-CIO for his success. Labor had also proven that it could defend its candidate against rivals, most notably Gary Hart. Simultaneously, the labor movement avoided the hyperfragmentation and factionalism that had been rampant in 1972, 1976, and 1980. Lane Kirkland observed: "Our motive in taking the new approach was designed as much to find a way to maintain trade union solidarity as it was to support any particular candidate. Because this was our major motive, we were wholly successful. We supplanted factionalism and division in the unions with a high degree of solidarity."[24] But whether this unity could last in the absence of a clear front-runner for the Democratic nomination remained an open question.

1988: The Struggle for Labor Unity

In light of its positive evaluation of the 1984 experience, the AFL-CIO seriously considered repeating its strategy in 1988. Although DNC Chair Paul Kirk asked union leaders to refrain from another federation endorsement, the key factor in their decision not to endorse was the absence of a candidate who stood out either as a closer friend of labor or as more electable than the others. There were, at the beginning, eight candidates to choose from: Massachusetts Governor Michael Dukakis, the Reverend Jesse Jackson, Colorado Senator Gary Hart, Arizona Governor Bruce Babbitt, Tennessee Senator Albert Gore, Jr., Illinois Senator Paul Simon, Delaware Senator Joseph Biden, and Missouri Representative Richard Gephardt. Although Hart remained anathema to most union leaders for his attacks on the AFL-CIO in 1984, most of the other candidates had their share of supporters within the labor movement. Internal polling and other forms of consultation undertaken by the AFL-CIO and the national unions suggested that the membership had widely varying preferences.[25]

This dispersion of support meant that unions might line up behind different candidates much as they had in 1972, 1976, and 1980. In order to prevent this outcome, federation unions reached agreement prior to the 1988 campaign that neither the AFL-CIO nor the national unions would endorse candidates or wage campaigns for them unless there was an official federation endorsement. The national unions could, however, encourage their members to serve as convention delegates for the candidates of their choice. Union strategists hoped that this arrangement would give labor a significant presence in each candidate's delegation to the convention without splitting the national unions into competing camps.

In that respect, the plan succeeded. With only a few exceptions, the national union headquarters all remained formally and substantively neutral in the nominating process. A spokesmen for Lane Kirkland later expressed satisfaction at the outcome: "We're so proud of ourselves for staying out together, for not gutting each other as we did in the Carter-Kennedy fight of 1980."[26] One of the few unions that effectively bypassed the federation guidelines was AFSCME, which achieved what was essentially a de facto endorsement of Michael Dukakis's candidacy. Although the union remained formally neutral during the primaries, the national headquarters encouraged and coordinated the activity of AFSCME locals working for Dukakis's nomination. In numerous states, AFSCME locals both rented office space to the Dukakis campaign and provided telephones and volunteers. In Iowa the state AFSCME assigned six full-time workers to help expand turnout through phone banks and mass mailings. Because of such efforts, some observers within the labor movement expect that AFSCME would have had special access to a Dukakis administration.[27]

Most national unions, however, avoided a commitment to a single candidate. In quite a few instances, union locals actually worked for more than one candidate. In Iowa the leaders of the state UAW issued a "recommendation" that members vote for Richard Gephardt, whose strong stance on trade issues made him a particularly attractive candidate among autoworkers. Nonetheless, the absence of an official "endorsement" of Gephardt by the union meant that local UAW leaders were still expected to offer assistance to members who sought to become delegates for other candidates. One local union leader commented, "This puts me in an awkward position: I'm for Gephardt, but I have to train Jackson people how to participate in the caucus if they ask. Instead of hammering away for one guy, we're going every which way."[28] Naturally, such fragmentation did little to increase the bargaining power of the labor leadership at the national level.

Although most unions ultimately found Dukakis an entirely acceptable candidate, there remained a strong current of support for Jesse Jackson. In the preceding years, Jackson had worked hard at improving his ties to union leaders, regularly walking picket lines and attending union demonstrations. These efforts paid off in 1988, when union locals in many states actively worked on his campaign. Jackson's support was particularly strong in New York City, where a growing minority membership facilitated his endorsement by many white union leaders from such unions as AFSCME, the CWA, the Longshoremen, the Teamsters, the Transport Workers, the Hotel and Restaurant Employees, and Local 1199 (of the Hospital Employees). Machinists President William Winpisinger even received approval from Lane Kirkland to put Jesse Jackson's name into nomination at the convention, and he delivered a fiery speech on Jackson's behalf.

Although the unions support were split among several candidates, their involvement did result in a very large number of union member delegates—the largest such contingent in the history of the Democratic Party.[29] The union delegates totaled approximately 1,000, about one-fourth of the 4,161 delegates at the 1988 convention. Of that number, 751 delegates were from AFL-CIO unions and 290 from the NEA. Among the AFL-CIO unions, AFSCME had the largest single contingent, with 200 delegates, followed by the UAW with 122. Dukakis had the support of an estimated 54 percent of the AFL-CIO delegates, while Jackson had the support of 25 percent.

But the large number of delegates did not in fact represent a high point in union power at Democratic conventions or in the nominating process. Because these delegates were dispersed among several candidates, the power of organized labor to determine the nominee was actually reduced. COPE Director Perkins observed: "When you have a concentrated effort behind a single candidate, your effort generates more influence. This time we have a lot of activity, but not that concentrated influence." [30] In the absence of a strong front-runner for the Democratic nomination, the labor movement clearly found it extremely difficult to unite and act together. The system thus continued to contribute to a fragmentation of union bargaining capacity.

Beyond Bossism

Because of the constraints inherent in the current nominating system, neither individual union leaders nor the AFL-CIO leadership can play the kind of highly autonomous power broker role they enjoyed in the past. This is not to say, however, that unions are less involved in the nominating process than before, or even that they are of less importance. Rather, the *bargaining terms* on which unions enter into the nominating process have been decisively altered. For one thing, in the new system many of the sources of power once tapped by the conservative wing of the labor movement have been sapped. The requirements of the reformed system demand that a union mobilize its membership to participate in primary elections or caucuses, and in general the more liberal wing of organized labor—dominated by the industrial, service, and public employee unions—is better capable of deploying its membership for such activity than are the conservative building trades unions, which are smaller and often lack a well-developed political apparatus.

At the same time, the AFL-CIO hierarchy itself also is left in a weaker position: with no members of its own to mobilize, it can exercise influence only indirectly, by affecting the behavior of affiliated unions. Kirkland was therefore forced to lead the federation by building consensus rather than through Meany-style bossism. Thomas Donahue, Kirkland's secretary-treasurer, compared the leadership style of the two men: "It was not that Meany suppressed discussion—he was just such a strong character that people got out of the habit. . . . With Lane, there is a conscious effort to make members feel they are the architects of policy." Journalist A. H. Raskin similarly observed: "Kirkland kept the Council going in the directions he considered constructive with no obtrusion of authoritarianism. He relied fundamentally on a framework of consultation, designed to give each member a sense of involvement in decision-making."[31] Even at its most assertive, Kirkland's new leadership role was confined to holding together a consensus around a candidate who was already a unified choice of labor (as with Mondale in 1984). Absent such unity, the activism of the liberal unions (even if limited by formal pledges of neutrality) was far more consequential in determining the nominee, as their involvement in the 1988 campaigns of Michael Dukakis and Jesse Jackson showed.

Overall, the more liberal, activist unions, such as NEA and AFSCME, seem to have done particularly well under the current rules of the nominating process. These two unions ranked first and second in the total number of delegates they brought to the 1988 convention. Thus, one close observer of the presidential nominating process, Byron Shafer, has argued that what distinguishes the successful unions in the current system is the "white-collar" character of their memberships.[32] More broadly, he views the primary system as aiding "white-collar" workers over "blue-collar" workers, since the former are allegedly more likely to participate in primary elections. Even after we put aside the antiquated and imprecise character of the terms used, this interpretation suffers from a number of problems. While unions such as AFSCME and the CWA do not represent industrial laborers, it is misleading to call their members "white-collar" if the characterization is meant to imply a privileged labor aristocracy of well-paid and highly educated professionals. AFSCME, in fact, represents many rather low-paid nonprofessionals, particularly service workers. Also, the one union that has consistently been ranked as equal in importance to AFSCME, the NEA, and the AFT in current nominating politics is the UAW, which, of course, remains thoroughly "blue-collar" in character.

The factors that explain why some unions do better than others in the nominating system are actually found in the level of motivation that unions bring to political activity. Unions representing employees that are especially likely to benefit from national-level political action are the ones most likely to make the extra effort required to get their members (white-collar or not) to vote in primaries. Thus, the most important commonality between the members of AFSCME and the NEA is not that all are white-collar but that all are public employees for whom political action is crucial if they are to advance economically. Likewise, industrial unions (such as the UAW) also have an interest in a wide array of federal legislation, ranging from trade issues to national health insurance. All this suggests that *any* large union that finds presidential politics important will, with sufficient effort, be able to exercise some influence over political outcomes, even if it possesses a blue-collar membership that is not predisposed to vote in primary elections.

The effect of the reformed system on union power in the Democratic nominating process is clearly mixed. On the one hand, the reformed system denies labor the relatively straightforward veto it appeared to have had in a broker-dominated system. At present, if a candidate that labor distrusts does well in the primaries (such as Gary Hart in 1984), labor has no way to squelch the candidacy behind the scenes. Thus, the current system increases the possibility that the unions will be confronted with an unattractive Democratic nominee. On the other hand, if labor is united and effective in caucuses and primaries, as it was in 1984, it can exercise a very strong influence within the nominating process. And even if unions distribute their support among several candidates, it is still likely that nominees will feel indebted to at least part of the labor movement for their nomination. Finally, it should be kept in mind that irrespective of the dynamics of the nominating process, the eventual nominee will always have a strong incentive to gain the support of the labor movement once the general election campaign commences.

On the whole, then, the opportunities for union power within the new system should not be discounted. Even though in some respects labor has lost political power over the last two decades, in other ways its position within the national Democratic Party is better than it was in the past. The long-standing dream of progressive unionists in the CIO and elsewhere during the postwar era was to realign the Democratic Party by expelling or transforming southern conservatives and corrupt party bosses. Walter Reuther described this strategy in the early 1960s: "The American labor movement is essentially trying to work within the two-party structure, but to bring about a basic realignment so that the two parties really stand for distinct points of view."[33] Paradoxically, despite the conservative shift in American politics in general, the national Democratic Party comes far closer today to Reuther's vision than it did some thirty years ago. The South is no longer a stumbling block for the nomination of liberal presidential candidates, and big-city bosses leading traditional party organizations are virtually nonexistent. Organized labor and African Americans have remained strongly positioned in the party, while their most virulent opponents have moved into the Republican Party or suffered defeat in the primaries. Labor's current competitors within the Democratic Party nominating process are generally not anti-union southerners but nonunion campaign consultants, wealthy fund-raisers, and various single-issue groups. It is not at all clear that this trade-off is a bad one for labor.

Arguably, it is also to the unions' advantage that the national party is a far more permeable institution, for both candidates and interest groups, than it has ever been before. Because of the proliferation of primaries and the decline of local party organization, it is far easier for a candidate disliked by mainstream elements in the party to nevertheless make a credible run for the nomination (as Jesse Jackson demonstrated in 1988). Thus, to indulge in an illuminating flight of fancy, if a popular union leader (say, one comparable in appeal to the Depression-era Mineworkers leader John L. Lewis) were to enter presidential primaries and run a media-oriented campaign, no party elites would have any real capacity to stop him (or her). Recognizing this logic, political scientist Graham Wilson was one of the few to observe as early as 1979 that "were COPE to back one candidate throughout primary election campaigns, it would face fewer organized rivals today than in the era of the Vietnam War. A participatory selection process in general favors an organization like COPE with money, organization, skill and numerous followers."[34] By the early 1980s Lane Kirkland, John Perkins, and other AFL-CIO strategists had recognized this truth as well, and the unified endorsement of 1984 was the logical result.

This judgment is, it should be noted, directly contrary to those analyses that view labor's position within the Democratic Party as so dismal that only a new and separate party can offer unions greater success within the political system. Kim Moody articulates the logic behind such a move when he laments that the decision by union leaders in the 1930s to work within the Democratic Party "disarmed labor for the future." He continues: "American labor possessed no independent party with which to seek power or obtain direct representation in the public arena. Labor was thus entirely dependent on the good will of the leadership of the Democratic Party."[35] Similar reasoning motivates the recent efforts by Tony Mazzocchi, a former vice president of the Oil, Chemical, and Atomic Workers Union, to organize a "Labor Party" that would eventually field union-supported candidates under a separate party label.

Although one can understand the frustration of Mazzocchi and Moody, the claim that unions have no bargaining leverage with Democratic office-holders is quite dubious. Jimmy Carter, for one, would be surprised to learn that labor unions lacked any independence and were entirely dependent on his "good will" for any influence they possessed. His campaign's frenetic effort in 1980 to prevent union defections to Ted Kennedy reveals a realm of union bargaining power that radical critics usually ignore: namely, the role of unions in Democratic primaries. As Edward Keating noted in 1923, "The primary law renders the formation of new parties unnecessary for the reason that whenever the people wish to renovate one or both of the old parties they may do so by the simple expedient of taking advantage of the primary."[36] Contrary to the lingo of left critics, there really is no such thing as a Democratic "party" that can be "entered" or "exited." Rather, there is only a set of candidates and their campaign organizations that compete for the use of the Democratic label. If labor can influence these candidates through strategic intervention in primaries then it does, in fact, influence the "party." And this is precisely what unions have done, with widely varying degrees of success, over the past fifty years. If unions want more union members elected to office, on the assumption that this would give them better representation, they should take a lead from the women's movement and advocates for racial minorities, and simply recruit members to run in Democratic primaries.

Labor's "dependence" on the goodwill of Democratic politicians is also less than critics imagine, for organized labor can vary the intensity of its support in the general election just as other Democratic Party constituencies do. The fear among politicians that union leaders and members will sit on their hands makes it highly likely that all Democratic presidential candidates will attend to the basic political and policy demands of the labor movement. And, indeed, all Democratic presidential candidates from John F. Kennedy to Bill Clinton have endorsed the bulk of the AFL-CIO's demands, including guaranteed union access to the executive branch, labor law reform, defense of the minimum wage, maintenance of the Davis-Bacon Act and other prevailing wage statutes, liberal appointments to the Labor Department and National Labor Relations Board, expansion of national health care, federal jobs programs, and so on. Once in office, Democratic presidents have deployed considerable resources to help the labor movement pursue these ends. When executive action alone was sufficient, Democratic presidents have rarely hesitated to take action in labor's favor, as dozens of pro-labor executive orders and NLRB appointments, from FDR to Bill Clinton, have repeatedly shown.

In constructing their political strategy, therefore, labor leaders are well aware that they possess a variety of useful bargaining resources and that these resources still regularly provide them and their members with substantial benefits. It is therefore highly unlikely that union leaders will ever find it in their own or their members' interests to seek the formation of a labor party (except insofar as such a call might serve as a temporary rhetorical threat to wield against Democratic politicians). While labor leaders may not have always made the most of their opportunities, nor fully maximized their bargaining power in any single episode of political conflict, they have not been irrational in seeking political power through the existing two-party system.

What union leaders *have* done, rather than waste their time on the chimerical pursuit of a labor party, is to make reasonable efforts to improve their bargaining position vis-à-vis Democratic Party politicians. As the story of union involvement in presidential nominating politics during the 1980s shows, such efforts have been twofold. First, unions have tried to increase the resources at their disposal, by educating and mobilizing their membership and by generating more money for campaign contributions and independent spending. Second, unions have tried to improve the quality of the promises or deals they can extract from politicians by better coordinating their political interventions. They have, in essence, attempted to turn the labor movement into a unitary actor that can be swung quickly and decisively behind a candidate as the political situation warrants.

Both of these undertakings have, however, run up against institutional constraints that are deeply rooted in the structure of American unionism. The high degree of decentralization prevailing within the labor movement—what I have called the fragmentation of bargaining capacity—has made it unduly difficult for unions to achieve the level of coordination necessary to maximize union bargaining power. With few real sanctions available to the central federation in order to compel political unity, efforts at coordination can easily trigger a crisis of representation that fragments power even further. At the same time, the institutional incentives that shape union leaders' quest to retain power within their organizations have often made them hesitant to fully mobilize their own membership to take advantage of the more open and plebiscitarian aspects of the political system. Such mobilization can threaten the status of leaders who depend on an unaccountable bureaucratic machine to maintain organizational control. These constraints, while not stymieing unions entirely, have clearly impaired the exercise of union power in nominating politics.

Still, it is entirely possible that in some future nominating contests the labor movement will converge on a single candidate early in the season, as it did in 1984. Should this occur, the unions are likely once again to be a kingmaker in the nominating process, much to the surprise of those who have written them off as moribund players in national politics. This possibility undoubtedly exercises a distinct influence over the thinking of Democratic Party politicians who contemplate a bid for the party's presidential nomination. In this manner, labor's influence in national politics is magnified by its continuing role in the nominating process.

7 *Labor and the Congressional Democrats*

What happened to the power of labor unions in Congress in the 1980s? For many authors, the answer is obvious: a collapse of political capacity and an ensuing exclusion from the policymaking process. Declining union representation in the workforce, economic restructuring, the decreasing appeal of liberal policies, increased business spending on campaign finance and political mobilization, greater suburbanization, the growth of "Reagan Democrats" among union voters, public animosity toward special interests, and, of course, Republican presidential victories—all contributed to a decisive reduction in union power.[1] Furthermore, when faced with organizational decline and severe political adversity, unions dropped their commitments to a broad program of social reform, pursuing instead a much more narrow and self-interested legislative agenda.[2] All of these developments are broadly seen as indications that the New Deal pattern of politics, with labor tied closely to the Democratic Party and pushing a pro–welfare state agenda, had finally met its demise.

In this chapter, I argue that the conventional view is misguided. Rather than a marked decline in union power, I find a surprising resiliency in labor's relationship with congressional Democrats. In some respects, labor's position in the party actually improved over the course of the decade. Furthermore, and partially because of these close ties to the Democratic Party, organized labor's issue agenda remained broad and diverse—indeed, labor's agenda was almost identical to that of the Democratic Party itself. This outcome, as we will see, had its roots in the consolidation of a distinct institutional configuration in both Congress and the labor movement. In each institution, bargaining capacity became more centralized. On the side of organized labor, the AFL-CIO achieved an exceptional degree of internal unity by the mid-1980s, leading to an improved capacity to bargain on the part of its top leadership. Within the House of Representatives, Speaker Jim Wright successfully concentrated power into his own hands, taking advantage of the previously unrealized potential of the congressional reforms of the previous decade. These developments brought into the legislative process the conditions for a form of centralized pluralism. The predicted results soon occurred: greater cooperation between unions and Democrats, more union legislative success, a broader union agenda, and an important role for unions in organizing and aggregating the liberal coalition.

Labor and the Democratic Leadership

The conventional wisdom, which argues for the diminished force of organized labor among congressional Democrats in the first half of the 1980s, uses that analysis to generalize about the entire decade. But the extraordinary conditions after the 1980 elections—the thorough political repudiation of the previous Democratic administration, a major Republican victory in the presidential election, Republican control over the Senate for the first time since 1954, the defeat of prominent liberal Democratic senators, and a gain of thirty-five Republican seats in the House—hardly seem to provide the best benchmark for identifying the *enduring* features of labor's role within Congress and the Democratic Party. With the defection of conservative southern Democrats (the so-called Boll Weevils) on key votes in the House of Representatives, as well as GOP control of the Senate (also with its share of Democratic voting defections), liberal, pro-labor Democrats had little opportunity to promote their own agenda. Plainly, the enactment of the central elements of the Reagan budget and tax cuts in 1981 would be very difficult to prevent.

Still, labor experienced considerable success in blocking the anti-union efforts of conservatives. Labor's opponents scored no victories in altering the legal framework of industrial relations, nor did they do any better in achieving other goals, such as curtailing wages on federal contracts, relaxing rules on the eight-hour day, creating new federal penalties for picket line violence, or easing laws governing equal employment opportunity and occupational safety. As Sen. Orrin Hatch (R-Utah), chair of the Senate Labor Committee from 1981 to 1986, complained during his tenure: "It is next to impossible to do anything on that committee without the approval of labor union leaders in Washington."[3] Hatch's comment recalls the old axiom that it is far easier to block legislation in Congress than to enact it, especially during a period of divided government. Ironically, this feature of the American political system, which has so often prevented passage of pro-union legislation, in this case allowed organized labor to weather the storm of the early 1980s with most of its statutory and regulatory protections still intact.

The latter half of the 1980s provides a different angle on the relationship between labor and the congressional Democrats, because only at this time were the Democrats able to go on the offensive against the Reagan administration and to articulate their own distinct agenda. If unions were to advance parts of their own program, their efforts would have to accompanied by a resurgent Democratic Party. The 100th Congress provided that context, for in the 1986 elections the Democrats regained control of the Senate and enlarged their majority in the House of Representatives. In anticipation of the 1988 presidential elections, the congressional Democrats sought new issues that would put the Republicans on the defensive. Thus, while the early 1980s present a picture of unions operating at the nadir of their congressional influence, the later 1980s show unions at work in a considerably more auspicious environment.

Labor's capacity to take advantage of this opportunity would largely depend on the kind of relationship that union leaders and lobbyists maintained with the Democratic leadership in the House and Senate, a relationship that in turn would be deeply affected by the reforms in congressional rules adopted in the early 1970s. As noted previously, these reforms were intended to weaken the power of committee chairs, usually southern conservatives, who regularly blocked liberal legislation supported by the majority in the Democratic caucus. Although for many reformers, especially in the House of Representatives, the ultimate goal was to increase the capacity of the majority party to put forth and enact a party program, the immediate effect of the reforms was almost the reverse: they encouraged an atomization and decentralization of power. Similar reforms in the Senate ensured that both chambers became more fragmented and individualized. Thus, the AFL-CIO's Andrew Biemiller complained in 1978 of "a breakdown in party discipline, particularly among members of the majority party, which weakened the role of the leadership." Biemiller claimed that this development also hindered congressional enactment of labor's program.[4]

There were several reasons why the more centralizing aspects of the reforms seemed to have little effect in House politics in the 1970s.[5] First, the Democratic Party remained seriously divided on policy issues, mainly along lines of North and South. Without policy consensus within the Democratic caucus, it was difficult for the leadership to take an aggressive stance on many issues. Second, the first Speaker after the reform process had been consolidated, Thomas P. O'Neill of Massachusetts, took a cautious attitude toward the enhancement of leadership power, choosing not to tap the full potential of the new rules. Third, because analysts and politicians still conceived of strong leadership solely in terms of the "boss" style dominant in earlier decades, the channels for effective party leadership under the new rules were overlooked. The evolution of a more consultative, accountable form of party leadership would not be fully appreciated until the 1980s.

Despite the push toward decentralization, latent within the rules was the possibility for an ambitious Speaker, under the right conditions, to consolidate power and play a leadership role not seen within Congress for decades.[6] It fell to Jim Wright (D-Tex.) to see these opportunities, and to take advantage of them. Elected as the new Speaker in January 1987, Wright sought, with the assistance of Majority Leader Thomas Foley (D-Wash.) and Whip Tony Coelho (D-Calif.), to formulate a more coherent Democratic Party agenda. The growing unity of House Democrats, caused primarily by the increased liberalization of southern Democrats and the subsequent relaxation of internal party antagonism, suggested that the Democratic caucus would be ready for a stronger brand of party leadership. Wright was ready and willing to provide it.

Wright described his legislative ambitions bluntly: "Reagan was the counterrevolution. I wanted to get the revolution going again."[7] The Speaker considered himself "a populist and an egalitarian" who maintained a strong commitment to an active governmental role in shaping economic development and providing a wide array of welfare state programs. At least in his own mind, Wright was trying to utilize the enhanced powers of the Speaker's office in order to rebuild the broad, inclusive alliance that had characterized the New Deal Democratic Party. Wright thus came into the Speaker's office with a larger conception of his role and a more aggressive commitment to a legislative agenda than had any of his immediate predecessors. "The House should develop a program of action . . . rather than leaving the making of policy to a fragmented group of 21 standing committees without any cohesion," Wright proclaimed. "There has to be a sense of coordinated policy, a cohesive pattern to what the institution does."[8]

In order to advance a cohesive Democratic legislative agenda, Wright sought to coordinate and deepen the existing ties between the House leadership apparatus and the labor movement. According to the *National Journal*, "Wright decided, when he took over the top leadership post, that operational changes were needed in how Democrats and labor dealt with issues of mutual interest."[9] Speaker Tip O'Neill had previously designated Deputy Whip Rep. Pat Williams (D-Mont.) as the labor whip, in order to have a fixed point of contact between the House whips and the labor lobbyists. Wright sought to further improve the quality of this relationship, encouraging closer coordination between union lobbyists and the highest levels of the House leadership. Representative Williams observed: "The Speaker wondered if we could develop a system for more order in the way in which we brought legislation to the floor. He also wanted to make sure that the legislation would pass when it reached the floor."[10] The goal was first to reach a consensus between the leadership and the labor movement on a set of bills and then to closely coordinate their lobbying activities in order to guarantee passage.[11]

The possibilities for leadership/labor coordination were also enhanced by changes in the AFL-CIO's own lobbying operation. Shortly before Wright became House Speaker, the AFL-CIO selected a new director of legislation:

Robert M. McGlotten, an African American who had been a lobbyist with the federation since 1974. McGlotten had a reputation as a flexible and highly skilled lobbyist. McGlotten replaced Ray Denison, who had served as director of legislation since former director Andrew Biemiller's retirement in 1980. The federation also chose a new associate lobbying director: Peggy Taylor, a former congressional staffer with seven years' experience as a union lobbyist. Thus, the AFL-CIO now had an African American and a woman in its two top lobbying positions—a marked departure from earlier patterns of white male dominance, and a change that would help the federation in its alliances with other members of the liberal coalition.

In keeping with the firmer alliance constructed with the House Democratic leadership, McGlotten sought to enhance the capacity of the labor movement to coordinate and prioritize its legislative activities on Capitol Hill.[12] This task was especially important because now a wide range of national unions was more deeply involved in Washington lobbying than had been the case in the 1960s, threatening a chaotic fragmentation of union political demands. To reach consensus on a delimited set of legislative goals, the most important union lobbyists relied primarily on a meeting every Monday afternoon. There they worked out compromises on the issues that would be given priority in the federation's negotiations with the House and Senate leadership. The goal was to maintain agreement by ensuring that the principal factions of the labor movement each had their interests represented on the list of the top five or six federation-endorsed issues. This afternoon meeting was supplemented by a larger gathering every Monday morning of the entire community of lobbyists from AFL-CIO-affiliated unions. The morning assembly was largely devoted to discussing tactical issues, disseminating information, and distributing lobbying assignments. A key result of these ongoing meetings was that McGlotten could maintain the support and confidence of the community of labor lobbyists and could thus bargain effectively on its behalf.

The effectiveness of the federation was also enhanced by the subsidence of the ideological and strategic conflicts among national unions, and between some national unions and the federation itself, that had disrupted labor unity in the past. By the 1980s the intensity of these conflicts—over foreign policy, the direction of social change, and internal decision-making procedures—had decreased within the labor movement, just as they had in the Democratic Party and society more generally. With the accession of Lane Kirkland to the AFL-CIO presidency and other personnel changes in the AFL-CIO's top staff, more opportunities arose for greater labor unity. Kirkland's more conciliatory and tolerant brand of leadership had prompted the return of the UAW to the federation in 1981; his commitment to a more active role within the Democratic Party appeased those unions, such as AFSCME and the Machinists, that had previously been appalled by the federation's proclamations (however disingenuous) of neutrality and nonpartisanship. Finally, in 1987 the Teamsters union, expelled from the AFL-CIO thirty years earlier for corruption, was allowed to rejoin, and in 1989 even the long-independent United Mine Workers returned to the fold.

With bargaining capacity increasingly concentrated both within the labor movement and within the House of Representatives, a relationship of close cooperation could be forged between the AFL-CIO and the party leadership. As reporter John M. Barry notes in his rich account of Wright's tenure as Speaker (based on day-to-day access to the leadership and to key meetings in the House), an informal deal was struck between the leadership and labor lobbyists: "cooperation for cooperation."[13] Labor would agree to coordinate its own agenda and strategy with that of the leadership, thereby creating a consensus around a shared set of legislative priorities. The AFL-CIO would then deploy its lobbying apparatus in support not only of "labor bills" but also of the broader range of issues that the leadership sought to advance. In return, labor's favored bills to the floor would be brought to the floor expeditiously and with the full support of the Democratic leadership and whip operation.

While the latter form of assistance might seem to be little more than a case of the leadership carrying out its formal duties, it usually involved facing the opposition of conservative and moderate Democrats who considered floor votes on controversial, labor-supported legislation an electoral liability. For example, Rep. Timothy Penny (D-Minn.) complained in 1988: "I think the leadership is pushing the labor agenda mostly because of the long-term relationship between the party and labor leaders. . . . We ought to be less confrontational and invite bipartisanship. I don't know why we are so unwilling to look for alternatives to achieve the same objectives with less controversy."[14] Another Democratic member was equally disgruntled: "Why do we have to keep voting on these things that have no chance of becoming law? Reagan is certain to veto it, even if the Senate ever gets off its ass and voted on it. Members are grumbling. Very few have the guts to confront the leadership, but there's resentment out there on the floor."[15] Such resentment would have little impact, though, for Wright had effectively centralized power and was now using it to push a liberal agenda, including labor bills, over the wishes of many rank-and-file members who had sought to avoid these controversial votes.

The closeness of the labor/leadership interaction is further illustrated in the informal daily contacts between Wright's key staff members and McGlotten and other labor lobbyists.[16] These contacts were so extensive that the community of labor lobbyists became in effect an arm of the Democratic leadership. Most interesting was the willingness of the leadership to share what was considered secret information with union lobbyists. The whips regularly prepared confidential, internal counts of where Democratic members stood on impending floor votes. Although members gave this information with the expectation that it would not be distributed even to other members, much less to outside interest groups, the leadership was willing to share it with the AFL-CIO. As Barry observes, "Internal whip counts were very sensitive; what a member told another member was confidential, and no one in the whip organization would share a member's name with a lobbyist. But they would tell McGlotten."[17] It became a regular practice for the whip operation to provide these counts to the top AFL-CIO lobbyists, who could then coordinate a lobbying campaign to pressure members who were not voting "correctly." The leadership also regularly sought to enlist the support of labor for a broad range of issues on the Democratic agenda, from progressive taxation to highway projects to trade legislation. In each instance, it was the ability of AFL-CIO lobbyist McGlotten to speak forcefully for a united labor movement, indeed his virtual "authority to make a commitment on the spot," as Barry describes it, that was crucial for his bargaining effectiveness.[18]

In the Senate, the situation was different in ways that reflected the basic differences between the two chambers. The party leadership in the Senate had fewer tools for exercising power, and neither Majority Leader Robert Byrd (Va.) nor, after 1989, Majority Leader George Mitchell (Maine) could achieve a concentration of bargaining capacity comparable to that enjoyed in the House. The changes of the 1970s had decentralized power in the Senate, just as they had in the House, but there the new provisions offered fewer opportunities for a more centralized party leadership. Majority Leader Byrd's role during the 100th Congress was especially weak, with Byrd making little effort to exert policy leadership. Majority Leader Mitchell did, however, act more assertively during the 101st Congress, endorsing a domestic policy agenda almost identical to that advocated by union leaders.

Union lobbyists were not as crucial in the Senate as in the House, because of the greater representation of rural states in the Senate and the absence of a powerful leadership organization to serve as an ally. Thus, although McGlotten and other union leaders had systematic access to Mitchell, the labor unions had nothing to work with equivalent to the whip operation. The key facts in the Senate were that the leadership was weaker, party unity was diminished, and the filibuster increased the powers of a (usually southern) minority to obstruct legislation. Union lobbyists could work closely with the leadership, but they could not achieve the kind of integral cooperation that had developed in the House.

The Resources of Organized Labor

What did labor have to exchange with the House leadership, and what made such a close alliance attractive to Speaker Wright and his allies? First, unions maintained an elaborate lobbying network in Washington, one that rapidly expanded in the 1980s as individual national unions developed their own political capacities.[19] This community of labor lobbyists included a number of individuals (including the AFL-CIO's McGlotten) with many years of experience in Washington and impressive reputations as knowledgeable and skillful players in the legislative process. Many had developed long and trusting relationships with the leaders of the Senate and House labor committees, with other key committee leaders, and with the principal figures in the Senate and House party leadership. The activity of these lobbyists was, moreover, backed up by well-funded research departments at the AFL-CIO headquarters and in many national unions—departments that provided union lobbyists with coherent and well-buttressed arguments in support of organized labor's policy demands.[20]

During the 1980s the AFL-CIO and the national unions also expanded their capacity to engage in so-called grassroots lobbying. It has often and correctly been stated that the labor lobbyists of the 1960s and even the 1970s were more proficient at insider, elite-oriented bargaining than they were at mobilizing their own membership to pressure Congress.[21] But this did not prevent the unions from expending considerable time and money during the 1980s setting up new institutional structures for generating pressure at the district level. The AFL-CIO alone spent over $400,000 a year in the late 1980s on grassroots lobbying. President Kirkland reported,

> In 1987 the AFL-CIO used an arsenal of grassroots weapons to build constituent pressure—Legislative Action Committees [LACs] in targeted districts, state federation teleconference strategy sessions with key members of Congress, mailgram campaigns, postcard and letter-writing efforts, face-to-face meetings with "swing vote" lawmakers, direct mail and phone bank outreach, call-in campaigns aimed at the local offices of federal legislators, plant gate hand billing, video technology and media support tactics.[22]

A recent academic study confirms this emphasis: "Labor lobbyists feel that LACs have been enormously helpful in getting legislation passed, more helpful than any device that the AFL-CIO has used in recent years."[23]

These resources took on an added importance because of the unions' approach to lobbying. Unlike most interest groups in Washington, unions are active on an extraordinarily wide range of issues, in domestic and foreign policy. In part because of this breadth, labor lobbyists are not as committed to a single issue and, therefore, a single vote, as are many other interest groups. Union leaders and lobbyists are also practiced at aggregating an array of interests within their organizations. Thus they tend to be both more accepting of compromise in the legislative process and more willing to work on issues that are not their first priority.

Most unions also maintained a commitment to the long-term health of the Democratic Party. J. David Greenstone notes in his analysis of AFL-CIO political involvement in the 1960s that unions identified with the party as an institution.[24] This remained the case in and after the 1980s. Most labor leaders believe that unions will have little influence in American politics unless the Democratic Party does well. They are, therefore, willing to subordinate their immediate interests and also to enlarge their definition of "labor issues" in order to enhance the prospects for the party. These factors made labor more useful to the Democratic congressional leadership than were other groups, fragmented and specialized, that populated the interest group universe in Washington. Moreover, organized labor is in lobbying for the long run. As Andrew Biemiller, the AFL-CIO legislative director in the 1960s and 1970s, once said, "The real secret of labor lobbying is that we never give up. If we are defeated in one Congress, we just come back in the next Congress."[25]

Finally, unions remained major financial investors in congressional elections, though labor's overall ranking in campaign donations has fallen since the 1970s. Much has been made, and rightly so, of the large increases in the number of corporate PACs and the subsequent rise in corporate campaign contributions in the 1970s and 1980s. Federal Election Commission (FEC) reports indicate that in congressional campaigns over this period, union PACs were easily outspent by corporate and trade association PACs.[26] In 1987–88, labor PACs spent $34.9 million in congressional elections, while corporate PACs spent $54.4 million and trade association PACs another $40.9 million. From 1977–78 to 1987–88, corporate PAC donations in congressional races rose more than 465 percent and trade association PAC contributions rose nearly 259 percent, while total labor PAC contributions grew only 242 percent. As David Sousa has demonstrated in recent research, labor's percentage of the PAC donations to all Democratic congressional candidates shrank from 52.8 percent in 1975–76 to 34.7 percent in 1987–88. Furthermore, Sousa shows that labor's percentage of the PAC contributions to Democratic House incumbents declined from 43.2 percent in 1977–78 to 31.3 percent in 1987–88 and that the same figure for Democratic Senate incumbents took an even more precipitous dive, from 47.6 percent in 1977–78 to a meager 18.8 percent in 1987–88.[27]

Important as these development may be, however, we should by no means conclude that unions completely lost their clout in campaign finance.[28] Indeed, many political operatives and members of Congress are convinced that union political money remains a more important resource for many unions than their members' votes.[29] In some ways, unions stabilized their position in campaign finance during the 1980s. As John T. Delaney and Marick F. Masters have recorded, between the 1977–78 and 1987–88 election cycles unions increased their total PAC contributions in federal races from $10,321,000 to $35,547,000 and their revenue per member rose from $0.86 to $4.47.[30] FEC data show that unions maintained a fairly constant share of total PAC receipts during the 1980s, if total PAC revenues (not just campaign contributions) are taken as the key unit of analysis.[31] In 1977–78 labor PAC receipts were 24.5 percent of the total, in 1983–84 they had sunk to 17.7 percent, but by 1987–88 they were back up to 20.6 percent. Over this same period, corporate PAC receipts rose from 21.8 percent of the total to 26.1 percent. While this was surely a negative change for labor, it hardly represents a collapse of union financial power. Part of the reason for the resiliency of unions in campaign finance was the use of a payroll check-off system, which allowed many unions—even some with declining memberships—to successfully increase the size of their PACs.[32]

Moreover, the amount of union money spent on congressional campaigns is not fully captured by FEC records of campaign contributions from union PACs. Much to the chagrin of Republicans, unions are clearly effective in deploying soft money—funds that are spent on nonpartisan internal communications, voter registration, and political education and that therefore do not have to be reported as contributions under the Federal Election Campaign Act. Although estimates of the amount of actual spending remain hazy, there is little doubt that unions spend many millions of dollars on such activities.[33]

Union money was also directed disproportionately to Democratic challengers and to Democratic incumbents facing strong opposition. Because unions have a broad agenda, their campaign donations follow a partisan and ideological orientation rather than the access or special interest strategy more characteristic of corporate or trade PACs.[34] In 1987–88, for example, 92 percent of union PAC contributions went to Democrats; although 64 percent of union PAC money went to incumbents, 21 percent went to challengers and 14.8 percent to open seat races.[35] Corporate PACs, by comparison, gave only 53 percent of their contributions to the Democrats in 1987–88 and gave 90 percent of their money to incumbents. Likewise, other business-affiliated PACs granted 82 percent of their contributions to incumbents.[36] These patterns of giving reveal that even in 1987–88, Democratic House challengers received 64.3 percent of their PAC contributions from unions; Senate challengers, 46 percent. In addition, much of the union money for Democratic challengers came very early in the campaign, helping to bolster candidates when they needed it most and thereby establishing a good early relationship between labor and the candidate.[37] On the whole, these investments ensured that many members of Congress felt they owed at least something to labor—which in turn guaranteed union lobbyists access, later used to promote not only their own issues but also those supported by the party leadership. In short, labor donated its money in a strategically effective manner that made certain that unions remained an important player in congressional campaign finance, despite a relative decline in total union giving compared with business PACs.

It was also of considerable importance, especially from the viewpoint of the party leadership, that union money flowed in large amounts to such Democratic Party institutions as the Democratic Congressional Campaign

Committee (DCCC), Democratic Senatorial Campaign Committee (DSCC), and the Democratic National Committee (DNC).[38] In addition, unions provided major funding in the late 1980s for the DNC's Project 500, an effort to boost Democratic strength at the state level in order to control the state legislatures that would in turn determine congressional redistricting following the 1990 census. These union contributions to party institutions helped the party leadership as it tried to gain influence over rank-and-file members of Congress. As California Representative Tony Coelho demonstrated during his tenure as chair of the DCCC, accumulated funds can be usefully deployed to individual members to create political debts to the leadership that may be long remembered. Conversely Coelho, despite his extensive ties to business, felt obligated to organized labor and strongly supported union efforts to secure plant-closing legislation, trade protection, and legislation protecting construction unions from nonunion competition.[39]

In addition to their activity in campaign finance and lobbying, unions also sought to deliver the votes of their members and those members' families in congressional elections. And there is considerable evidence that unions actually succeeded in this task fairly well.[40] Sousa's work on union voting behavior is especially instructive. Based on the American National Election Studies, he shows that through the 1980s union members voted disproportionately for Democrats in House elections, that union voters were much less likely to split their tickets by voting for Democrats for Congress and Republicans for president, and that unions were especially successful in keeping their white and middle-income members from defecting from the Democratic fold (especially in comparison to their nonunion counterparts). Sousa flatly concludes: "The suggestion that there are droves of 'Reagan Democrats' in labor unions and labor union households is simply wrong."[41]

During the 1980s, labor unions retained sufficient financial, organizational, and, to a more limited extent, electoral resources to be able to engage in effective bargaining with the Democratic leadership and many members of Congress. Union lobbyists were available to help the leadership in lobbying recalcitrant members, especially those members who felt loyal to unions or beholden to them for votes and money. John Barry has described the resulting mentality of members of the House toward labor (and business): "Members did not like making enemies of either organized labor or the business community. *Those people would raise money against you. Hell, they'd even run somebody against you.*"[42] It is on the basis of considerations such as these that labor unions, like their business opponents, maintained systematic access to key congressional players.

We should note, too, that during this time the labor movement's role was also enhanced by the slow process of the nationalization of the congressional Democratic party. By all accounts, those southern Democrats who have remained Democrats have faced increasing incentives since the 1960s to become more liberal, not more conservative (a fact that helps explain recent defections among southern Democrats to the GOP). The key causal factor at work here is the entry of African American voters into the political arena and especially their influence, along with that of teachers and other union members, in southern Democratic primaries. These developments have made the Democratic Party in Congress more homogeneous, as conservative Democrats in the South have been displaced by Republicans or by fairly liberal Democrats. The region's realignment along lines more in keeping with the national Democratic Party has diminished the significance of anti-union sentiment within the congressional party, especially in the House.[43] The party leadership could thus act more forcefully on liberal issues and serve as a more reliable ally for organized labor.

What Did Labor Gain?

To what extent did unions actually advance any of their policy goals as a result of the alliance with the Democratic leadership? Of course, labor's capacity to realize its agenda was sharply limited by Republican control of the presidency up to 1993. Still, we can identify several areas where the labor/leadership alliance succeeded in setting the terms of debate and even in enacting legislation over Republican presidential opposition.

During the 100th Congress (1987–88), a notable example of the labor movement securing valuable leadership support is provided by the evolution of the legislation requiring advance notification of plant closings, which was passed into law in June 1988. The bill mandated sixty days' advance notice to employees before a layoff or plant closing that involved fifty or more workers. It was strongly opposed by business lobbyists, who viewed it as the first step toward a series of new labor standards mandating severance pay, health benefits, and family and medical leave. A spokesperson for the National Association of Manufacturers declared: "This is the biggest labor-management battle of the year, absolutely. This is the very beginning. If they get notice now, they'll come back with consultation and information disclosure. Instead of creating jobs, it's going to reduce the ability of companies to create jobs. What we're going to here is the Europeanization of our economy."[44] Although the final bill was not as far-reaching as the early proposals endorsed by union lobbyists (which had mandated that employers engage in "good faith" consultation with union representatives), its passage was still a victory for the labor movement over business opposition. As one labor lawyer observed, the new law constituted "an initial encroachment into the manner and timing of management actions to make important business changes."[45]

The politics surrounding the passage of the bill are especially noteworthy. Originally attached to the 1988 omnibus trade bill, the advance notice proposal was strongly opposed by President Reagan, who vetoed the entire trade bill on May 24, 1988, rather than allow the measure's enactment. The Democratic leadership then chose to promote a freestanding plant-closing bill, which passed in both chambers by veto-proof margins and became law without the president's signature. Although many members of Congress at first viewed the bill as another example of an inside deal between the leadership and labor that had little resonance with the general public, opinion polls showed it to be quite popular, with approval ratings of nearly 80 percent. Union lobbyists also launched a major grassroots campaign in support of the bill, and they viewed its eventual passage as proof that unions could mobilize at the district level in order to influence the course of congressional action. But despite the bill's evident popularity and potential as a 1988 election issue, it is certainly questionable whether labor could have encouraged timid members to vote on the measure at all without the strong support of the House and Senate party leadership.

Union lobbyists worked closely with the House and Senate leadership on several other important issues during the 100th Congress. Early in 1987, when the House leadership sought to override President Reagan's veto of a highway construction reauthorization bill, union lobbyists were mobilized to help secure the necessary two-thirds majority. Speaker Wright hoped to use the early veto override to establish the strength of the Democratic Congress vis-à-vis the Republican president. Wright met with Robert McGlotten, chief lobbyist for the AFL-CIO; Owen Bieber, president of the UAW; and Thomas Donahue, secretary-treasurer of the AFL-CIO, and in return for his promise of support for their positions on trade issues he obtained their help.[46] Barry, who had day-to-day access to Wright, describes the Speaker's dialogue with the union leaders:

> Wright told them he did support their position [on trade], then added, "Now let me ask you something. This highway veto, it's a high-stakes roll of the dice. And auto people ought to be interested. The Building Trades. It's very important. The Republicans figure this will create a Reagan resurgence."
>
> The highway bill was not an AFL-CIO priority—at least it had not been—but McGlotten replied, "I'll get right on it."[47]

A better example of the symbiotic nature of the labor/leadership exchange, wherein each side traded support for respective key issues, would be hard to find.

In return for such assistance, Wright not only promoted the plant-closing bill but also advocated labor's views on the 1988 Trade Act, including the so-called Gephardt amendment. The amendment was Missouri Representative Richard Gephardt's effort to impose tougher penalties for unfair trade practices by requiring countries with consistent trade surpluses with the United States to reduce those surpluses by 10 percent a year. The amendment was crucial for the AFL-CIO and especially for the manufacturing unions suffering membership losses as their industries contracted in the face of foreign competition. Although the Gephardt amendment narrowly passed the House with the support of organized labor, the leadership apparatus, and some sectors of the business community, it did not win approval in the Senate. Despite this setback, union leaders were pleased to see in the final trade bill a number of provisions that the AFL-CIO had specifically endorsed, including a provision defining the abuse of workers' rights abroad as an unfair trade practice, the allocation of funds for a program to retrain dislocated workers, and an extension of the existing trade adjustment program. Lane Kirkland announced with satisfaction that the bill had "at long last targeted habitual unfair trade practices by our foreign competitors and set sanctions against them."[48]

Other bills enacted on which labor and the leadership worked together successfully during the 100th Congress included those covering new restrictions on the use of polygraphs by employers, the reversal of the Supreme Court's Grove City decision undermining civil rights laws, fair housing legislation, catastrophic health insurance (later repealed), welfare reform, and reparations to Japanese Americans interned during World War II. Unions were also a major force in the battle against the confirmation of Judge Robert Bork as a Supreme Court justice, providing considerable financial resources and technical assistance to groups leading the anti-Bork campaign.[49]

Evaluating this diverse record through an analysis of the AFL-CIO's designated "key congressional votes," Marick Masters, Robert Atkin, and John Delaney have identified rising percentages of union success in the late 1980s, in keeping with the argument advanced here.[50] In 1988 the AFL-CIO won on 92.8 percent of its key votes in the House, compared to only a 46.7 percent victory rate in 1981. In the Senate the AFL-CIO's rate of success rose from 21 percent in 1981 to 57.1 percent in 1988. Although an analysis based on AFL-CIO key votes is of limited value because the issues chosen from year to year reflect more the vagaries of the congressional agenda than organized labor's priorities, these percentages are still suggestive of the very congenial environment for labor in the late 1980s. Indeed, many have viewed the 100th Congress as one of the most productive for labor since the time of the Great Society. David Price, a Duke University political scientist who served in that Congress, notes that "strong leadership in the House was a critical part of the equation." Lane Kirkland's conclusions were similar: "On many of these issues, labor's successes and labor's agenda could not have been accomplished without the support of the Democratic leadership of Senate Majority Leader Robert Byrd and House Speaker Jim Wright."[51]

Furthermore, these accomplishments were hardly limited to a narrow or parochial labor agenda. The breadth of labor's commitments was displayed in the active support by AFSCME and the Service Employees International Union for an array of proposals sometimes grouped under the label "family issues." The two main pieces of legislation in this category were a bill providing increased federal support for child care and the Family and Medical Leave Act, which would require that employers allow employees to take time off to care for family medical problems. Union lobbyists viewed these issues as well-suited for use against the Republicans in forthcoming elections and as effective tools in improving the image of labor unions. "These bills will help bring us back into the mainstream," a top AFL-CIO official commented.[52] Both bills were ultimately passed by Congress, and both were vetoed by President George Bush in 1990 (although the Family and Medical Leave Act was later enacted during the Clinton administration).

Proposals such as family and medical leave, plant-closing legislation, and mandated employer health benefits were all indicative of a trend toward increased union support for legislation requiring employers to provide certain kinds of benefits for their employees. This development suggests that unions were seeking to achieve through legislation what might otherwise have been pursued through collective bargaining. Indeed, one analyst has suggested that "there appears to be a concerted drive on the part of unions to shift industrial relations from the plant to the legislative hall wherever and whenever possible."[53] Such legislative initiatives have the attraction of providing more in the way of welfare state benefits without requiring increased federal spending—a notable virtue at a time of huge federal budget deficits. There are dangers in this approach as well, however: new mandated benefits and universal labor standards may further reduce the demand among employees for union representation. Thus far, unions have been willing to take the risk.

There are several reasons why the unions maintained a broad agenda even during a time of adversity. One important factor was the increase in the number of women and minorities in the unions, which fueled pressures on union leaders to work closely with the representatives of these groups and to endorse the issues of greatest importance to them. Also, labor's commitment to the Democratic Party linked its agenda symbiotically with that of the party leadership. This interchange inevitably contributed to a broadening of labor's agenda, even as it committed the party leadership to many of labor's more specialized issues. Moreover, the *costs* of lobbying on a wide range of issues are not high. Unions do, after all, already have a large and impressive lobbying apparatus in place, and it does not take vast resources to add a few more issues to an already lengthy list. Although it is true that the breadth of the unions' agenda diverts some of labor's political capital to issues that are not central to unions as institutions (such as family and medical leave), labor's visibility on these issues helps keep current the political debts owed by members of Congress and other interest groups, which in turn serves labor's long-range interests.

As one consequence of maintaining a broad agenda, labor revitalized close ties with other liberal interest groups and social movements. The protracted conflict with the liberal wing of the Democratic Party over issues of war, race, gender, ideology, and political reform had, by the mid-1980s, largely been resolved, as unions cooperated regularly with women's groups (e.g., labor support for child care and comparable worth legislation), environmentalists (e.g., the alliance built against the free trade agreement with Mexico), African Americans (e.g., labor support for the Civil Rights Act in the 101st and 102nd Congresses), and homosexuals (e.g., union lobbying against amendments to the Americans with Disabilities Act that would have allowed employers to discriminate against food servers with AIDS). The animus and hostility that were so evident in the late 1960s and most of the 1970s diminished with changes in the leadership of the AFL-CIO and the rise of a new generation of national union leaders, especially in the growing public employee unions.[54] In short, by the end of the decade, the liberal/labor coalition was probably as healthy as it had ever been in its somewhat checkered history.

These alliances helped the labor movement as it again proposed legislation intended to enhance the status of unions in industrial relations. Starting in the mid-1980s, the AFL-CIO sought new legislation outlawing the permanent replacement of economic strikers. During that decade permanent replacement was a tactic increasingly used by employers seeking to forestall effective strikes. With the strong support of Speaker Thomas Foley (who assumed that office after Wright's 1989 resignation), and backed by a major grassroots campaign by the AFL-CIO, this legislation reached the floor of the House during the 102nd Congress and was passed by a comfortable margin, 247–182, on July 17, 1991. However, as the fate of labor law reform efforts in the 1960s and 1970s might lead one to predict, the bill fell victim to a filibuster in the Senate, when the attempt at cloture failed by a vote of 57 to 42—3 votes short of the supermajority needed to end debate. The five Democrats who joined the Republicans in voting against cloture were from the South—Terry Sanford (North Carolina), Ernest Hollings (South Carolina), and Dale Bumpers and David Pryor (Arkansas)—and, in the case of David Boren (Oklahoma), a border state. Conversely, the five Republicans who voted for cloture were all from northern or Pacific states: Robert Packwood and Mark Hatfield (Oregon), Ted Stevens (Alaska), Arlen Specter (Pennsylvania), and Alfonse D'Amato (New York). Labor's failure to end the filibuster signaled that despite the trends toward liberalization among southern Democrats, the regional disparities in the strength of the labor movement remained a potent obstacle to realizing labor's legislative goals.

This defeat thus revealed the enduring limits on labor's position within Congress, and indeed the historical limits on its incorporation into the American political system. These limits were hardly novel in character. In fact, the overall pattern of labor's success and failures in Congress in the late 1980s (and into the 1990s) was similar to that of earlier periods. Labor still retained sufficient resources to play its traditional role of helping to advance those parts of the Democratic domestic policy agenda, such as the family leave bill and plant-closing legislation, that distributed benefits to broad constituencies.[55] In this respect, the role of labor was not appreciably different from that described by Greenstone in the 1960s, when he noted that unions sought to bring "centralization, cohesion, and unity" to the congressional Democratic party in order to facilitate passage of a broad welfare state agenda.[56] Unions in the 1980s were also usually successful in preserving existing special interest measures (such as prevailing wage statutes) that provided them with concentrated benefits while dispersing costs more widely. Where unions invariably failed was in achieving passage of legislation that would enhance union organizing or otherwise redistribute power specifically to unions. While the impact of southern Democratic defections on such bills could be successfully managed in the House, such opposition had catastrophic effects in the Senate, where the filibuster rule inevitably exaggerated the power of cohesive minorities.[57]

The most obvious difference from the past was the increased liberalism of the House Democratic caucus, primarily because southern conservatives were playing a decreasing role in the party as a whole. The obstacles once posed by southern Democratic committee chairs were rendered less relevant by House reform and by the growing number of northern liberals with seniority, who increasingly came to control committee chairmanships. The greater homogenization of the Democratic Party in the House made it possible for the Speaker to be a stronger and more aggressive leader. Indisputably, this more centralized leadership redounded to labor's benefit. Labor was able to build a strong relationship with the Democratic congressional leadership and to help set the congressional agenda in the latter half of the decade. In this double sense, then, institutional rules and procedures mattered. Labor benefited from the new possibilities for strong leadership and greater party discipline in the House, but remained stymied by the antimajoritarian features firmly ensconsed in the Senate. When the next Democratic president came to Washington, it would be on this uneven terrain that unions would pursue their policy agenda.

8 *The Clinton Administration: The Legacy of the Past*

With the arrival of Bill Clinton in the White House, labor leaders found new cause for optimism about their prospects in national politics. The return of unified party government, along with Clinton's calls for domestic policy activism, suggested that forward movement on labor's key issues was again possible. Even so, union leaders had doubts about Bill Clinton's commitment to the union cause and his capacity to deliver major legislative accomplishments. Like Jimmy Carter, Clinton had limited experience with labor unions, hailed from a southern "right-to-work" state, and presented himself as a new Democrat with few commitments to traditional New Deal orthodoxy. Nevertheless, during the campaign Clinton had endorsed the union position on many issues and had assured labor leaders that he would respect the norms of access and consultation expected of Democratic presidents. Perhaps more reassuring was that Clinton seemed like a politician in the LBJ mold: sometimes unscrupulous, to be sure, but still an idealistic man with grand ambitions, a heartfelt belief in activist government, and, most important, an ability to get things done and concentrate political power. In short, Clinton was a man with whom one could bargain and whose political profile did not appear markedly different from that of other postwar Democratic presidents.

In this chapter I argue that the first Clinton administration did in fact have much in common with earlier Democratic administrations. Although Bill Clinton may have fashioned himself as a new Democrat, he was first of all a Democrat, and that identification brought with it certain norms, commitments, and obligations that even the most clever of Democratic presidents would find it hard to avoid. As a result, the administration acted to promote the interests of unions as organizations and to advance legislation that unions strongly supported. Naturally, there remained decided limits on what the administration could provide the unions, but these limits were not new or in any way surprising. As had been the case during earlier Democratic presidencies, unions generally succeeded in the House of Representatives, were stymied by the filibuster and conservative coalition in the Senate, and depended on the president to help pass liberal legislation and make pro-union appointments. There was nothing in this basic configuration that would not be recognizable to a labor lobbyist of the 1960s or before.

Theoretically, we ought to be able to explain the dynamics of labor's role in the 1990s using the same tools that we applied in earlier periods. Thus, a key question is the extent to which bargaining capacity was concentrated within the labor movement and the Washington community. As noted previously, the Democratic Party in the House of Representatives was by the early 1990s more unified and centrally led than it had been in decades. In the Senate, however, the traditional decentralization of power and the special authority granted to minorities through the filibuster still threatened to derail labor's agenda. Under these conditions, the best hope for enacting progressive legislation remained in effective presidential leadership. Labor leaders needed and wanted a strong president who could concentrate as much power as possible into his own hands, and then use that power to promote a Democratic Party agenda. But while Clinton had immense political skills, it was not clear whether he would be able to triumph over the forces of fragmentation and particularism that remained so pervasive in the capital.

Within the labor movement, the degree of unity at the beginning of the Clinton presidency was considerably higher than it had generally been during the 1970s. As AFL-CIO president, Lane Kirkland had brought almost all of the nation's major unions into the federation—including the UAW, UMW, and Teamsters—and provided a low-key style of leadership that while hardly inspiring, at least did not alienate the principal union factions. Equally important, the heated conflicts over political strategy and policy that had once bitterly divided the labor movement had now largely receded. Thus, although Kirkland was no union boss in the manner of a George Meany, he and the federation's top lobbyists appeared capable of bargaining effectively and persuasively with elected officeholders for the labor movement. Kirkland's control over economic resources, such as the behavior of the national unions in collective bargaining, was no better than that of his predecessors, but for reasons that will become clear, this would prove of little consequence for labor's political involvement in the 1990s.

Thus, at least some of the ingredients for liberal policy success were in place: an ambitious and activist president, relatively high party unity and strong House leadership, and a unified labor movement capable of working closely with Democratic allies in Congress and the executive branch. Would this be enough to establish a high level of cooperation between the unions and Democrats? And how long could any of it last?

Nominating and Electing the President

Labor's relationship with President Clinton would be determined in part by the nature of union involvement in the 1992 presidential nominating process. As in 1988, the preferences of the national unions were too widely dispersed to allow a unified labor endorsement early in the season. With both Iowa Senator Tom Harkin and Arkansas Governor Bill Clinton drawing considerable support, and with many unions still undecided, the AFL-CIO Executive Council voted to abstain from an early endorsement and to allow the national unions to support candidates of their own choice. While this decision allowed a large number of union members to eventually be elected as delegates to the national convention, it also opened the door to a thorough (and all too familiar) fragmentation of labor's bargaining capacity.

The candidate that initially attracted the most union backing was Senator Harkin. With his traditional New Deal message, criticisms of free trade, and advocacy of strong pro-union changes in the labor law, Harkin was supported by many industrial unions that had suffered economically in recent decades. Most unions, however, adopted a "wait and see" attitude: if Harkin did well, surviving into the later primaries held in major industrial states, they might deploy more resources on his behalf—but they showed little interest in investing vast resources into a ship that might never get out of port. The wisdom of such calculations was confirmed when Harkin performed poorly in New Hampshire and most of the subsequent primaries. By mid-March, the senator had withdrawn from the race altogether.

Even before Harkin's withdrawal, several important unions had lined up behind Bill Clinton. The American Federation of State, County, and Municipal Employees (AFSCME), the American Federation of Teachers (AFT), the Hotel and Restaurant Employees Union, and the Retail, Wholesale, and Department Store Union all announced their early support for the Arkansas governor. AFSCME was especially adept at using its large size and immense resources to obtain privileged access to Clinton during both the primary season and the ensuing general election campaign.[1] The National Education Association (NEA) also endorsed Clinton early, joining with the AFT in citing Clinton's electability and his opposition to tuition credits for private schools. Ironically, despite his self-identification as a "new" Democrat, Clinton thus gained the most support from public sector unions with a strong vested interest in big government. Meanwhile, the more conservative building trades unions largely sat out the nominating process altogether.

The other announced candidates were liked even less by unionists. Former Massachusetts senator Paul Tsongas and Nebraska Senator Bob Kerrey had little appeal. Indeed, Tsongas opposed passage of striker replacement legislation, which had already passed in the House of Representatives and was supported by almost all Senate Democrats. Former California governor Jerry Brown did gain the support of many local union leaders after Harkin's withdrawal, but his protest candidacy was never taken seriously by the national union leadership.

Thus, as the primary season progressed Clinton increasingly benefited from labor support, especially in the important New York primary. Clinton's triumph in New York was attributed in large part to the mobilization of public employees by AFSCME and the AFT, as well the support from such private sector unions as the International Ladies' Garment Workers Union and the Hotel and Restaurant Employees.[2] As Clinton went on to additional primary victories, his candidacy easily secured the endorsement of other unions, including the UAW, the Service Employees International Union (SEIU), and the Mine Workers. In rallying around Clinton's campaign, the national unions acted strategically, hoping to unify the party quickly behind a candidate they saw as the inevitable nominee. In May 1992 the AFL-CIO itself officially endorsed Clinton, and it encouraged other party factions to do the same.

In some ways, the outcome in 1992 was not too dissimilar from that in 1960, despite all the changes in American politics in the intervening period. In 1960 Hubert Humphrey played a role comparable to that of Tom Harkin in 1992: the traditional heartthrob of the liberals—an ardent defender of the old-time religion, but an unlikely victor in the general election. John F. Kennedy, in contrast, was not as close to the labor movement and was deemed more unreliable in his politics, but union leaders still swung their support behind his candidacy after the early primaries showed that he was the most electable choice. In similar fashion, Clinton garnered more union support as he succeeded in the primaries, despite his mixed record on union issues in Arkansas. And in both elections the most distrusted of the candidates—Lyndon Johnson in 1960 and Paul Tsongas in 1992—were forced out of the race as serious contenders well before the convention.

Also common to both periods was that union leaders were more interested in supporting an electable Democrat than in securing the nominee who was most "correct" on union issues. As one AFSCME leader put it: "We believe that we need to be about winning in 1992. . . . If we went for Harkin we probably could get 90 percent of our agenda. If we went for Clinton we probably could get 85 percent of our agenda. But it's Clinton who, in my opinion, can get us to the White House."[3] This kind of pragmatic bargaining stance was familiar, having guided unions in 1960 and in earlier years, and it now produced a similar result: the nomination of a mainstream Democrat willing to support labor on most of its key issues.

In the general election, Democratic presidential nominees have typically downplayed their union connections in favor of broad appeals to the electorate, particularly to swing voters. Union leaders do not protest, because they recognize that an explicitly pro-union campaign by the nominee could be counterproductive. Thus, in return for discreet pledges of support from Democratic candidates, the unions have provided financial and organization assistance. The tacit bargain is made with the expectation that a Democratic president will, at a minimum, agree to sign pro-union labor law bills, support increases in the minimum wage, work for health care reform, provide unions with reliable access and consultation, and support prevailing wage laws for federal contractors.

This classic pattern was repeated during the 1992 general election. Clinton made the rounds at a few labor union conventions and strongly endorsed legislation to prevent the hiring of permanent replacement workers during strikes. His support for the North American Free Trade Agreement (NAFTA), although contentious, was accepted as in keeping with the traditional commitment of Democratic presidential candidates to free trade. Moreover, disagreements over trade were offset by Clinton's decision to place health care reform at the center of his campaign and by his call for an increase in the minimum wage. Clinton also promised to allow unions access to the policymaking process and to protect union interests in the administration of labor law and the operation of the Labor Department. Yet, like earlier Democratic nominees, Clinton did not advertise his pro-union commitments when giving speeches to the general public or articulating broader campaign themes.[4]

For their part, the AFL-CIO and national unions put their campaign machines into high gear, making new efforts to register union members and to bring them to the polls, and disbursing millions in "soft money" to Democratic party coffers.[5] The Teamsters union alone, for example, which had previously endorsed Republican candidates, spent $4 million promoting Democratic candidates and claimed that it had registered 100,000 new Democratic voters among the union's membership.[6] At the same time, the AFL-CIO's Committee on Political Education refined its strategy by concentrating its voter mobilization efforts on only the registered Democrats among the union membership and on nonunion swing voters in the community, instead of targeting union members at large.[7] This new approach avoided the danger that COPE might inadvertently generate votes for the opposition as it went about mobilizing union members for its preferred candidates. In the aftermath of the election, union leaders claimed that these efforts were vital in helping to deliver the crucial swing states of Ohio, Michigan, and Pennsylvania for the Clinton/Gore ticket. Eleven million out of 44 million Democratic presidential votes came from union households, and the 55 percent of unionists voting for Clinton was well within the range common in other postwar elections.[8]

Thus, Clinton entered office with debts to the unions for their electoral, financial, and organizational support. To be sure, unions were not as central to the Democratic coalition in 1992 as they had been in 1960 or 1948, if for no other reason than the proliferation of new interest groups and social movements in American politics in the intervening decades. Still, none of these other groups possessed anywhere near the financial resources and ongoing organizational capacity generated by the unions. Organized labor remained a uniquely important player in the process of electing a Democratic president, and Democratic presidents supported union issues in return.

Access and Appointments

The importance of the union/Democrat relationship was soon confirmed in the administration's first appointments and the subsequent access to top officials that union leaders enjoyed. For many reasons, leaders of the AFL-CIO and its affiliated national unions have an interest in meeting regularly with executive branch policymakers, ideally including the president himself. It is quite significant, therefore, that the record of the Clinton administration in this regard was closer to the cordiality of the Johnson administration than the tension of the Carter administration.

Virtually all union leaders claimed to be deeply satisfied with the quality and quantity of their access to policymakers. Robert McGlotten, the AFL-CIO's chief lobbyist in Washington prior to his retirement in 1995, said, "I've been to the White House about 40 times in the last nine months. Before I was there about twice in 12 years." AFSCME President Gerald McEntee, who was invited to dinner at the White House and for a ride on Air Force One, noted that "Our experience has been the absolute opposite of [what it was with] Reagan and Bush. With these people, we have input and influence." According to George Kourpias, president of the Machinists union, "[Clinton] has opened up his office. We have Cabinet officials we can visit with. We sit at his table. So we are well satisfied."[9] AFL-CIO President Lane Kirkland had regular lunch meetings with presidential adviser George Stephanopolous, and they were sometimes joined by Secretary of the Treasury Robert Rubin.[10] Other union presidents with especially close ties to Clinton included John Sweeney of the SEIU, Albert Shanker of the AFT, Arthur Coia of the Laborers, Lynn Williams of the Steelworkers, and Keith Geiger of the NEA.[11] As one journalist observed, "The presidents of large national unions got their calls returned for the first time in twelve years, and found themselves socially and politically back as 'players' in Washington."[12] The president himself told the AFL-CIO convention, "I feel like I'm home, and I hope you feel like you have a home in Washington."[13] On questions of access, then, the available evidence suggests that the Clinton administration handled its relations with union leaders with aplomb.

Similarly, many of the administration's key appointments were acclaimed by the labor movement. The most important single appointment was that of the secretary of labor. President Clinton's nomination of Robert Reich, a lecturer at Harvard's John F. Kennedy School of Government, was initially viewed by some commentators as detrimental to the unions, for Reich had no previous direct experience with the labor movement. One columnist argued, for example, that Reich was "the first post-industrial secretary of Labor. Reich will be the first appointee in years without strong ties to the Labor Movement." He would be "an advocate for 'symbolic analysts' rather than hard hats," whose selection meant "the end of an era in U.S. politics and labor relations."[14]

Such claims soon proved exaggerated, however, as union leaders found Reich a reliable defender of labor's position on many issues, and an accessible and sensible manager of the department's affairs. Reich was soon singing the praises of the labor movement in no uncertain terms: "Labor unions of America, your country needs you now more than at any time in its history. . . . None of us can afford an America that is divided, that is splitting apart. You are an enormous part of the answer," Reich declared.[15] Within a month of his appointment, the *Wall Street Journal* reported that "union leaders now find Labor Secretary Reich the perfect choice."[16] On numerous measures, including such special interest concerns as the Davis-Bacon Act (setting prevailing wage standards for federal construction projects) and the issuance of an executive order banning the permanent replacement of strikers by federal contractors, Reich was credited with successfully promoting the union position within the White House.[17] He also appointed a number of prominent unionists to high-level positions within the Department of Labor. At the AFL-CIO convention in 1993, Reich quipped about these and other appointments: "I'm amazed there's anybody left in this room."[18]

At the White House, a number of key officials also had union ties. Joan Baggett, the deputy director for political affairs, had spent more than a decade as political director for the International Union of Bricklayers and Allied Craftsmen, and Howard Paster, the administration's chief congressional lobbyist, had previously worked as legislative director for the UAW. Harold Ickes, appointed White House deputy chief of staff in 1994, was both a political and biological descendant of New Deal liberalism and had worked as legal counsel for a number of unions prior to his White House appointment. Clinton's choice to head the Democratic National Committee, David Wilhelm, was a former AFL-CIO researcher who had maintained a close relationship with the unions in his later career as a campaign manager and consultant.

These appointments gave unions a wide range of contacts within the Clinton administration. In fact, the Clinton record on appointments would seem to be as good if not better than that of previous Democratic administrations. Of course, Democratic administrations have never been full of union officials, and no union leaders have had all their preferences on key appointments honored. Even during the Kennedy administration, for example, the president spurned George Meany's list of union leaders he wanted as labor secretary, appointing instead Arthur Goldberg, general counsel for the Steelworkers, whom Meany had never favored.[19] It is entirely possible that unions may be seeing *more* of their leaders appointed to executive branch positions today than ever before, perhaps because the contemporary union leadership generally has a higher level of professional education.

Labor in the Legislative Process

As history shows, there is a typical pattern of union involvement in the legislative process. Unions always defend their own "special" interest in labor laws and such parochial endeavors as the Davis-Bacon Act or various forms of trade protection.[20] At the same time, they also work to support a broad program of social reform with widely dispersed benefits (a commitment visible in union lobbying on such issues as Social Security, federal aid to education, unemployment benefits, progressive taxes, civil and voting rights, etc.). Especially in this latter endeavor, the ends of organized labor and those of the Democratic Party can become indistinguishable. As a result, union leaders and lobbyists frequently think and act in decidedly partisan terms, hoping to strengthen the coherence of the party as an electoral and legislative institution. When Democrats have occupied the White House, unions have regularly supported the president's agenda against opposition on Capitol Hill, thus playing a role in bridging the separated powers that is analogous to the functions usually ascribed to political parties.

During the Clinton administration, this was still basically the prevailing pattern: overall, the unions provided meaningful support for key elements of the administration's agenda. The president's ambitious health care plan and economic program, as well as such lesser initiatives as the Family and Medical Leave Act and the "motor-voter" bill, all benefited from energetic union lobbying, often coordinated directly with the White House and congressional Democratic leaders. Partly as a result of this alliance, legislation long on the common agenda of labor and the liberal Democrats was finally enacted. Nevertheless, unions encountered many of the same old obstacles as before, as pro-union and other liberal legislation was regularly blocked by the conservative coalition filibustering in the Senate.

At the beginning of the Clinton administration, it appeared that the legislative output over the next four years could well be impressive. Although the Democrats had made no gains in the Senate and actually lost ten seats in the House, they retained sizable majorities of 258 to 176 in the House and 57 to 43 in the Senate. Furthermore, trends within the Democratic Party suggested a much higher potential for unified party governance. The congressional party was increasingly united ideologically, which facilitated stronger party leadership and the development of common themes and strategies to use against the Republicans. Speaker Tom Foley was not as aggressive nor as ambitious as Jim Wright, but he still had at his disposal the enhanced power of the Speaker's office in the postreform House, as well as the elaborate whip operation overseen by the energetic and spirited Representative David Bonior.

As congressional specialist Barbara Sinclair observes, "The congressional Democratic party of the early 1990s was different from the party that Carter, the last Democratic president, confronted—in ways mostly favorable to Clinton."[21]

The Senate was a different story, however, as the powers available to the party leadership were much more limited and the opportunities for individual participation—and obstruction—correspondingly more abundant. Senate Majority Leader George Mitchell would often find it quite difficult to deliver the votes of his fellow senators in support of the president's agenda. Most problematic was the filibuster. Sinclair notes that "Extended debate has become more frequent, and increasingly senators are willing to use that power on issues of lesser importance."[22] With a Democratic majority three votes short of the total needed to invoke cloture, the passage of legislation would usually require at least some Republican support as well as very large Democratic majorities. Moreover, the Senate leaders could not control floor scheduling or block irrelevant riders as effectively as their House counterparts. Senators were usually more jealous of their individual prerogatives and intent on capturing the media's attention, even at the cost of partisan unity and legislative productivity. Finally, the very nature of the Senate as an institution had negative consequences for organized labor. With increasingly unequal populations among the various states, a constitutional system that granted all states equal representation also delivered disproportionate influence to the lightly populated rural areas where unions were weakest.

Notwithstanding such perils, at the beginning of the Clinton administration the forces of liberalism prevailed, allowing quick passage of several bills that had long been supported by organized labor and congressional Democrats. Indeed, the most notable early successes were on issues in which labor and its allies had invested considerable resources in preceding years, building a solid foundation for the new administration's accomplishments. A prominent example was enactment of the Family and Medical Leave Act, which had originally passed Congress in 1992 with strong labor support, only to be vetoed by President George Bush. AFSCME and the SEIU, both with large female memberships, had been key proponents of the legislation, providing financial resources, interest group coordination, and personnel for the lobbying drive. The passage of the bill early in the Clinton administration thus reflected a direct overlap between the interests of labor and the administration's desire for legislative success, and the new law's importance was repeatedly touted by President Clinton during his 1996 reelection drive.

Similarly, the so-called motor-voter law, containing a set of measures intended to increase voter registration, benefited from its very strong union support during the preceding decade. Union leaders saw the proposal as benefiting the Democratic Party and liberal causes by increasing registration and turnout among low-income and minority voters. Although proponents of the legislation were confronted by a filibuster in the Senate, Republican opposition was successfully overcome by various concessions and intense lobbying, and the measure was signed into law by President Clinton in mid-March 1993. The AFL-CIO also secured early presidential support for a revision of the Hatch Act in order to ease restrictions on political activity for federal and postal employees. This bill was quickly passed by the House in March 1993, went on to Senate approval in July, and was signed by President Clinton in the fall. Like the motor-voter law, Hatch Act reform was part of a joint union/Democrat effort to expand the political capabilities of a key party constituency—in this case the federal employees who had such a direct interest in large and activist government.

The unions also supported the president's 1993 economic package, an ambitious set of measures intended to shrink the budget deficit through higher taxes on corporations and the wealthy, as well as through budget cuts in defense, health care, agricultural crop subsidies, the federal civilian workforce, and other programs. In keeping with the president's campaign pledges, the package also included new investments in public infrastructure, basic research, low-income housing, environmental restoration, education, and job training. While the AFL-CIO expressed concern about the "disproportionate sacrifices imposed on federal workers" in the plan, it was pleased with the call for more job training and with the new proposed spending on highways, bridges, and water treatment plants (which promised to bring high-wage employment for the building trades).[23] But to labor's dismay, the president's investment plans were cut significantly by a Congress (especially the Senate) that interpreted the 1992 elections as sending a message of deficit reduction above all.[24] Congress also shifted the budget in a more conservative direction by eliminating a proposed energy tax, reducing funds for "empowerment zones" to promote inner-city development, scaling down the earned income tax credit for low-income taxpayers, and approving cutbacks in federal entitlements.

Most distressing for the unions, though, was the fate of what on the president's economic agenda they liked most: the $30 billion economic stimulus package. Originally proposed along with the overall budget plan, the package was intended to help create 500,000 jobs through tax incentives for new investment and enhanced spending on such items as highway construction, mass transit, extended unemployment benefits, and Community Development Block Grants. The stimulus proposal was the part of the president's program that was closest to the expansionary tradition of postwar liberalism, and it soon aroused much opposition from congressional Republicans as well as more conservative Democrats. Still, after intensive lobbying by the administration, organized labor, and other liberal constituencies, the measure passed the House in a highly partisan vote, with only three Republicans in favor. In the Senate, however, a Republican-led filibuster resulted in the bill's demise. In the end, the only part of the stimulus package left intact was a relatively small $4 billion extension of unemployment benefits. Thus, while the labor/president alliance had succeeded in the House, it could not overcome the obstacles in the Senate.

After the budget battle, the most crucial issue on the administration's domestic policy agenda was health care reform, the success or failure of which would determine whether the Clinton administration would be able to lay claim to achievement on the scale of such Democratic heroes as Johnson and Roosevelt. Could unions do for the president's plan what they had done for Medicare in the mid-1960s? The administration apparently had hopes that labor could be an important partner in what would be, under even the best of circumstances, a politically difficult initiative. In an early effort to recruit union support, Hillary Clinton met with AFL-CIO officials in March 1993 to promote the administration's forthcoming plan, and the president himself also made numerous phone calls to key union leaders.[25] "The President has asked the AFL-CIO to carry a heavy part of the burden of advancing his health care reform program," AFL-CIO President Lane Kirkland said. In response, the federation vowed to spend at least $4 million on a massive lobbying effort, and AFL-CIO Legislative Director Robert McGlotten declared: "To show our support is earnest, we have said we will be out there in the field and ready to hit the ground running."[26]

As part of this commitment, the AFL-CIO sought to rally grassroots support for the president's program. The federation and several of its affiliates participated in the Health Care Reform Project, a coalition of business, labor, consumer, and provider groups led by Sen. John Rockefeller (D-W.Va.). The coalition coordinated media events, television and radio advertising, the targeting of members of Congress, and the deployment of activists to key states and districts. The AFL-CIO's own activities included assigning organizers from the national unions and the federation staff to stimulate and coordinate local lobbying campaigns. At the height of the federation campaign in July and August of 1994, fifty-three full-time and thirty-two part-time organizers were working in twenty-eight targeted states. In addition, in 1993 and 1994 more than 180 meetings were held with members of Congress by the AFL-CIO's Legislative Action Committees, composed of union activists organized for lobbying at the district level. Telephone banks were also organized to make follow-up calls to union members who had received direct mail encouraging them to write or call Congress. The federation reported that it sent out 1,254,500 brochures supporting health care reform, and that the affiliated unions independently sent out at least as many.[27] Through its efforts alone, AFSCME claimed to have generated 350,000 handwritten letters to members of Congress. In terms of sheer size, then, the union efforts seemed at least comparable and perhaps superior to those organized on behalf of Medicare nearly thirty years before.

Still, the effectiveness of the union effort is open to question. In a detailed study of the struggle for health care reform, journalists Haynes Johnson and David Broder conclude: "The unions played the old politics. They planned rallies across the country . . . with balloons, placards, crowds of workers, and speakers shouting out their pleas to act, now, for reform. The opponents played the new politics. While the Labor Day union rallies were staged to ignite enthusiasm for reform, the conservative group Citizens for a Sound Economy used the electronic airwaves to reach a wide audience." [28] Barbara Sinclair similarly observes that "Proponents were never able to pay for extensive television advertising or to mount the sort of grassroots campaign in every district that the NFIB [National Federation of Independent Business] was able to carry out." [29] As such statements suggest, one problem confronting labor was that in the 1990s there were far more groups active and deploying resources in the political system than had been the case as recently as the late 1970s. By some estimates, the total number of health care–oriented interest groups active in Washington rose from under 300 in the early 1980s to over 800 by 1993.[30] Thus, the millions that unions spent promoting the idea of health care reform seemed almost puny next to the huge and very expensive mobilization of interests affected by the administration proposal.

The intensity of the union effort was also reduced by the labor movement's own disunity. Some unions had decidedly mixed feelings about key aspects of the administration's reform, concerned about its effects on their members who already possessed impressive health benefits. The politically strong American Postal Workers Union, for example, insisted on continuing its own health insurance program and demanded an exemption from the Clinton plan. Paul Starr, who took direct part in formulating the administration plan, observes that "unions saw it as taxing high-cost health plans—the kind some unions still enjoy—without the guarantee of coverage 'that can't be taken away.'" The union reluctance further contributed to a key problem Starr identifies: "While the antagonists had great clarity of purpose, the groups backing reform suffered from multiple and complex fractures and were unable to unite." [31] Timing was another problem: the health care battle came shortly after unions had devoted much time, energy, and money to the campaign against passage of NAFTA. Many unionists were angered by the Clinton administration's support of NAFTA and, exhausted by the fight, found it difficult to summon enthusiasm for yet another crusade.[32]

While the defects of the union effort may not have been the main cause for the health plan's eventual defeat, they did show that labor alone could not overcome the many other obstacles in the way of such a reform. With President Clinton's small margin of victory in the presidential election, his short or nonexistent coattails in the congressional elections, and his limited popularity with the general public, the prospects for victory were slim to begin with. Indeed, despite major union support, Medicare had only passed in the mid-1960s under extraordinary circumstances: truly massive Democratic congressional majorities, support from an exceptionally skilled president elected by a landslide, and stunning economic growth. In the absence of these conditions, even the strongest of union efforts might not have made much difference.

Liberal prospects were, of course, dimmed even further when Republicans gained control of Congress in the 1994 elections. But despite this far more adverse context, labor still was able to effectively promote its agenda. The most prominent success story was the cooperation between unions and the Clinton administration to secure passage of a $0.90 minimum wage increase in the summer of 1996. Labor unions were the key players in building support for the initiative, as they had been for minimum wage increases in the past. The AFL-CIO spent $2 million on television and radio ads directed at twenty House Republicans who had expressed opposition to the increase. Of those targeted House members, half ultimately voted with the majority in favor of the bill.[33] Over the Fourth of July holiday the federation also spent $100,000 in radio advertisements directed at senators opposing the wage raise. The final success of the bill demonstrated a high level of coordination between Democrats in Congress, the Clinton administration, and the leadership of the labor movement. The Democratic leadership seized on it as a near-perfect election year issue, and Secretary of Labor Robert Reich personally walked the corridors of the Senate lobbying for the measure.[34]

In stark contrast to these examples of cooperation was the confrontation in late 1993 between President Clinton and the labor movement over passage of NAFTA. The free trade agreement between Mexico, Canada, and the United States, which was strongly opposed by the AFL-CIO and all its affiliated unions, spurred the greatest opposition among unions in import-sensitive industries. At times, the antagonism between labor and the Democratic supporters of NAFTA grew quite volatile. The most notable flare-up occurred in early November when President Clinton attributed his difficulty in gaining support for the agreement to "the vociferous, organized opposition of most of the unions telling these [House] members in private they'll never give them any money again, they'll get them opponents in the primaries, you know, the real roughshod, musclebound tactics."[35] The president further charged, "At least for the undecided Democrats, our big problem is the raw muscle, the sort of naked pressure" applied by labor.[36] Almost as soon as he made these comments, however, Clinton sought to tone them down, insisting that union leaders "are my friends. I just don't agree with them on NAFTA." But his criticisms still generated much ill-feeling among union leaders, who complained that he was speaking in "code words" implying union corruption and Mafia ties. "The president took what I described as a cheap shot at us. That's how the acrimonious part of this fight begins," AFL-CIO Secretary-Treasurer Thomas R. Donahue said, emphasizing, "I cannot exaggerate the depth of feeling on the issue"[37]

In the aftermath of NAFTA's passage in mid-November, there was much talk that unions would withhold campaign contributions from Democratic members of Congress who had voted contrary to the union position. The

AFL-CIO did in fact cut off financial support to the Democratic National Committee and the Democratic House and Senate Campaign Committees, but it kept the action essentially symbolic by lifting the ban after only three months. For a short time even Lane Kirkland acted miffed, putting off President Clinton's requests for a meeting and traveling instead to Europe for a few weeks. "The President has clearly abdicated his role as the leader of the Democratic Party," Kirkland declared.[38] It was only after a forty-five-minute meeting between Kirkland and Clinton in December 1993 that the two leaders reconciled, and started planning a joint strategy to enact health care reform.[39] Soon, most union leaders were again cozy even with the Democratic members of Congress who had voted the "wrong" way. *Business Week* reported in February 1994 that "the unions have mostly forgotten their threat to retaliate against pro-NAFTA Democrats . . . and the AFL-CIO has quietly dropped a ban on contributions by affiliated unions to the Democratic National Committee."[40]

Why didn't the passage of NAFTA lead to a more serious rupture in union support for the Democrats? For one thing, support for labor's position among congressional Democrats was actually quite impressive. Against the wishes of a president from their own party, House Majority Leader Richard Gephardt and Democratic Whip David Bonior actively opposed NAFTA, and they were joined by a large majority (156 to 102) of House Democrats and 27 out of 55 Democratic Senators. And most of the defections that did occur among House Democrats were by members from the South, who backed the treaty 53–32—compared to a three-to-one ratio of opposition to NAFTA in the rest of the Democratic caucus.[41] Few observers had expected the unions and other opponents to come as close as they did to derailing the treaty.

Second, conflict between Democratic presidents and the labor movement over trade is hardly a new phenomenon. As David Mayhew has noted, "Nearly every president since Hoover, regardless of party, has promoted free-trade policies largely successfully against resistance in Congress, although the resistance in 1993 was unusually spirited."[42] Unions knew before Clinton was elected that he favored NAFTA (as well as extension of the General Agreement on Tariffs and Trade), and his support was not therefore interpreted as a violation of a previous agreement or understanding.

Third, and perhaps most important, NAFTA was only one of many issues on the agenda of organized labor, and few unions wished to sacrifice their broad agenda for NAFTA alone. As then-COPE Director Richard Walsh asked: "If there is only one issue that matters and if you lose it, where do you go then? How many times can you draw the line in the sand?"[43] Also, many of the unions growing in political importance were based in the public sector and thus were not directly affected by the NAFTA outcome. The political director of the AFT downplayed union threats to disown renegade Democrats: "It has never happened before, and it probably never will happen, that the entire labor movement at the end of an election makes a decision on one vote."[44]

Given such comments, it is understandable that DNC Chair David Wilhelm would observe in the midst of the NAFTA battle that "over the long haul, this is an issue we agreed to disagree on. The relationship will be as strong as ever coming out of this debate."[45] In fact, the NAFTA conflict had far fewer lasting consequences than many predicted at the time, producing much less bad blood than had conflicts over economic policy during the Carter administration. Ultimately, the two sides still needed each other very much: labor knew that the administration and most congressional Democrats supported the union position on the vast majority of issues, and the Democrats knew that they acutely needed union organizational and financial support. Thus, *both* sides were forced to accept the implications of DNC Chair Wilhelm's observation that "even the best of marriages have disagreements."[46]

Labor Law Reform and Implementation

Every Democratic administration since Franklin Roosevelt's has taken significant steps to help labor unions maintain their organizational integrity, and the Clinton administration was to be no exception. Thus, President Clinton immediately took action in several areas to assist the unions' efforts to preserve their economic and political effectiveness. The easiest steps were those that involved no more than an executive order. Shortly after his inauguration, in a move redolent with symbolism, Clinton lifted a ban on the rehiring of the air traffic controllers originally fired by Ronald Reagan in 1981. The president also rescinded two executive orders by President Bush. The first required federal contractors to post notices informing union workers that they could ask to have any union dues money spent on politics returned to them, and the second forbade federal agencies and contractors from requiring workers on federally financed construction projects to be members of unions. These were small measures, perhaps, but they signified a real shift in direction from that of the preceding twelve years.

The real battles, however, would—as always—be fought over the question of statutory revisions of the nation's labor law. During the Clinton administration, this issue would be broached differently than before; in March 1993 a special presidential commission was charged with considering major reforms in this area. Appointed jointly by Labor Secretary Robert Reich and Commerce Secretary Ron Brown, the Commission on the Future of Worker-Management Relations was set up to examine three issues: whether new methods or institutions should be developed to encourage labor-management cooperation and employee participation; what changes, if any, should be made in labor law and collective bargaining to increase cooperative behavior, improve productivity, and reduce conflict and delay; and what, if anything, should be done to help resolve workplace disputes without resorting to the courts or federal agencies.

Chaired by John Dunlop, the commission's nine other members included former labor secretaries William Usery (who had served under President Ford) and Ray Marshall (from the Carter administration), former UAW president Douglas Fraser, former commerce secretary Juanita M. Kreps (another Carter-era figure), and Paul Allaire, the chief executive officer of Xerox Corporation. In addition, four professors were members: Richard Freeman of Harvard, William Gould of Stanford Law School, Thomas Kochan of the Massachusetts Institute of Technology, and Paula Voos of the University of Wisconsin. When Gould left to become the new chair of the National Labor Relations Board (NLRB), he was replaced by Kathryn C. Turner, chair and CEO of Standard Technology, Inc. Despite some employer representation, this clearly was a union-friendly commission. The four academics all had records of strong support for labor law reform, as did most of the other commission members.[47] The Chamber of Commerce expressed dissatisfaction with the commission's membership and predicted that if it tried to readjust "the labor-management balance, we are in for a period of real conflict and distrust."[48]

But the commission's final report disappointed unionists and business leaders alike. Issued in late 1994, it called mainly for a set of incremental changes in the labor law in order to reduce "conflict, fear, and delays." Among the more important recommendations were new regulations to ensure speedy elections after employees express a desire to be represented by a union; better access for union organizers to private workplaces; prompt injunctions against unfair labor practices; strengthened procedures, including outside mediation, to encourage "first contracts" after a union has been recognized; and fewer exemptions from existing labor law for supervisory or managerial employees. The AFL-CIO complained that the "commission failed to recommend strong enough protections for workers who . . . currently face strong employer opposition."[49] At the same time, conservative commentators complained that the commission's final report "looked backward to the 1930s and 1940s" and focused too much on "rejuvenating the trade union."[50]

Despite its moderate tone, the commission's report neither stimulated major legislation nor fostered any consensus on the direction for reform. As the AFL-CIO noted, "By the time the Dunlop Commission issued its final recommendations . . . the Republicans had taken control of Congress, and despite the strenuous protests of the labor movement the Commission chose to trim its sails and produce the most modest of recommendations. Even those recommendations were dead on arrival."[51] The report was ignored, in large part because organized labor was the only constituency consistently and strongly supporting any changes in the law. Although some business leaders did fear that prevailing interpretations of the National Labor Relations Act (NLRA) might stifle new forms of labor-management cooperation, they clearly did not find such constraints sufficiently onerous to invite a compromise with labor, especially if it meant accepting pro-union changes in labor law.[52] And in the absence of clear signs of economic and societal disruption, blame-avoiding and reelection-seeking members of Congress were unlikely to pursue any legislative efforts that would bring an epic confrontation between labor and management.[53] The unions had been trying to achieve labor law reform for four decades with no success, and nothing in the current environment made pro-union change in the labor law appear any more attractive or necessary to those who had scuttled such ventures in previous years. In any event, such calculations were rendered thoroughly irrelevant when the Republicans gained control of Congress in 1994, thus eliminating any hopes for labor law reform for many years to come.

Ironically, the only legislation actually influenced by the Dunlop Commission was a Republican effort to undermine the existing restraints on employer-dominated workplace organizations—so-called company unions. The commission had called for "clarification" of the NLRA so that new forms of "labor-management cooperation" would not be declared illegal. Several NLRB rulings had implied that labor/management committees that considered productivity and other workplace issues might constitute company unions, long prohibited under the NLRA. Because of these rulings, several nonunion firms were prompted to disband long-standing employee participation programs.[54] Thus, the commission recommended clarifying the NLRA so that "nonunion employee participation programs are not found to be unlawful simply because they involve discussion of terms and conditions of work or compensation where such discussion is incidental to the broad purposes of these programs." At the same time, the commission concluded that "the law should continue to make it illegal to set up or operate company-dominated forms of representation."[55]

Union leaders were thoroughly dismayed that the report suggested *any* changes in this area of the law, which they saw as opening the door to an eventual legalization of employer-dominated organizations in the workplace. In fact, just as labor leaders had feared, after the Republicans gained control of Congress the House Economic and Educational Opportunity Committee (formerly the Education and Labor Committee) endorsed a proposal known as the Teamwork for Employees and Managers (TEAM) Act, designed to give management the right to establish employee organizations to discuss workplace issues—including wage, hours, and working conditions—outside of union settings. In effect, the bill would revise (unionists would say "repeal") section (8)(a)(2) of the NLRA—the section specifically outlawing company unions. The bill passed the House in September 1995 by a vote of 221 to 202 and was approved by the Senate in July 1996 by a vote of 53 to 46—both votes were well short of the two-thirds majority needed to override a presidential veto. Shortly thereafter it was vetoed by President Clinton, despite the efforts of 600 chief executive officers who signed a letter calling for the president to support the legislation.

Although the Dunlop Commission inspired no pro-union legislation, one important piece of union-backed legislation did make its way to the floor of Congress prior to the GOP takeover. This was the Workplace Fairness Act, as supporters dubbed it, intended to prevent employers from hiring permanent replacements during strikes. The legislation was designed to overturn a 1938 Supreme Court decision that held that during strikes over *economic* issues (i.e., not unfair labor practices), employers could choose to retain replacements hired during the strike as permanent employees. The strikers would not be formally "fired," but they could only regain their jobs when vacancies appeared due to normal attrition. Unionists viewed the use of permanent replacements as a drastic measure that thoroughly disrupted the balance between management and labor. Union leaders concluded that if they were to regain the initiative in collective bargaining and reestablish their credibility among nonunion workers, the use of permanent replacements would have to be banned.

As noted in the previous chapter, an earlier version of the Workplace Fairness Act was approved by the House of Representatives in July 1991, only to be defeated a year later in the Senate. Despite the addition of a Democratic president, the outcome would be similar during the 103rd Congress. On June 15, 1993, the Workplace Fairness Act passed the House, 239–190, but was then blocked in the Senate by a filibuster supported by the conservative coalition. A move to invoke cloture was defeated on July 13, 1994, with labor only garnering a 53–46 vote. The defeat revealed the same old pattern: six southern Democrats—Dale Bumpers and David Pryor of Arkansas, Ernest F. Hollings of South Carolina, Harlan Mathews of Tennessee, and Sam Nunn of Georgia—joined border-state Democrat David Boren of Oklahoma to vote with forty Republicans against labor. The three GOP votes for cloture came from Alfonse D'Amato of New York, Arlen Specter of Pennsylvania, and Mark Hatfield of Oregon. This result suggests that rumors of the conservative coalition's death are a bit premature—certainly on labor issues the alliance seems alive and well.

But the similarities with past union defeats ran deeper: just as Lyndon Johnson and Jimmy Carter had been criticized by unionists for lackluster efforts on behalf of labor law reform and for not even delivering the votes of Democratic members of Congress from their home states, so Clinton was attacked for not delivering the support of Arkansas's two Democratic senators and for a generally unimpressive lobbying effort.[56] The *New York Times* reported that the bill "never inspired the midnight phone calls and political arm twisting the White House had lavished on other difficult political issues, like the North American Free Trade Agreement or last year's budget."[57] In this respect, the similarities with the Carter administration's exhaustion of much of its political capital on the Panama Canal Treaty, also shortly before a labor law vote, were striking. Overall, the pattern of labor defeat was remarkably persistent: three times in thirty years, Democratic presidents from the South endorsed labor law reform, provided consistent (but rarely intense) lobbying support, and eventually were defeated by the conservative coalition as it took advantage of the Senate filibuster.

Despite this outcome, in the aftermath of the failure of the striker replacement bill President Clinton could, and did, utilize the executive powers at his disposal to bring about policy change in a pro-union direction. In March 1995 he issued an executive order barring the federal government from doing business with any firm that permanently replaced its workers during a strike. The U.S. Chamber of Commerce denounced the move as "a gross abuse of power," and Sen. Nancy Kassebaum (R-Kan.), who headed the Senate Labor and Human Resources Committee, similarly declared: "The executive branch should not attempt to use the federal procurement process to make major changes to our labor law."[58] The federal courts would agree with Kassebaum, as the Supreme Court eventually let stand a federal appeals court ruling that Clinton's order had violated the NLRA by creating a new industrial relations requirement applying only to federal contractors. Thus, in the saga of the striker replacement issue we see labor once again stymied by two of the most antimajoritarian elements of the American political system: the Senate filibuster and the Supreme Court.[59]

But despite these obstacles, Clinton's capacity to assist organized labor was not exhausted. Most important, the president could still make appointments to the National Labor Relations Board. While in his first year in office, Clinton appointed three new members to the five-member board, changing its character significantly and causing a marked pro-union shift in public policy.[60] The most important appointment was that of William B. Gould IV, who won Senate confirmation in March 1994 as the new board chairman. Gould was a Stanford law professor and the author of numerous books and articles strongly endorsing pro-union labor law reforms. His most recent book, published in 1993, was titled *Agenda for Reform* and included a critique of Reagan-era NLRB appointments as "one-sided and promanagement."[61] Gould's nomination drew much opposition, including that of the National Association of Manufacturers, the Chamber of Commerce, and the National Federation of Independent Business. Expressing Republican skepticism about the appointment, Senator Kassebaum said she was "greatly troubled by the lack of confidence that exists in the business community for this nominee."[62] Gould would ultimately be confirmed only after a bitter nine-month struggle, at the close of which he received more nay votes (38) on the Senate floor than had any previous Clinton nominee.

The anxiety of conservatives about Gould's appointment was not unfounded, for Gould was explicit about his goal of recasting the direction of labor law set in the 1980s: "My overriding goal has been to bring the board back to the center and to establish or re-establish its credibility as an impartial arbiter for labor and management. It is well-known that there was in the Reagan-Bush era a systematic attempt to reverse as much labor law doctrine as possible so as to make it difficult for unions to have a fair opportunity to test employee sentiment at the ballot box."[63] Under Gould's leadership, the Clinton-appointed NLRB majority pursued several initiatives intended to improve the board's effectiveness. Most significant were a series of procedural changes that expedited the processing of cases brought before the NLRB. During the 1980s union leaders had complained about a huge backlog in the consideration of unfair labor practice charges, often leading to delays that lasted several years and were, in their view, quite injurious to employee rights. Indeed, in 1984 a high-water mark of 1,647 pending cases was reached, far above the historical average of 400 to 600 cases per year.[64] By granting the NLRB's administrative law judges more flexibility, and by streamlining the board's own decision-making procedures, Gould was able to bring the backlog of cases down to 397 by March 1996, the lowest figure in over two decades.

The board also dramatically increased its use of injunctions to stop violations of the National Labor Relations Act. These injunctions, which were almost exclusively directed against employers, often required that discharged union supporters be immediately reinstated. The board authorized a record 126 injunctions from March 1994 to March 1995, in contrast to only 42 injunctions during fiscal year 1993 and 26 in 1992. To justify the large number of injunctions, Gould pointed out that "It's created a climate in which more parties are inclined to be more law-abiding than would otherwise be the case because they know that under this board we are serious about prompt and vigorous law enforcement."[65]

The reaction of the business community to the new NLRB initiatives and to Gould himself was vehemently negative. The Labor Policy Association, an association of 225 major corporations critical of union power and existing labor law, charged: "Under his leadership, the board has been the most politicized in recent memory. No matter what the facts, no matter what the precedent, the employer loses."[66] The *National Journal* reported that "Gould has all but become Public Enemy No. 1 to some in the business community."[67] Regardless of such attacks, Gould remained an outspoken defender of collective bargaining and a vocal critic of legislative efforts he considered inimical to it. He castigated the Republican's TEAM Act as a measure that "is really designed to promote the existence of what used to be called company unions and sham unions."[68] The criticism of the NLRB, he said, grew from the fact that "there was a substantial element in this country that rejects the basic purposes of the National Labor Relations Act."[69]

The evolution of the NLRB under Gould's leadership clearly demonstrated that the Clinton administration was interested in shifting public policy in a more pro-union direction. Because union efforts to reform labor law were defeated in the Senate, organized labor was left dependent on executive orders and appointments for protection. In many ways, then, and despite the massive battles on trade, the president could do more for labor than could Congress. Such an outcome fits well with the general point that a fragmentation of power in national politics tends to hurt labor, while a concentration of power into an institution directly responsible to majority will redounds to its benefit. As liberals had long appreciated, a strong president still held the last best hope for progressive policy change.

The Sweeney Rebellion

While the relationship between labor and the Democrats was similar to that which prevailed in the past, an unexpected new development needs to be explained: the dramatic schism within the labor movement during 1995 that led to the sudden removal of AFL-CIO President Lane Kirkland. The rebellion had several causes, the most immediate and obvious of which being the lackluster leadership provided by Kirkland after the mid-1980s.[70] Kirkland had begun impressively—planning the AFL-CIO's reentry into Democratic Party presidential politics in the early 1980s, beefing up the federation's lobbying activity on Capitol Hill, and arranging the reaffiliation of such unions as the Teamsters, Mine Workers, and UAW. But by the end of the decade his innovative energies seemed spent. Kirkland frequently appeared more interested in foreign policy than domestic affairs, and he rarely made any effort to shape public debate. More important, he also failed to recast the federation as a force capable of reversing the decline in union membership or of addressing the massive changes in industrial relations. And in the view of many union leaders, the failures on NAFTA, health care reform, and striker replacement were at least partly attributable to weak leadership.

The above factors alone, however, were unlikely under normal circumstances to spur an effort to replace the nation's top union official. As George Meany's continued incumbency during his own period of fading effectiveness attests, weak leadership alone had never before provoked the removal of an AFL-CIO president. Several things were different in 1995. Most crucially, the internal demographics of the labor movement had changed. The liberal public employees unions had expanded in size, now surpassing even such industrial-era behemoths as the UAW and United Steelworkers, while the craft unions that had been the traditional bulwark of union conservatism had stagnated or declined. As many of the craft unions experienced major changes in their membership base and leadership, they became far more willing to consider innovative techniques in both collective bargaining and politics. Also, within the labor movement as a whole, white men were now a minority (albeit only slightly), numbering 8,178,000 versus 4,971,000 white women, 2,519,000 blacks (male and female), and 1,357,000 Hispanics (male and female).[71] While these changes at the base were only slowly making their influence felt at the higher reaches of the national union hierarchies, a change in the spirit and tenor of the unions as mass organizations was unmistakable.

In this context, the startling outcome of the 1994 congressional elections took on a decisive importance, shattering much of the remaining support for Kirkland's tenure. During all the years of Republican and conservative advances, from Richard Nixon's success in 1968 through Republican presidential victories in the 1980s, the House of Representatives had always been a dependable redoubt: the last line of defense against efforts to undermine labor's legal protections. With the loss of the House in 1994, labor was suddenly thrust into its most perilous political situation since the passage of the Taft-Hartley Act in 1947. Labor's opponents need only win back the presidency, a possibility that in early 1995 seemed quite likely, and they would be in a position to pass anti-union labor laws and new measures limiting union political activity. For a union leadership accustomed to finding safe haven in the House Education and Labor Committee and the Democratic congressional leadership, the results of 1994 were terrifying. In response, a dose of strong and sophisticated leadership was required, and one question quickly came to mind: Could a curmudgeonly, old, and increasingly isolated Lane Kirkland really provide it?

For many union leaders, the answer was clear: Kirkland had to be replaced. This view was most strongly articulated by Gerald McEntee of AFSCME and John Sweeney of the SEIU, presidents of unions with long liberal and activist traditions, enormous and lucrative bases in the public sector, and an abundance of women and minority members.[72] These two leaders had started discussing the possibility of replacing Kirkland as early as the end of 1993, and by the summer of 1994 they were actively plotting his ouster. In the aftermath of the November elections, their efforts took on a new intensity and became increasingly plausible and attractive to other members of the AFL-CIO Executive Council. After Sweeney and McEntee revealed to the *Washington Post* in January 1995 that a challenge to Kirkland was imminent, they were joined by nine other union leaders in constituting what they called the "Committee for Change."[73] By February, Ron Carey of the Teamsters, Richard Trumka of the Mine Workers, George J. Kourpias of the Machinists, Owen Bieber of the Auto Workers, George Becker of the Steelworkers, Arthur Coia of the Laborers, Frank J. Hanley of the Operating Engineers, and Sigurd Lucasson of the Carpenters had all put their unions behind the plan to oust Kirkland at or before the October 1995 AFL-CIO Convention.

Although from the beginning it was evident that the dissident union leaders commanded sufficient votes to displace Kirkland, it was also clear that they lacked one key prerequisite for success: a viable candidate to run as Kirkland's replacement. The dissidents first chose to approach Secretary-

Treasurer Tom Donahue, the AFL-CIO's second-highest-ranking official. Although himself a protégé of Lane Kirkland, Donahue was widely viewed as more energetic, innovative, and flexible than his mentor, and the dissident unions hoped his candidacy would serve as a viable first step toward deeper reform. It was also expected that at age sixty-seven, Donahue would serve for only a few years, thus leaving the path open for a more effective and ambitious leader to rise to the top before the turn of the century. Such calculations were dashed, however, when Donahue refused to publicly challenge the man alongside whom he had loyally served for nearly two decades. Rather than running for the presidency, Donahue eventually decided to leave the labor movement altogether, announcing on May 8 his intention to retire at the end of his term in October 1995.

The rebels thus turned to the SEIU's Sweeney as the most appropriate candidate to directly challenge Kirkland. President of a growing and innovative union with strong footholds in both the service industries and public sector, Sweeney was by disposition a conciliatory force in the Executive Council and had maintained amiable relations with its various factions. Sweeney had also established himself as an energetic and reform-minded leader of his own union, and it seemed likely that he could bring the same spirit to the stale corridors of the federation. Although rarely a compelling public speaker, he was quite willing to voice the demands of the labor movement in the news media, and the SEIU had pursued increasingly sophisticated public relations strategies under his leadership. At first a reluctant candidate, Sweeney eventually put aside his own reservations about publicly and personally challenging Kirkland: by late May it was clear he was planning a run for the federation presidency.

While Sweeney was laying the groundwork for his own campaign, Kirkland's base in the Executive Council was rapidly crumbling. By June, ten more unions had joined the campaign against Kirkland, and it was now obvious that the twenty-one unions that had come out in opposition to his presidency would be able to control a majority of the delegates at the October convention. Facing the virtual certainty of his public repudiation, Kirkland announced on June 12, 1995, that he would resign effective August 1, three months prior to the formal end of his term. As the *New York Times* put it, "Labor's Giant Leader" had finally been brought down.[74] His action was all the more stunning because all prior federation presidents had been removed from power only because of death or serious illness.

With Kirkland out of the race, Thomas Donahue's main reason for his original decision not to run for the AFL-CIO presidency had disappeared, while the political context had changed dramatically. With Sweeney now leading a spirited and unified opposition, Donahue's brand of leadership, with its emphasis on continuity with the main policies of the Kirkland era, lacked any support among the dissident unions. Thus Donahue quickly reassessed the situation. With the strong backing of Lane Kirkland, Donahue chose to reverse his earlier plan to retire and announced, also on June 12, that he would now pursue his own campaign for federation president. But this time, Donahue cast his lot not with the dissidents who had previously courted him but with those forces that had remained loyal to Kirkland during the preceding six months of political turmoil. With the support of these forces, Donahue was installed as interim AFL-CIO president at the Executive Council meeting in August, and Barbara Easterling, an influential vice president in the Communication Workers of America, was elected the new secretary-treasurer. Donahue and Easterling agreed to run a joint campaign for election to full two-year terms at the fall convention.

Meanwhile, on June 13, the day after Kirkland's resignation, Sweeney officially announced his own candidacy for the presidency, as well as the slate of candidates that would jointly contest all the top leadership posts. For the office of secretary-treasurer, the rebels nominated Richard Trumka, who had been elected president of the Mine Workers in 1983 at age thirty-three and who was widely respected both for his rhetorical skills and his effective handling of several major strikes against coal operators. In addition, the slate pledged to create a new post—executive vice president—that would be responsible for mobilizing women and minorities and for better utilizing the city- and state-level labor federations. As a candidate for this new position, the slate recruited Linda Chavez-Thompson, a regional vice president of AFSCME. With Chavez-Thompson's selection, a Latina woman was brought into a high-ranking position within the dissident campaign, which now advertised itself as providing "A New Voice for American Workers."

This convoluted chain of events set the stage for an epic battle between Sweeney and Donahue over the leadership and direction of the federation. Ironically, Sweeney and Donahue had both started as unionists in the SEIU and were long-standing friends, and Donahue had served as Sweeney's mentor through much of the latter's career. But despite their similar backgrounds, the differences in strategy and style between the two candidates would grow increasingly distinct as the campaign proceeded. The plan to remove Kirkland had not begun with much radical intent, but the dynamic of insurgency pushed the opposition forces to develop new themes to justify their campaign. With Kirkland gone, replaced by the more articulate and energetic Donahue, the reformers would have to offer something more profound than their previous complaints about the lackluster and unimaginative leadership of a single individual. Thus Sweeney promised major reform in the federation's structure and a far more active role for the AFL-CIO in coordinating the labor movement's response to its economic and political troubles. Within the federation, the New Voice slate pledged to broaden the participation of union leaders, most notably by expanding the Executive Council from thirty-five to fifty-four members. To reverse the decline in union density, Sweeney wanted the federation to be much more actively engaged in training new organizers and in elaborating coordinated interunion strategies to organize workers in particular locales. In contrast to Donahue, who expressed greater interest in recruiting white-collar professionals, Sweeney emphasized the organizing of low-wage workers and minorities. Although the involvement of the federation in foreign affairs was not an issue in the campaign, the Sweeney camp was much more inclined to reduce the federation's spending on foreign affairs and scale down its various activities abroad.

As the demands for change became more insistent, Donahue responded with his own reform program, which also endorsed an enhanced AFL-CIO role in politics and organizing. Donahue called for the expansion of associate membership status for employees without a collective bargaining contract; greater political mobilization by the AFL-CIO; more federation support for strikes; better use of talk radio, cable television, and the Internet; and the appointment of a special committee to consider changes in the federation's "entire structure, governance, and decision-making process."[75] These efforts were hindered, however, by Donahue's loyalty to and identification with the old regime of Lane Kirkland. When Donahue insisted during the campaign that Kirkland's tenure as federation president had been "immensely productive," he only alienated further those union activists distressed by recent declines in union density, defeats in collective bargaining, and GOP victories in national politics.

Whatever lingering hopes the Donahue forces had for victory were further dispelled by the astute strategy developed by the New Voice slate to gain the backing of a majority of delegates at the October convention. Since each union was granted a number of delegates proportional to its membership, and since those delegates almost always voted as a bloc in accordance with the preferences of the union president, it was quite possible to assemble a winning coalition by gathering together the leaders of the largest unions, even if this group did not constitute a majority of the union presidents in the federation. The New Voice slate did precisely that, deriving much of its support from such giant unions as AFCSME, the Teamsters, the SEIU, and the UAW. Still, in order to win, the slate would also have to secure the support of several craft unions, as well as the votes of delegates representing state federations and local councils of the AFL-CIO. In addition, New Voice needed to retain the support of union leaders and delegates as they faced the various inducements offered by the Donahue campaign (which included all the patronage possibilities available to an incumbent AFL-CIO president). To achieve these ends, the slate initiated a spirited campaign to rally support among both the rank and file and the secondary leadership of the major unions, complete with T-shirts, posters, leaflets and handbills, and even videotaped campaign speeches, all developed with the assistance of a professional public relations firm. Donahue and his allies also organized a well-funded campaign and hired their own public relations firm. As the campaign intensified, the two sides utilized the national media extensively, appearing jointly on NBC's *Meet the Press*, NPR's *Talk of the Nation*, PBS's *News Hour*, C-SPAN's programs, and elsewhere.

When the final votes were counted at the October convention in New York City, Sweeney triumphed with the support of 34 unions, representing 7,286,837 million members—57 percent of the federation's membership. Donahue gained the votes of 42 unions, representing 5,716,165 members, or 43 percent of the total. Sweeney's victory by a decisive majority signaled a major shift in the federation's internal balance of power. Not only had the public employee unions grown dramatically, thus gaining much greater weight in federation voting, but the Teamsters and Laborers, two traditionally conservative unions long riddled with corruption, had recently elected new, and relatively liberal, leaders who joined the Sweeney camp with some enthusiasm. (Ironically, the changes in the Teamsters union was a direct consequence of the Bush administration's decision to seek a federal court order requiring free, fair, and, most important, direct elections for the office of Teamster president. The result was the election of Ron Carey, who then shifted the union much closer to the Democratic Party than it had been in many decades.) Finally, such old CIO unions as the UAW, USW, and UMW were, for once, all firmly in the federation and all on the same side in an internal dispute. Despite their diminished size, these three industrial unions alone represented well over a million workers and contributed much to Sweeney's success.

Paradoxically, given the more conservative tenor of American politics in general, the victory of the Sweeney coalition also registered the triumph of the more liberal—even social democratic—wing of the labor movement for the first time in the history of the federation. This was symbolized during the campaign by Sweeney's decision to join the Democratic Socialists of America, the successor organization to the section of the Socialist Party led by the late Michael Harrington and a group much reviled by Kirkland and his allies at federation headquarters. Moreover, many of the unionists most involved in the New Voice coalition had cut their teeth on student, civil rights, and antiwar organizing during the 1960s. They were, in short, the descendants of the New Left, and the Sweeney victory now allowed this generation of activists to finally gain a secure position in the federation itself.

More generally, the leadership change was a victory for the segments of the labor movement that had been on the losing side in internal conflicts ever since the 1950s. The CIO unions had come into the federation internally divided and outnumbered, and Walter Reuther had found himself so isolated that he eventually chose to take the UAW out of the AFL-CIO altogether. In 1972 the more liberal unions could not prevent George Meany from forcing AFL-CIO neutrality in the presidential race, nor were they any more successful in encouraging a more accommodating federation attitude toward the liberal social movements of the time. Even during the 1980s, the legacy of the Meany era was felt in the federation's obsession with anticommunism, its distrust of other activist organizations, and its residual skepticism about more militant forms of mobilization and protest. In a dramatic departure from this pattern, Sweeney's election victory represented the victory of the "left" in an internal showdown. Virtually every one of Sweeney's proposals echoed concerns voiced by Walter Reuther during the 1960s. Nearly three decades after he led the UAW out of the federation, the cogency of Reuther's critique had at last been recognized.

The 1996 Elections

Despite its reformist rhetoric, the Sweeney victory did not bring about any immediate reorientation in the main elements of the AFL-CIO's political strategy. The origins of that strategy were deeply rooted in the structure of labor's incorporation into the American political system, and it was unlikely to be altered by a leadership change alone. What the new leadership did initiate was a greater intensity in the pursuit of the essentially traditional and realistic strategy of electing Democratic candidates. An early sign of labor's renewed vigor was the role of the AFL-CIO and affiliated unions in the January 1996 special election in Oregon, called to fill the Senate seat left vacant by the resignation of Republican incumbent Bob Packwood. The labor movement poured volunteers, money, and staff into the campaign on an unprecedented scale, facilitating a narrow win by Democratic candidate Ron Wyden.

This victory emboldened labor operatives, led by the new Sweeney-appointed COPE Director Steve Rosenthal, to plan an even more ambitious intervention in the November congressional elections. In March 1996 the federation approved a special $35 million political fund, devoted mainly to the goal of displacing Republican members of Congress—especially those freshmen elected in 1994. Of this amount, $25 million would be spent on radio and television advertising and $10 million on political organization, including the deployment of 131 full-time political coordinators to direct union volunteers. The additional long-term goal, according to Rosenthal, was to establish in key congressional districts a base of 100 to 150 union activists, available to be mobilized for both electoral and lobbying purposes.[76] The cost of this effort, which was billed as an "issue advocacy" expenditure rather than a direct campaign contribution, was borne by a new per capita assessment by the federation on the affiliated unions. The national unions in turn raised the money out of each union's general treasury funds or, in some cases, directly from increases in membership dues.

Although news accounts emphasized the remarkable size of the AFL-CIO's outlays, the $35 million was just a fraction of the total amount spent by labor unions in the federal elections.[77] In addition to the special fund, the federation also contributed large amounts directly to individual campaigns through its PAC operated by COPE. At the same time, the national unions were making independent "educational" expenditures, used to communicate to their members and the general public, and their PACs made direct contributions to candidates and soft money contributions to the Democratic Party. Federal Election Commission data showed total union PAC campaign contributions in the 1995–96 election cycle of $49 million, union soft money contributions to the national parties of $9.5 million, and other independent expenditures of at least $6.7 million—all *on top of* the special $35 million fund. House Democrats received 48 percent of their PAC donations from unions, up from 36 percent in 1994.[78]

This spending was deliberately and skillfully arranged to deploy labor's funds most potently. Thus, although the money spent out of union general treasury funds (rather than PAC treasuries) was not supposed to be used in coordination with partisan campaigning, in fact it always ended up in districts where it was most needed to advance the Democratic Party's strategy to regain control of the House. There is abundant evidence that, in practice, the labor movement's "independent" expenditures were highly partisan in intent.[79] Indeed, Senate testimony by former White House deputy chief of staff Harold Ickes in October 1997 revealed an even closer level of cooperation than many had imagined. According to Ickes, on November 15, 1995, less than a month after Sweeney's election, President Clinton met with Sweeney, Secretary-Treasurer Richard Trumka, and Labor Secretary Reich in order to discuss plans for retaking the House of Representatives and stimulating the longer-term revitalization of the labor movement. Even at this early stage, the union leaders promised to spend at least $20 million more than they had in the 1993–94 election cycle. On December 5, 1995, another high-level meeting took place between White House Chief of Staff Leon Panetta, President Sweeney, Sweeney's own chief of staff, Gerald Shea, and AFSCME President Gerald McEntee. Among the topics discussed were AFSCME's decision to spend another $10.5 million on the 1996 campaign, the need for Democratic congressional unity in the upcoming election, and the nature of labor's involvement at the congressional district level.[80]

The Republicans were appalled at the labor movement's intensified involvement and its strategic coordination with Democratic operatives. One Republican media consultant went so far as to state that the unions were "the single biggest factor in congressional races nationwide, far outstripping any impact that the Clinton/Gore campaign will have on the political environment for individual Congressmen. They have completely set the terms of the debate, because when you put that much advertising up that early, you change everybody's numbers."[81] Meanwhile, the Republican and business response seemed disorganized and uncoordinated. For months labor advertisements went largely unanswered over the airwaves, and Republican candidates complained that the response by the Republican National Committee was completely inadequate. In a mood of growing anxiety, leaders in the business community formed a new alliance they called "the Coalition," set up specifically to counter the AFL-CIO's enhanced role. The group included about forty of Washington's most effective business lobbies, including the U.S. Chamber of Commerce, National Federation of Independent Business, National Restaurant Association, National Association of Manufacturers, and National Association of Wholesaler-Distributors. One of its main goals was to undertake a coordinated fund-raising drive with a goal of at least $20 million to set against the increased labor spending. Yet by the end of the campaign season the Coalition ended up with a mere $5 million specifically to battle the union juggernaut (although total spending of business in the election would eventually exceed that of the unions, by as much as six-to-one).[82]

Still, on election day the congressional Republicans seemed to have little to complain about, losing only nine seats in the House and actually gaining two more in the Senate. Although union leaders clearly found the results disappointing, there were still some aspects of the electoral outcomes that were to their liking. Most important, of the forty-four freshmen Republican specially targeted by the AFL-CIO, twelve were defeated, while all twenty-seven of those not targeted were reelected—clear evidence, from the federation's perspective, that their intervention could have a major impact on electoral outcomes.[83] This interpretation has been strongly supported by the findings of political scientist Gary C. Jacobson, one of the foremost contemporary students of American congressional elections. Jacobson concludes unequivocally that "labor's independent campaigns against Republican incumbents did help Democratic challengers, and quite substantially."[84] According to his calculations, those Republican freshmen targeted in the AFL-CIO campaign typically experienced an 8 percentage point drop in their share of the vote in comparison to those freshmen left untargeted, even if the electoral circumstances of the candidates were otherwise quite similar. Jacobson estimates that had labor not intervened, only two rather than twelve freshmen Republican would have been defeated.

Unionists derived considerable satisfaction as well from Democratic successes in several high-profile races that drew national attention. Walter H. Capp's defeat of Rep. Andrea Seastrand (R-Calif.) and Deborah A. Stabenow's victory over Rep. Dick Chrysler (R-Mich.) both occurred in congressional districts where the unions had poured in large amounts of money and numerous volunteers.[85] Union leaders observed that in congressional races nationwide, 62 percent of union members voted for Democrats and only 35 percent for Republicans, in contrast to 45 percent and 53 percent respectively among voters in nonunion households. This outcome was significantly better than that in 1994, when congressional Republicans secured 40 percent of the labor vote. In addition, union households accounted for 24 percent of the electorate, up from 19 percent in 1992, and unions claimed to have mobilized an extra 2.5 million votes for Democratic congressional candidates.[86]

Finally, the AFL-CIO maintained that the real origins of the Republican's success lay in their adoption of a more mainstream stance on economic and social policy questions. The GOP maintained control of the House, unionists insisted, only because they moved closer to labor's positions on the minimum wage, education spending, and health insurance reforms. The views of the labor establishment were thus summarized well a few days after the 1996 election by commentator Guy Molyneux: "Labor's goal was a Congress less threatening to the interests of workers and their families. Today, a smaller and more subdued GOP majority knows it must coexist with a Democratic president for four more years."[87] Even better, all this had been accomplished without precipitating an anti-union backlash, as had so often happened before when unions tried to flex their muscles in the political arena. The lack of an identifiable backlash probably reflected the declining credibility of anti-union rhetoric when the movement seemed so clearly on the defensive. In any case, labor's success suggested that unions could intervene in more visible and aggressive ways in national politics in the future without experiencing the costs that such efforts had previously incurred.

All of this activity may count as a renewal of the old alliance of labor with the Democratic Party, but there was one area of significant change in 1996: it lay in how the federation spent its money in electoral politics. By choosing to spend much of the special $35 million fund on its own advertising campaign, the AFL-CIO was able to better control the content of its message than had been possible under the more passive strategy of simply funneling union money into a candidate's campaign treasury. Much of the AFL-CIO advertising sought to promote such issues as the minimum wage, Medicare, Social Security, and education, even if these were not necessarily key parts of the agenda of the candidate in whose district they were advertising. Sweeney later described the reasoning behind this approach: "We must stop giving money to political parties who won't give unions the respect we deserve, and we must stop supporting political candidates who won't support working families. It is time for us to begin spending our money on our own media and on grass-roots lobbying around the issues that matter most to workers."[88]

But the main strategic goal of the AFL-CIO even after the Sweeney takeover remained a traditional one: to support the Democrats in their quest to control Congress and the executive branch. For their part, the congressional Democrats were headed toward a greater dependency on organized labor, as the business support (read "dollars") once guaranteed them by incumbency flowed to the new majority party in Congress. Now that the congressional Democrats and labor were sharing the experience of minority status and a common enemy, their alliance became even closer. Thus, this long-standing and historic bond between one of the world's oldest labor movements and an equally venerable political party seemed destined to continue well into the next century.

Persistence of Cooperation

When viewed in historical perspective, the relationship between the unions and the first Clinton administration revealed little that was new. The few areas of change were found in the greater intensity of conflict over foreign trade and in labor's somewhat reduced centrality as an agent capable of mobilizing support for major social reforms. Other elements of the relationship remained constant: union leaders maintained privileged access to the White House and executive branch policymakers, acted as agents in support of important parts of the president's legislative agenda and economic program, received White House support for labor law reforms and a pro-union administration of existing labor law, and coordinated electoral strategy closely with the White House and Democratic Party operatives. In Congress the unions worked closely with Democratic leaders to push a common agenda and plan electoral strategy. And, as so often in the past, unions were most likely to be blocked in the Senate, where the conservative coalition was able to utilize that body's antimajoritarian rules to its own advantage.

The level of cooperation between the administration and labor was occasionally quite impressive, although always limited by the continuing dispersal of power in the Washington community. Despite the disagreements over trade issues, unions remained a generally reliable ally on health care reform and helped promote the president's economic and social policy agenda. But as Lane Kirkland's power deteriorated in the mid-1990s, his control over the political resources of the labor movement also dwindled, and his ties to the administration grew more sporadic and uncertain. However, his successor, John Sweeney, was able to establish a new degree of bargaining capacity in a labor movement that was rapidly expanding its political resources. Thus, by mid-1996 a new cycle of cooperation had begun, as evidenced in the coordinated push for a minimum wage increase and the joint effort to take control of Congress away from the Republicans in the November elections.

There is one last comparison with the politics of earlier Democratic administrations that can profitably be drawn. During the Johnson and Carter presidencies, the most enduring cause of conflict in the administration/labor relationship was disagreement over how to best deal with rising inflation. In contrast, President Clinton did not have to seriously worry about inflation at all during this period and therefore felt virtually no pressures to recruit union leaders in the unhappy and institutionally challenging task of restraining the material aspirations of their own membership. Wage and price guideposts, which had been so prominent in the 1960s and 1970s, were now long-forgotten policies. Although under these new conditions quasi-corporatist trade-offs—and the opportunities for special access and policy benefits that they presented—were no longer on the agenda, the unions were ultimately much happier to play a political game that did not require the manipulation of their economic resources. The constant friction over labor's engagements in collective bargaining that marked both the Johnson and Carter years was thus avoided, making the long-standing liability of labor's fragmented control over its own economic resources much less relevant in the 1990s.

Conclusion: Organized Labor at the End of the Twentieth Century

The notion that organized labor was an inconsequential and spent force in national politics was, at least for most observers, decisively refuted by the intense involvement of the AFL-CIO and its affiliated unions in the 1996 elections. Others may have found more convincing the success of the unions in opposing "fast-track" trade legislation in the fall of 1997. In either case, recent events have largely confirmed the claim of this book that unions have maintained an impressive amount of political power.[1] Furthermore, the evidence has shown that the portrait of constant and unmitigated union decline was always exaggerated. Even at the high point of conservative power during the Reagan and Bush administrations, unions retained considerable influence in Congress and among Democratic presidential aspirants. This power reflected the labor movement's successful production and deployment of valuable political resources in federal elections and in the congressional legislative process. Thus, Democratic politicians interested in getting elected, staying elected, and influencing legislative outcomes still found it useful to seek the resources that labor had to offer.

In order to complete the analysis, we are left with three tasks: first, to evaluate the explanatory power of the analytical framework devised in Chapter 2, and to compare this framework to possible alternative approaches; second, to discuss the significance of these findings for our broader understanding of the nature of change and development in postwar American politics; and third, to speculate about the likely course of union political action in years to come.

Evaluating the Framework

This study has advanced a distinctive analytical framework, at the core of which has been the idea that the *exchange value* of the political and economic resources generated by organized labor is deeply affected by *institutional* conditions: namely, the degree to which bargaining capacity is centralized within the labor movement and the national state. I believe that while this theory cannot account for everything in the history of unions in national politics since the 1960s, it does explain the main dynamics of cooperation versus conflict more fully than any of the available alternatives. I do not claim, and have not argued, that the centralization of bargaining capacity is the *only* factor operating to explain these outcomes. Still, institutional factors have a persistence over time that allows them to serve better as explanatory variables than other factors do. Thus, for the purposes of constructing a *theory* of unions in national politics, an institutional approach has much to recommend it.

At this point, one last review of the argument is in order. I have presented evidence showing that when bargaining capacity was appropriately concentrated among top Democratic Party officeholders and their counterparts within the labor movement, the odds for union/Democrat cooperation and successful enactment of labor-endorsed legislation increased markedly. In contrast, when the fragmented structures of American unionism were allowed to have their "natural" effects, the labor movement all too easily fell into incoherent and squabbling cacophony as it split into parochially oriented segments of the labor market. Thus, in the absence of decisive leadership from federation headquarters, the labor movement is rarely able to deploy its bargaining resources—whether they are derived from the workplace or the voting booth—in a manner likely to command the respect and cooperation of national politicians. Likewise, left to its own "natural" logic, the American constitutional order cultivates separated institutions that neither share nor produce much power. Indeed, the fragmenting and deadlock-producing tendencies of the American political system have been identified time and again in analyses that compare the United States to other democratic political systems.[2] The point seems conclusive: stasis and disunity are very easy to create within both the labor movement and the American political system.

To counteract these tendencies, wise and forceful leadership is required. Of course, neither the labor movement nor the Democratic Party has consistently enjoyed this rare commodity. Still, when ambitious leaders were effective in concentrating power into their own hands (i.e., in creating more centralized bargaining capacity), the results were impressive. Lyndon Johnson and George Meany proved in the mid-1960s that such a centralization of power could be quite fruitful—even if their experience also showed the potential for a crisis of representation when that power came to be seen as lacking in democratic accountability. Similarly, Jim Wright and Lane Kirkland (with the assistance of their designated agents) showed that the trick could be still pulled off even in the late 1980s, when a cohesive labor movement allied with a stronger congressional Democratic leadership produced significant progress on the liberal agenda. Both Wright and Kirkland, who explicitly saw themselves as the successors of Johnson and Meany, managed to achieve some centralization of bargaining power without triggering much of a backlash from their own constituents. In contrast, the travails of Jimmy Carter and George Meany in the late 1970s illustrate the consequences of a weak bargaining position: neither was very successful in concentrating power or delivering on his promises (limited as they might be), and the result was the mutual, sullen withdrawal and corresponding decline in cooperation that the theory advanced here would predict.

Then there is the case of the Clinton administration. The relationship between President Clinton and Kirkland never became quite as much of a spectacle in disorganization and confrontation as the Carter/Meany show was by 1980, but neither did it reveal the kind of close cooperation witnessed in earlier periods. Neither Kirkland, whose power was clearly on the wane by the early 1990s, nor President Clinton, who came into office with much less than an electoral majority, could achieve or maintain a dominance in their respective organizational spheres comparable to that achieved by President Johnson and George Meany in the mid-1960s. The two leaders (and, more broadly, the administration and the federation) were thus seriously constrained in what they could consistently offer to each other in political negotiations. As the Clinton administration hovered somewhere between the cooperation of the mid-1960s and the discord of the Carter years, its degree of policy success, unsurprisingly, also fell in the middle range.

This précis of the argument again draws our attention to how important institutional factors have been in structuring the perceptions, incentives, and choices confronting unionists and politicians. When the institutions of the labor movement and the national political system resembled the ideal-type of centralized pluralism, unions found it easier to forge cooperative relationships with key Democratic politicians. Moreover, these ties encouraged union leaders to broaden their political agenda and adopt a larger definition of their own self-interest. Thus, no account of unions in politics is going to get very far if it does not start with a deep-rooted appreciation of the distinctive institutional structures of American unionism and of the larger political system in which it functions. As the proponents of a "New Institutionalism" in the social sciences have shown, institutional structures clearly can have a causal impact, generating outcomes that are not fully explainable in terms of ideas and interests alone.[3]

This does not mean that there are no rival explanations for the variations in the degree of cooperation between unions and Democrats. One obvious alternative is to find the source of variation in the influence of economic factors, specifically rates of economic growth and the extent of international competition facing U.S. industry. From this perspective, Lyndon Johnson was able to be friendly with the unions because he had the money to do so, in an economic climate that was conducive to big government and federal intervention and regulation. With the decline of U.S. economic dominance and slower rates of economic growth, it is not surprising that later Democrats would clash more often with organized labor.

This view, of course, is not entirely contrary to the account provided here. In fact, I have emphasized the importance of the level of inflation in generating conflict between Democratic presidential administrations and organized labor during the 1960s and 1970s (and in reducing it during the 1990s). But there are two problems with a focus on economics alone. First, it is entirely conceivable that the fight against inflation might have produced *more* cooperation, not less. This possibility is suggested by the formation of the National Accord during the Carter administration, as well as by the intensification of corporatist experiments in Western Europe in the 1970s. That cooperation ultimately failed in the United States was more an indication of *institutional* weaknesses, both in the labor movement and the state, than of any unavoidable logic of the economy. Second, economics cannot account in any way for the intensification of cooperation with the Democratic congressional leadership in the 1980s or 1990s, a development that reflected institutional factors and political developments that had little or nothing to do with economic change.

A second alternative approach is to focus on ideology and personality as the key factors. In this view, Meany and Johnson got along well because they thought the same way and related to each other well personally, while Carter and Meany feuded because they did not. I have referred to these idiosyncratic factors from time to time in the case studies; certainly in the case of the Carter administration they were important. But if institutions had not already been in considerable disarray, such conflicts clearly would not have gotten so far out of hand. As the evidence in Chapter 5 shows, at every turn the antagonism between Meany and Carter was worsened because neither was very effective at controlling the resources nominally at his command. That weakness inevitably heightened the possibilities for misunderstanding, disillusionment, and scapegoating, thus encouraging conflict even prior to the eruption of personal antagonisms.

We should also note that while ideology and personal ties may help promote cooperation, such efforts are unlikely to get off the ground absent the necessary institutional conditions. The interest of both AFL-CIO lobbyists and House Speaker Jim Wright in working together more closely may have stemmed from shared ideology, but the success of that cooperation ultimately depended on the centralization of bargaining capacity by both Wright and top AFL-CIO lobbyists. Similarly, the cooperation between labor and Democrat leaders with backgrounds and personalities as diverse as Jim Wright's, Tom Foley's, and Dick Gephardt's shows the long-term causal importance of partisanship, resources, and institutional capacity over other factors.

A third position would be that resources matter but institutions are secondary. Unions were strong and elicited the cooperation of officeholders when they possessed a large quantity of valuable resources, weak and ignored when they did not. Thus, in this view the centralization or decentralization of bargaining capacity is irrelevant. However, the facts fail to support this approach: unions still possessed huge resources during the Carter years, in some ways more than during the Johnson years, yet experienced far more conflict with the administration. That conflict was rooted in the impact of new policy problems in the context of decentralized institutions and had little to do with a sudden drop in the significance of union resources. Conversely, the growth of cooperation in the House in the late 1980s mainly reflected better institutional control over a fairly stable quantity of resources. Resources do matter, but their use is deeply affected by institutional conditions that develop according to their own distinct logic and time line.

I do not mean the above critique to imply that there are no analytical tensions or anomalies presented by the application of my model to the historical case studies. In my view, one of the more interesting theoretical anomalies relates to the changing institutional location of centralized pluralism. The model in Chapter 2 argues that a strong Democratic president + strong federation leadership = cooperation. Yet, more recently, the equation might be put another way: strong Democratic congressional leadership + strong federation leadership = cooperation, but at the expense of a Democratic president (especially on trade legislation). Thus, by the late 1990s labor's historic focus on the Democratic presidency as the most dependable source of support for pro-union policy change is showing signs of deterioration. But the importance of this point should not be exaggerated. Conflicts over trade aside, the goal of the labor leadership still seems to be a strong Democratic president, and there are obvious constitutional reasons why the construction of cooperative relationships with the congressional leadership cannot ever fully displace the construction of a good relationship with the chief executive.

As such calculations suggest, the American political system presents union leaders with a highly complex institutional game board, lending itself to a diverse array of strategies. It will therefore be particularly interesting to observe how unions operate in the new form of divided government initiated in the 1990s. This new configuration seems to be based on a hard-line Republican majority in Congress, an increasingly liberal Democratic caucus (especially in the House), and a Democratic president tempted by the allures of "triangulation" between these two poles. For students of labor's role in national politics, this new setting for the elaboration of union political strategy provides rich opportunities for empirical research and theoretical refinement.

Is the "New Deal Order" Really Dead?

The historical narrative in this book has revealed surprising areas of consistency in labor's role. Briefly, this continuity has five characteristics:

1. Unions still operate almost exclusively through the Democratic Party, and union political behavior can still be understood in terms of the maintenance and deepening of this partisan commitment.
2. Union leaders still maintain a highly cooperative relationship with the Democratic congressional leadership, and they draw on this relationship in promoting a broad program of social reform in addition to more particular demands.
3. Unions still maintain considerable influence in presidential elections and the Democratic Party's presidential nominating process, enabling unions to secure the support of the party's nominee on almost all of their key issues.
4. Once elected, Democratic presidents continue to make key appointments desired by labor, to grant labor privileged access to the executive branch, to promote many of the most important causes on labor's legislative agenda, and to help unions maintain their economic and political viability.
5. Aggregate union political resources, as measured in terms of financial reserves, membership voting behavior, and organizational capacity, have generally remained stable; in some respects, they have increased.

This evidence of continuity poses a problem for an influential body of analysis that might be called the "New Deal is dead" school. Among the proponents of this view are historians Steve Fraser and Gary Gerstle, who argue that "however much its ghost still hovers over a troubled polity," the New Deal "as a dominant order of ideas, public policies, and political alliances" decisively came to an end with the election of Ronald Reagan in 1980.[4] In an edited volume published in 1989, these authors develop the concept of a "political order," by which they mean an enduring set of relationships among political ideologies and programs, policymaking networks, and economic elites. They argue that American politics from the 1930s to 1970s is best understood in terms of the rise and fall of a "New Deal order" that possessed "an ideological character, a moral perspective, and a set of political relationships among policy elites, interest groups, and electoral constituencies that decidedly shaped American political life for forty years."[5] Organized labor was a crucial player in this order, both in constructing and in maintaining it. However, the failure of the labor movement to organize the South ultimately weakened American liberalism, as did the inability of liberal Democrats to create a more universalistic welfare state that would appeal deeply to middle-class voters. In the 1960s and 1970s, the order was further damaged by protracted conflicts over foreign policy and the appropriate role for new social movements based on race, gender, age, and sexual orientation. Growing economic dislocation and decay, manifested in rising inflation, stagnating living standards, and unmanageable budget deficits, made things even worse. Thus, by the late 1970s the New Deal order was merely a shell of its former self, and the labor movement was left as a residual force, declining in "numbers, economic strength, and political influence" and incapable of maintaining its historic ties to the Democratic Party.[6]

A similar conceptualization of a midcentury "political order" has been advanced by political scientist David Plotke. He defines a political order as a "durable mode of organizing and exercising political power at the national level, with distinct institutions, policies, and discourses."[7] Using this concept, Plotke charts the rise and fall of a "Democratic political order" created during the New Deal by Democratic party elites operating in alliance with organized labor and other newly mobilized constituencies. This order "fused democratic and modernizing elements in a progressive liberalism that advocated government action to achieve economic stability, enhance social security, and expand political representation." Plotke views organized labor as a "powerful interest group supportive of and intertwined with the Democratic order."[8]

In the long run, though, labor was weakened by a process of postindustrial transformation that was set in motion by the very policies of the Democratic order itself. As the order successfully orchestrated high rates of economic growth and innovation, the traditional bastions of unionism in heavy industry were undermined and workers took on new identities as consumers and suburbanites. Unions and other Democratic constituencies also grew overly dependent on the state itself for protection and resources. Weakened by statism and socioeconomic change, the Democratic political order experienced a crisis in the late 1960s because of growing racial conflict, the emergence of new social movements, and intense disagreement over the Vietnam War. Under these pressures, the Democratic order finally collapsed in "a spectacular political unraveling," clearing the way for Republican efforts to construct a new order on its ruins.[9] Thus, like Fraser and Gerstle (and many others), Plotke concludes that the life functions of the Democratic political order (or "regime") have been terminated.

But how convincing are such claims? Certainly, most will agree that the New Deal electoral coalition was fractured by the events of the 1960s and has never been the same since. Crucially, the success of the civil rights movement in ensuring voting equality for African Americans virtually guaranteed the destruction of the "solid South" that had formerly provided such a strong base of support for the Democratic Party. Most would also agree that by the 1970s the New Deal faith in the federal government as the most appropriate entity for solving all social problems no longer had much popularity or credibility. And few would dispute that the interest group system changed significantly, as corporate elites that were once friendly to the Democratic Party and its policies took refuge elsewhere, and organized labor confronted a hyperpluralist proliferation of new activist groups on both the Left and Right.

Nevertheless, the present work has unearthed extensive evidence of continuity in labor's role in the Democratic Party at the national level. Indeed, if we accept Plotke's description of a political order as "a durable configuration of institutions and discourses that frames choices by political agents," then we cannot agree that the old order has deteriorated to the degree claimed.[10] Many of the institutions and discourses that framed *labor*'s political choices during the 1990s were not novel at all but rather entirely consistent with the long-term pattern over many decades. If the Democratic or New Deal order were dead, labor would have been excluded from the congressional and presidential wings of the Democratic Party, its legal protections would have been abolished, and it would have become irrelevant in the political calculations of elected officeholders. None of this has happened. Unless and until it does, the terms of labor's incorporation remain basically similar to what they were more than fifty years ago (though the overall political environment is not, to be sure, as congenial to labor's political demands as it once was).

For all these reasons, the "political order" or "regime" framework, with its emphasis on across-the-board and interconnected shifts in the power of key players, provides few tools for understanding the discrete ups and downs in labor's situation. At best, these broad theories help us identify the outer limits on union power and the sources of the larger environmental factors that have made political life more difficult for unions and their allies. These theories do seem, for example, to aid our understanding of why American liberalism has been on the defensive in so many areas since the 1960s. But the fact remains that the hard shell of the labor/Democrat alliance—its deep resiliency to attacks from Republicans and conservative opponents within the Democratic party—simply is not predicted by those accounts that want to find a neat concordance of political outcomes across diverse policy areas and institutional settings.[11] The labor/Democrat alliance may have had its origins in the historic events of the 1930s, but it has outlived the political order that spawned it.

Of course, those in the "New Deal is dead" school could provide a response. They would probably say that the evidence of continuity assembled in this book is based only on events or issues that are trivial or irrelevant. The relationships and policies I have explored—such as labor's involvement with the congressional leadership, or President Clinton's appointments to the National Labor Relations Board—are not very important in their own right, and therefore do not contradict the claim that the old order is dead. In any case, they would say, the "political order" perspective does not require that there be a total transformation of everything when an order collapses. Naturally there may be lags in various institutions and policies. After all, the old order was thoroughly entrenched, and it is to be expected that its supporters will resist change.[12] Thus, critics will argue that the elements of continuity that I identify should be seen for what they really are: the leftovers of the old regime, not elements indigenous to the current system or period.

We might find this response compelling, were it not for the signs of the active reproduction—even intensification—of the labor/Democrat relationship during the mid- and late 1990s. The Clinton administration's very pro-union appointments to the NLRB and the Department of Labor, its support (albeit lukewarm) for labor law reform, its successful advocacy of enhanced regulation of the workplace (the Family and Medical Leave Act and stricter OSHA enforcement), its pride in enacting a minimum wage increase and expanded earned income tax credit, and its continued cultivation of and consultation with labor leaders—all suggest an ongoing commitment to maintaining labor as an "organized constituency" of the Democratic Party (to use David Greenstone's term for labor's role in the mid-1960s).[13] Likewise, the AFL-CIO's expanded intervention in the 1996 election and the coordination of its own legislative agenda with that of congressional Democrats and the Clinton administration show a similar commitment to continuing the labor/Democrat relationship. If anything, the purification of the congressional Democratic party through the departure of its southern and more conservative wings leaves labor in a better—not worse—position than it was before, *at least within the party itself*. Similarly, the weakening of southern barons and northern machine bosses in the presidential nominating process has only bolstered the role of unions in selecting the Democratic nominee—a point made manifest in the aggressive, almost desperate, efforts made during 1997 and 1998 by both House Minority Leader Richard Gephardt and Vice President Gore to secure union support.

The persistence—even growth—of union power in Congress was especially obvious in November 1997, when President Clinton was forced to withdraw his proposal to renew "fast-track" trade legislation. The fast-track provision, first approved by Congress in 1974, restricts the power of Congress to amend international trade agreements, thereby strengthening the president's hand in international trade negotiations. Clinton's pursuit of the measure was part of his larger commitment to expanding free trade, especially with Latin America and Asia. Thus, when the bill came before the House, the labor movement organized a major campaign in opposition. Working closely with House Democratic leaders, especially Minority Leader Gephardt, the AFL-CIO and affiliated unions organized intensive telephone, mail, and grassroots lobbying in twenty key congressional districts, and spent at least $1.5 million on television advertising.[14] The AFL-CIO also allied with an array of liberal interest groups, including Ralph Nader's Public Citizen, the Sierra Club, Friends of the Earth, the National Farmer's Union, the Humane Society, and the Pure Food Campaign. By mid-November, with whip counts showing that at least 225 members (163 Democrats and 62 Republicans) would vote against the measure, Clinton was forced to shelve the proposal indefinitely. What was particularly startling was that Clinton was unable to win the support of even a quarter of the House Democratic caucus, in contrast to the 40 percent that had voted for NAFTA in 1993. Given the AFL-CIO's key role in organizing the opposition, few doubted that the victory registered labor's growing political clout.[15]

The factors cited above as indicators of labor's power, it should also be noted, are of the same type as those used by analysts who discern a collapse in union power. Presidential appointments to the NLRB and Department of Labor, presidential actions on workplace regulation and welfare state programs, and the degree of consultation with union leaders have all regularly been taken as appropriate gauges of labor's power during the Reagan-Bush era. Accordingly, it is entirely appropriate to employ them in evaluating labor's current status. If the attacks on labor during the 1980s count as evidence of the success of the right wing, then the efforts to help labor in the 1990s must in turn demonstrate the continuation of New Deal–style relationships. President Clinton's choice, for example, to let the Teamsters' strike in August 1997 against United Parcel Service take its natural course, as well as his support of the efforts by his new secretary of labor, Alexis Herman, to encourage a reasonable settlement, was highly praised by grateful labor leaders. Such an outcome surely deserves to be accorded as much attention and analytical importance as the executive branch's hostile reaction to the air traffic controllers' strike in 1981.

Likewise, the many barely publicized but very important decisions that the Clinton administration regularly made in labor's favor must be taken into account when evaluating the labor/Democrat relationship. A good example would be the decision, made directly by President Clinton after meetings with the leaders of public employee unions, to deny federal approval to a plan by the state of Texas to privatize the administration of the state's welfare system—a measure that, if approved, would have hurt thousands of employees represented by AFSCME, the CWA, and the SEIU. In fact, anyone who peruses the record of the Clinton presidency will discover numerous actions of the federal government that, while lacking the sex appeal of major legislative battles, contributed much to the defense of the everyday interests of unions and their members. The point was made succinctly by William Hamilton, political director of Teamsters union, in an internal memo dated March 14, 1996: "We ask for and get, on almost a daily basis, help from the Clinton administration for one thing or another."[16]

Finally, in evaluating the idea that the New Deal legacy is moribund, we must recall that despite the best efforts of Presidents Reagan and Bush and the post-1994 Republican congressional majority, there has been no real transformation in public policy. While the New Deal *electoral coalition* may indeed have fragmented, and its ideology fallen into disrepute, New Deal *programs* have remained largely intact.[17] For example, the National Labor Relations Act, whatever its fundamental flaws from the union standpoint, survived the 1980s with no legislative amendments, thus opening the way for a significant revitalization effort by the Clinton-era NLRB. Likewise, the minimum wage (as embodied in the Fair Labor Standards Act) still exists, and it continues to be raised. Other preexisting regulations of the employment relationship, such as the Occupational Safety and Health Act, the Employee Retirement Income Security Act (protecting the security of pensions and other retirement benefits), and Title VII of the Civil Rights Act (with its major impact on private sector hiring and promotion practices), survived the Reagan-Bush era. Furthermore, entirely new efforts at workplace regulation were initiated, including the Americans with Disabilities Act, the Worker Adjustment and Retraining Notification Act (plant-closing legislation), the Family and Medical Leave Act, and restrictions on employer use of polygraph tests. In short, the comprehensive "rollback" of the interventionist state simply has not occurred, and attempts to exclude labor from the policymaking process have failed.

This outcome can also be seen as evidence for the resiliency of the phenomenon known as "interest group liberalism." As its foremost critic, Theodore Lowi, has noted, at the heart of this practice is a commitment to the "legitimation of organized groups and their formal as well as informal inclusion in the policymaking process."[18] In interest group liberalism, every group has a place, and that place is not to be denied or slighted by the conflicting demands of either rival groups or the broader public interest. All economic interest groups are thus granted some share of the budgetary or regulatory pie, and accorded some degree of protection from market forces. Commonly, this results in a form of functional representation, as illustrated in such citadels of clientelism as the Departments of Labor, Commerce, and Agriculture.[19] These arrangements reflect the logic of a system in which power is distributed "by the maxim of to each according to his claim" and the regime itself is legitimized by "reserving an official place for every major structure of power."[20]

Some have suggested that the conservative revival of the 1980s threatened interest group liberalism by weakening its major constituencies and forcing a new budgetary discipline, thereby making its future untenable.[21] But the story of labor's continued insertion into the policymaking process, despite the decline in union density, provides good reason for believing that the taproot of interest group liberalism retains considerable vitality. Furthermore, that these long-standing interest group accommodations are so resilient goes a long way toward explaining why the efforts to construct a new conservative political order have proved relatively anemic: there has simply been too much to dislodge—indeed, far too much—for any effort at radical reconstruction to succeed.[22]

The Future

What, then, is the future likely to hold for the labor movement in national politics? The prognosis for the next ten to fifteen years is this: the unions will continue to survive in roughly their current form as major but not dominant players in the Democratic Party. The public sector unions will continue to grow (albeit at a slower pace than they did in the 1960s and 1970s), inevitably gaining greater strength within the decision-making bodies of the federation. This fact alone will guarantee a deep AFL-CIO commitment to national politics and the advancement of the Democratic Party. Yet the private sector unions will also continue to devote much energy to politics, helping to elect Democrats and lobbying for those protections and benefits that they cannot achieve through collective bargaining.

These claims are buttressed by the continuing union efforts to improve their political capabilities. In September 1997, for example, the AFL-CIO convention approved a five-cent increase in the per capita tax levied on each union. The resulting money ($12 million over two years) will pay for a federation effort to register four million members of union households by 2000 and to recruit at least 2,000 unionists to run for public office at the local, state, and federal levels. The convention also approved a new television advertising campaign intended to improve labor's public image. Such efforts will be aided by the trend toward union mergers, seen most impressively in the plan of the Machinists, Steelworkers, and Auto Workers to soon form one massive union based in the metalworking industries. As a result of these mergers, which are strongly supported by President Sweeney and his allies at federation headquarters, unions are likely to be better-funded and better-administered than they were in the past—and, in all likelihood, considerably more effective in the management of their political programs. In this way, at least some of the institutional fragmentation that has long bedeviled union political action will be partially relieved.

Still, all this activity will largely constitute a new mobilization for an old strategy. That strategy, set long ago, is to work within the electoral and legislative processes of the Democratic Party. Thus, it is extremely unlikely that labor will make any serious efforts to create its own political party (although it may occasionally flirt with the idea in order to scare Democratic politicians into taking its demands more seriously). Instead, the union movement will continue to enmesh itself more deeply in the Democratic Party at all levels and will further improve its ties with those left-liberal constituencies that emerged out of the conflicts of the 1960s and 1970s. It is reasonable to expect, therefore, that labor will work at maintaining internal Democratic unity and will eschew the divisive rhetoric and tactics of bygone years. Organized labor has finally made its peace with the 1960s, a fact confirmed in John Sweeney's ascension to the federation presidency in 1995.

As a result of these efforts, the major candidates for the Democratic nomination in 2000 will seek out the support of organized labor, and it is entirely possible that the president elected that year will be a Democrat with very close ties to the unions. That such an outcome might even be conceivable, after decades of intensive assault from so many quarters, can only be considered an impressive achievement for the labor movement. More generally, that the labor/Democrat relationship should survive as well as it has, some sixty years after the launching of the New Deal, testifies to the enduring power of that political transformation—still the Big Bang of our modern political universe—to structure political behavior. A crucial part of that new system of power, and one distinguishing it from all that went before, was the construction of a close bargaining relationship between national Democratic Party officeholders and the national labor leadership. Neither a "barren marriage" nor an altruistic union, the ensuing relationship was a rational exchange of political commitments that has provided regular benefits for both sides—and seems likely to do so for many years to come.

The paradox is that this political resiliency—even vitality—comes at the very same time that private sector union density continues its inexorable decline. How much longer can the unions continue to generate political power if the membership base is stagnant? Is there a threshold point, a percentage below which unions will be unable to take compensating action? The answers to these questions are unknown, and in this sense unions are indeed "at the crossroads," as one scholar has recently put it.[23] It is clear that at some point, the unions have got to staunch the loss of membership. Eventually decline will decisively undermine union power, though the moment of crisis may not arrive for another decade or perhaps much longer. The current efforts at revival thus become all the more interesting and important. If the foregoing arguments are correct, then the future character of the Democratic Party will be decided by the success or failure of such initiatives.

Finally, perhaps we should not find the paradox of union power in the midst of decline entirely surprising. History records that political upheavals have often been generated not by the action of ascendant social classes but by the defensive actions of classes or strata as they wane. In the late nineteenth century, American farmers caused much turmoil in the political system, even as the inescapable nature of their decay was becoming obvious. Likewise, peasant rebellions throughout the world have often been driven by the actions of rural producers that sensed, and feared, the coming transformation of their way of life. By a similar logic, the political potency of American unionism may persist, even strengthen, as it seeks to protect its industrial sector members from the imminent ravages of a postindustrial economy. This dynamic, combined with the continuing union presence in the public sector and parts of the service sector, ensures that the unions will continue to make forceful political interventions. The final chapter in the history of labor's role in national politics still remains to be written.

Postscript: Labor Approaches the Post-Clinton Era

The resolution of the 2000 presidential election was perhaps the strangest and most unpredictable spectacle that anyone could have imagined. The prognostications of the pundits were turned topsy-turvy as Al Gore decisively won the national popular vote tally, only to be denied an electoral vote triumph due to a defeat in Florida by the astonishing margin of just a few hundred votes. As the post-election battles over Florida's electoral procedures wound their way through the nation's courts, complete with rowdy street demonstrations and vitriolic partisan attacks over the airwaves, the usual landmarks of American electoral politics seemed far from view. In the midst of the chaos, however, the role of organized labor was the very picture of constancy. In the 2000 election, as in so many others in the past, the labor movement stuck to its old and traditional, but also tried and true, strategy of endorsing Democratic party candidates and working actively for their election. Although commentators in the press had made much of the brief flirtation by some union leaders with the presidential candidacy of consumer advocate Ralph Nader, by fall 2000 the leadership of the labor movement—and, it turned out, the rank and file as well—was strongly unified behind the campaign of Vice President Al Gore. The labor-Democrat alliance thus endured, much in the same form it always has, albeit with the technical adjustments that changing times always demand.

While the fundamentals of the relationship remained unchanged, several issues were raised by the increased prominence of union political action in the late 1990s. One question was how labor actually went about trying to influence electoral and legislative outcomes. What kinds of tactical choices were made, and how did union leaders try to maximize the impact of their limited resources? Second, was the AFL-CIO's renewed effort at voter education and mobilization—the very centerpiece of the program adopted by the new federation leadership installed in 1995—reflected in improved union-member voting turnout and behavior? Third, did all this activity pay off in better government policy? What, if anything, did labor get out of its expensive alliance with Democratic officeholders? Finally, as labor faced what was, on paper at least, its worst-case political configuration—a Republican-controlled Congress and presidency—what would be the likely future of the labor-Democrat alliance?

The Final Years of the Clinton Administration

The last several years of the Clinton administration were, from the standpoint of the labor-Democrat relationship, relatively uneventful and straightforward. With the Republicans in control of the House and the Senate and the president stymied by perpetual investigation and, finally, the great Monica Lewinsky scandal of 1998–1999, little labor-supported legislation of any type was advanced. Yet, with the departure of House Speaker Newt Gingrich after the 1998 congressional elections and the growing confusion and unpopularity of the congressional majority, the Republicans, too, were unable to advance a significant legislative agenda. It was back to gridlock as usual in Washington, with the notable exception of trade legislation, where the labor movement experienced a disappointing setback that belied its 1997 success in defeating fast-track trade authorization.

The most intense legislative debate for organized labor in this period was undoubtedly the struggle in spring 2000 over granting permanent normal trading relations (PNTR) to the People's Republic of China. This provision would allow Chinese goods the same low-tariff access to U.S. markets as products from most other nations, without the existing requirement that the policy be reviewed on an annual basis. The Clinton administration, with strong Republican support, enthusiastically endorsed the PNTR bill, arguing that freer trade with China would foster economic growth in the U.S. and Asia and encourage liberalizing trends in Chinese society—all ultimately to the benefit of U.S. national security. The AFL-CIO, led by its import-sensitive industrial unions, castigated the policy as an ill-conceived measure that would lead only to the increased exploitation of Chinese workers, an exodus of high-paying industrial jobs from the U.S., and the strengthening of the country's undemocratic, Communist rulers.

Labor tried mightily to stop the legislation, organizing letter-writing campaigns, visits by union members to Capitol Hill, local protest rallies, and television ads in key congressional districts. For its part, the Clinton administration went all out for the bill, with the president meeting with more than one hundred members of Congress and traveling to key congressional districts in the Midwest and California. The administration also engaged in a furious game of deal-making, offering individual lawmakers assistance with myriad local problems and issues that could be impacted by federal policy. The administration's efforts paid off in May 2000, when the bill passed the House of Representatives by a wide margin, 237 to 197. With Senate approval a virtual certainty, this vote meant the end of labor's aspirations to squash further trade liberalization with China. While 138 Democrats—nearly two-thirds of the House caucus—had voted against the bill, the outcome was still a stinging defeat for the labor movement. Union lobbyists had believed they had a good chance of victory, based on both their earlier success in blocking extension of fast track trade authority and the apparent revival of anti-free–trade sentiment as reflected in the protests against globalization at the November 1999 Seattle World Trade Organization (WTO) meetings. But as was the case with the earlier NAFTA battle, labor was unable to overcome President Clinton's aggressive lobbying, the corporate community's impressive unity, public indifference, and the perception that serious issues of national security and geopolitics—not just tariff agreements—were at stake.

Clinton's intense efforts in support of a bill strongly opposed by organized labor revealed once more the limitations that have always been part of the union-Democrat alliance. Indeed, the aftermath of the House vote brought an almost exact repeat of the recriminations that followed passage of NAFTA in 1993. "I am deeply angry that the president, whom working families elected, chose to divide progressive elected officials and their constituencies," said AFL-CIO President John Sweeney.[1]

The UAW went further, with President Stephen Yokich releasing a written statement declaring, "We have no choice but to actively explore alternatives to the major political parties. It's time to forget about party labels and instead focus on supporting candidates, such as Ralph Nader, who will take a stand based on what is right, not what big money dictates."[2] Leaders of the Teamsters and Steelworkers also claimed that they would take retribution against congressional Democrats who had "betrayed" labor's trust.

But, as always, these were truly idle threats, intended more to assuage internal union constituencies and perhaps scare a few gullible Democrats than to foreshadow a real change in union strategy. As in 1993, after a few months of complaining and threatening, even the discontented industrial unions fell back into line, soon supporting the same old congressional Democrats and, indeed, the vice president of the very administration that had done so much to pass the offending legislation. Writing in the midst of these machinations, Rahm Emanuel, a former senior adviser to President Clinton, captured the logic of the situation as seen from the White House: "Just as a labor backlash did not develop after NAFTA, so none will come after PNTR. Nobody really believes that the AFL-CIO will defeat a Democratic member with so much riding on the outcome of the 2000 election. Labor won't spend $20 million to $30 million to regain the necessary six seats for control of the House, just to lose that investment by defeating a pro-PNTR member."[3] Such was the longstanding nature of the labor-Democrat alliance—no one should have been surprised.

As this episode (along with labor's well-publicized support for the Seattle protests against the WTO) demonstrated, trade remains a sore spot in the labor-Democrat alliance, especially at the presidential level. The commitment of Democratic presidents to preserving the United States's position as the dominant force in international relations has brought with it a strong devotion to a policy of trade liberalization. As the unchallenged global hegemon, a serious (as opposed to cosmetic) turn to protectionism by the U.S. is out of the question, and neither Democratic nor Republican executives are likely to sacrifice the strategic position of the U.S. in the global order in order to gain a few more votes in Michigan and Pennsylvania.

Notwithstanding its persistence, the trade conflict remains eminently manageable, for labor leaders and their Democratic allies have far more in common than not. Indeed, even as new legislation was largely stymied in the latter years of the Clinton presidency, the administration continued to issue executive orders and new regulations intended to benefit workers and unions. In late 2000, for example, the administration released new ergonomics workplace safety regulations that had been strenuously opposed by business groups. Clinton also announced new rules designed to prevent federal agencies from awarding contracts to firms that violate labor and environmental laws—an effort once again to use the federal contracting power to compel employers to fully obey existing labor law. Such measures, bound to be opposed (and perhaps revoked) by the new Bush administration, were reminders of just why labor has maintained its traditional Democratic commitments, despite the recurring disputes over how to regulate the international economy.

From 1998 to the 2000 Election

In 1998 and 2000, the labor movement pursued the same goal it had in 1996: to retake Congress for the Democrats and, in 2000, to keep a Democrat in the White House. The congressional elections of 1998 were of some significance, as they revealed certain technical innovations that the labor movement would pursue even more energetically in 2000.[4] As the AFL-CIO prepared its strategy for 1998, it sought to draw the salient lessons from its experience of renewed mobilization in 1996. One drawback to the intensive effort of that year was that it stimulated new Republican efforts to weaken union power by restricting labor political spending. The proposal that the GOP favored required that unions receive written permission from individual union members before spending their dues money on any kind of political activity—a provision that would surely undermine the effectiveness of union political intervention. While labor beat back these efforts in both Congress and the states, the intensity of the GOP reaction suggested that labor interests might be better served by tactics that were less provocative than the high-profile, self-consciously aggressive style of 1996.

The new plan for 1998, therefore, was to come in "under the radar screen," as labor operatives put it, by discreetly mobilizing union members and local communities without at the same time alerting labor's adversaries that they were the target of a massive, nationally orchestrated campaign. In addition, union officials concluded that the television advertising used in 1996 was too diffuse in its impact, activating not only union supporters but also many union opponents. To avoid these problems, the AFL-CIO's operatives adopted a strategy they called the "ground war," which would supplement and in some cases displace the TV- and radio-based "air war" of 1996. Steve Rosenthal, the AFL-CIO's political director, announced that labor would put more of its money and resources into independent educational activities directed toward union members rather than the old tactic of making large contributions directly to campaigns, which union activists now derided as "checkbook" politics. Rosenthal especially encouraged one-on-one communications between union activists and individual members which, while extremely labor intensive, could best take advantage of the unions' pre-existing organizational structures. The surprisingly successful performance of congressional Democrats in the 1998 elections confirmed union activists' belief that intensive efforts at issue-based, grassroots mobilization would be the secret weapon that labor could wield to retake Congress and elect a Democratic president in 2000.[5]

The first task of the 2000 election season for labor strategists was to see to it that the Democratic party converged early around a viable presidential nominee. By the summer of 1999 it had become clear that the only serious candidate willing to challenge Vice President Al Gore for the party nomination was former New Jersey Senator Bill Bradley. The narrowing of the nominating contest to a duel between Bradley and Gore came only after House Democratic Leader Dick Gephardt—a longtime labor favorite—had withdrawn earlier in the year. Sensing the difficulty in challenging a sitting vice president for the party nod and attracted by the likelihood that he could become Speaker of the House after the 2000 elections, Gephardt abandoned his presidential bid in favor of leading the House Democrats into the 2000 campaign. Bradley, meanwhile, sketched out a role for himself as a liberal insurgent, gaining the early support of former Labor Secretary Robert Reich and liberal Minnesota Senator Paul Wellstone. While Bradley did not depart from the free-trade orthodoxy of the Clinton administration, he did articulate a critique of recent economic developments that might have attracted considerable labor support.

But from the beginning it was clear that AFL-CIO President Sweeney strongly preferred Al Gore, who also had the support of such key unions as AFSCME and the Communication Workers of America. There were several arguments in Gore's favor. First and foremost, he seemed the most likely candidate to secure the support of other key party elites and mass constituencies, and thus the most likely to emerge as the victor even without labor's endorsement. If labor could move the process along more quickly and gain credit with the eventual nominee while doing so, there was little obvious downside to an official endorsement. And if such a maneuver foreclosed any serious primary challenges, this was all to the better, for such internal party conflict only increased the likelihood of a general election defeat. For these reasons, Gore's backers in the labor movement argued strongly for an early AFL-CIO endorsement—well before the first caucuses and primaries—so that the vice president could tap the massive resources of the labor movement when they counted most.

Second, Gore had demonstrated that he was a reliable politician with a sincere respect for the labor movement. As a Senator from Tennessee, his COPE rating had been good (indeed, comparable to Senator Bradley's), despite the weakness of the state's labor movement. As vice president, Gore had made it a point to be accessible to union leaders and had insisted that they be included in relevant deliberations in the executive branch. For the status- and protocol-conscious union leaders this record was important and reassuring, but, perhaps most significant, Gore had demonstrated during his tenure as vice president that he strongly supported the right of workers to form labor unions and the need for proper legal protections for unions as institutions. He strongly opposed GOP efforts to limit union political spending and to promote such schemes as the TEAM act authorizing a version of company unions. As vice president he had joined picket lines and intervened to support strikes and collective bargaining efforts. He had spoken out in support of the NLRB, Medicare, and OSHA and against efforts by the GOP Congress to cut these programs back. In short, Gore's credentials as a pro-labor Democrat were about as good as any Democratic presidential nominee since the New Deal. Finally, and notwithstanding his lackluster reputation as a campaigner, his experience in national politics suggested he would run a solid campaign in the general election.

Not all union leaders, however, were persuaded by this logic. There were two main sources of discontent. The first was the old bugaboo trade. The unions that had been most opposed to NAFTA, the WTO, and PNTR were also the unions angriest at the Clinton administration and most dissatisfied with the free-trade stance of the presumptive Democratic nominee. The Autoworkers, Steelworkers, Teamsters, and Machinists saw much to dislike in Gore's trade stance and were eager to find ways to punish the administration without directly threatening the general election outcome: one way to do so was to delay or prevent an early federation endorsement of the nomination of the current vice president. The second problem, and one that grew in importance in the fall of 1999 as Bradley's campaign gained steam, was the perception that Al Gore had serious problems as a campaigner. He failed to excite the Democratic base, including the union rank and file, and apparently turned off the much sought-after swing voters. With Texas Governor George W. Bush, the likely Republican nominee, way ahead in the polls and with signs that restive Democratic primary voters might bolt to Bradley in Iowa, New Hampshire, and elsewhere, a number of union leaders were reconsidering the wisdom of any early endorsement.

These concerns all came to a head as the AFL-CIO convention prepared to meet in Los Angeles in October 1999. Sweeney had much earlier decided that it was at this convention that the federation should officially announce its endorsement of Al Gore. Now the convention was taking place at the very moment that Gore's candidacy was threatened by the rising popularity of Bradley. In this context, a decision to delay the endorsement would be seen by the media and other party elites as a sign that Al Gore was in very serious trouble. Conversely, a decision to endorse Gore at this crucial juncture would be seen as a major boost to his troubled campaign and an indication that his standing with the core constituencies of the party remained strong.

It was, finally, John Sweeney who made the difference for the Gore campaign. Sweeney insisted that Al Gore had been there for labor over the past eight years and that it was now time to pay him back for his loyalty. Sweeney went all-out in support of the vice president, pressuring key union leaders in the days and hours preceding the convention. In making such an active and open commitment to Gore, Sweeney put his own reputation and that of the federation on the line. Ultimately, by making the endorsement an issue of personal loyalty and the federation's prestige, he made it all but impossible for most union leaders to vote against a Gore endorsement.

On October 12, 1999, the AFL-CIO convention endorsed Gore with little open dissension, although such prominent unions as the UAW, Teamsters, Steelworkers, and Mineworkers still remained formally neutral. After the vote, Sweeney triumphantly introduced the Vice President to the assembled delegates. In his acceptance speech, Gore vowed to fight for a ban on permanent replacement of strikers, to oppose school vouchers, and to include provisions for worker rights and environmental protection in future trade agreements (although he left it vague how these would be enforced). He expressed his support for union organizing in terms that were unequivocal: "I believe that the right to organize is a basic American right that should never be stopped, never be blocked, and never be taken away. Let me tell you, that right needs to be strengthened today." He promised that as president he would veto all antiunion legislation and stand firmly against any Republican efforts to "take back the country to an antiunion, antiworker past." And he endorsed longstanding Democratic party arguments—dating to the New Deal and before—in defense of labor's role in the workplace: "If there is a heavy hand on the part of an employer who is not respecting employees, who is not sensitive to their families or to their needs, then there ought to be a check and a balance against that heavy-handed power in the form of an unhampered right of employees to join together and speak as one voice as a group."[6] With such words, Gore had strayed far from the New Democrat emphasis on markets and individual consumer choice as the main vehicles for social progress.

The next order of business for the AFL-CIO was to ensure that labor actually came through for Gore in the crucial early caucuses and primaries. The movement's large apparatus of money, staff, and volunteers quickly swung into action.[7] For the Iowa caucuses, the AFL-CIO and other national unions sent thirty-five full-time organizers to the state and made at least 30,000 phone calls to union members. The AFL-CIO worked with the Iowa State Education Association to send four separate mailings, one of which included a five-minute video featuring John Sweeney promoting Gore's candidacy, to 25,000 union households. A group of political scientists studying the caucuses report that "the AFL-CIO and affiliated unions actually brought a tractor-trailer to Iowa City and parked it outside the Gore headquarters just off Interstate 80. Inside the trailer was a 'war room,' with computer systems, telephones, and a sophisticated phone-banking plan."[8] But most important was simply labor's ability to bring out volunteers and members willing to attend the caucuses for a few hours on a winter's night. Bradley's amateurish (albeit well-funded) campaign posed no challenge to this operation, and the results were clear on caucus night, when Gore beat Bradley 63 percent to 35 percent, with union voters comprising 33 percent of the turnout.

Labor was also an important factor in New Hampshire, despite the low union density in the state. Union volunteers made more than 5,000 union house visits and hand-delivered videos reviewing Gore's "longtime support for working families." Labor's grassroots effort generated seven contacts for each union household and was followed up in the days before the election by multiple telephone calls and yet more outreach in the form of get-out-the-vote drives. On Election Day members of union households were 24 percent of the turnout and cast their vote 62 to 37 percent for Gore, providing crucial help in securing Gore's 53 percent to 47 percent victory over Bradley.[9]

With these defeats, Bradley's campaign was effectively over, left only to await its final demise after the various state primaries on March 7 and 14. Organized labor had done its job well (but not without a good deal of help from Bradley's own curiously lackluster campaign and poor electoral strategy). At the August Democratic convention, labor delegates were 1,500 strong (of 4,368) and represented the largest single interest-group block (just as they had for several decades). President Sweeney, AFL-CIO Vice President Richard Trumka, and AFSCME President Gerald McEntee all spoke from the convention podium. While this was not the first time that union leaders took such a visible role, it was a notable departure from the conventions of the 1960s and before, when union officials operated almost completely behind the scenes and disclaimed any direct involvement in party activities.

By 2000, labor's incorporation into the party apparatus was complete. In engineering the endorsement of Gore, Sweeney had established himself as the unrivaled power broker for the political resources of the labor movement—a fact that did not go unnoticed or unappreciated by either Gore or other Democratic politicians. For the first time since labor's 1984 intervention on behalf of Walter Mondale, the federation had made an early endorsement in a contested nominating process. Sweeney had thus delivered the AFL-CIO for the vice president at the hour of maximum peril for the Gore campaign. Had a Gore administration materialized, this record would have enabled Sweeney to maintain a level of access and political importance perhaps not seen since George Meany's heyday in the 1960s.

Despite all this, in the summer of 2000 there was still some question (and much media speculation) about whether labor votes and resources would really flow to the Gore campaign in the general election to the extent necessary to generate a decisive victory. Most worrisome were the indications that some union members and even prominent union leaders were attracted to Green party presidential candidate Ralph Nader. By early August, however, the UAW and Steelworkers had endorsed Gore, and the United Mine Workers and Teamsters finally came around in September. America's labor movement had once again returned to its longstanding political home.

The Ground War

In the general election, the AFL-CIO pursued its usual strategy of mobilizing union members and allied constituencies through the deployment of large quantities of money, staff, and volunteers. As in 1998, the federation encouraged the use of the member-to-member strategy, which union officials argued was extremely effective in converting workers to the Democratic side and then mobilizing them to vote on election day. Simply taking the time to personally ask members to vote and providing them with the information necessary to vote the right way was proving highly beneficial.[10] The federation said that 76 percent of union members who received election-related information in 1998 voted for the labor-backed candidate, as compared with 58 percent among those who did not receive information.[11] Thus, the goal in 2000 was clear: to drive up the percentage of union members contacted, with the reliable expectation that turnout and Democratic votes would increase correspondingly. If things went as planned, the Democrats would keep the White House and trim, or perhaps even eliminate, the GOP's 223 to 210 House majority and its 54 to 46 majority in the Senate. The AFL-CIO said it would spend at least $46 million on the mobilizing effort, which of course would be combined with the spending of the various national unions. The 2000 campaign promised to be one of labor's most well-funded and orchestrated election efforts ever.

Labor operatives immediately adopted a special focus on a number of the key states deemed to be in play in the 2000 presidential election: Ohio, Pennsylvania, Michigan, Wisconsin, New Jersey, Missouri, and Florida. With the exception of Florida, all of these states had a higher union density level than the national average, and some, of course, had longstanding, powerful union movements. In each state, the AFL-CIO worked with state and local federations and individual national unions to implement the now well-tested "ground war" strategy. In Pennsylvania, for example, union organizers divided the state into five geographic zones and began meeting in August with every local union president in the state, seeking to identify a network of activists within each local and workplace.[12] In Florida, labor put huge efforts into mobilizing retired union members, sending out mailings claiming that Bush's privatization proposals threatened their Social Security benefits and that Gore's plans would reduce the cost of prescription drugs.[13] In the Midwest, the UAW for the first time negotiated a holiday with automakers for election day, allowing the membership to vote more easily and enabling union activists to work on get-out-the-vote campaigns. Michigan Governor John Engler called the holiday "the largest single corporate contribution in American history," an agreement that "dwarfs the other money in politics."[14]

Across the nation, the AFL-CIO developed targeted mailings with different themes for different regions and groups of workers. In Midwestern states, a major difficulty was the intensive effort by the National Rifle Association to convince unionized workers that they should vote primarily on the basis of their identity as gun owners and thus support Republican nominee George W. Bush. Much as labor had fought against similar appeals by George Wallace in 1968, the AFL-CIO waged its own campaign to convince workers that Al Gore posed no threat to legitimate gun ownership. While the NRA insisted in its literature that "there is no longer much meaningful difference between Democrats and Republicans when it comes to policies that affect union workers," labor emphasized the Gore advantage on such bread-and-butter issues as workplace safety and Social Security. "Al Gore doesn't want to take away your gun, but George Bush does want to take away your union," the AFL-CIO declared in a special flier distributed to workers in Ohio, Michigan, and Pennsylvania.[15]

That most expedient of union political techniques—direct financial contributions to a candidate's campaign and to state and national party committees—was also well-utilized in 2000, notwithstanding labor's use of new modes of political mobilization. Federal Election Commission reports showed that as of October 2000 unions had contributed more than $60 million to federal candidates and political parties (93% to Democrats), an amount that already surpassed the $59 million spent during the entire election season in 1996 and the $48 million spent in 1992. The largest contributions came from some of the traditional top players in union campaign finance: AFSCME ($5,123,214), SEIU ($3,573,664), CWA ($3,299,264), IBEW ($3,133,840), and UFCW ($2,662,407). (These figures do not, it should be noted, include independent labor spending on educating and mobilizing union members, such as the $46 million that the AFL-CIO pledged and the additional quantities by individual national unions.)[16]

According to the AFL-CIO's own calculations, its 2000 mobilization added 2.3 million people in union households to the voter rolls—up from only half a million new voters in 1998. The federation said that in total more than 1,000 coordinators (compared with 400 coordinators in 1998) were assigned to train and organize hundreds of thousands of union volunteers to help educate and mobilize union members, with an additional 500 coordinators joining the effort in the final few weeks. Union activists under federation auspices made eight million personal phone calls (up from 5.5 million in 1998) and sent out 12 million pieces of mail—not including the phone banks and mailings conducted by individual union affiliates and state labor federations. An estimated 100,000 union members volunteered their time at work sites and phone banks and in precinct walks to support Democratic candidates. To energize union members during the final weeks, the federation sponsored a "People Powered" bus tour, in which more than 20 union leaders boarded buses that rolled through 25 cities in Pennsylvania, Kentucky, Ohio, Michigan, Washington, West Virginia, and Oregon. Labor sent sound trucks blaring political messages into black and Latino neighborhoods. "No other group in America has built a longlasting structure that can turn out hundreds of thousands of activists in every township in the U.S.," crowed Sweeney after the election.[17]

Polling data indicate that the labor effort had the desired effect. Union households made up a record high 26 percent of voters, up from 23 percent in 1996 and 1998 according to a national survey of union members conducted by the polling firm Peter Hart Research Associates, and voted for Gore 61 percent to 33 percent (compared to a national Gore vote of only 48 percent).[18] Union households and the high turnout and overwhelming support for Al Gore by union members played a pivotal role in many states, including Michigan, Pennsylvania, Wisconsin, and Washington. In Michigan, for example, union households accounted for 43 percent of all voters and were crucial in the election to the Senate of Democratic congressional representative Debbie Stabenow. Labor efforts were also critical to the successful senatorial campaigns of Jon Corzine in New Jersey, the late Mel Carnahan in Missouri (Carnahan's widow pledged to accept an appointment to his position), Bill Nelson in Florida, and Maria Cantwell in Washington. Along with a $9 million voter registration and turnout effort by the

NAACP, labor's efforts were credited with turning the tide. Around the country union members also mobilized in record for other key elections, winning the state senate in Colorado, defeating two ballot initiatives that restricted union political spending in Oregon, and defeating voucher initiatives in California and Michigan.

Ironically, then, labor had achieved much of what it had hoped for: the major swing states of Michigan, Pennsylvania, New Jersey, and Wisconsin had all gone for Gore. Moreover, by most accounts, Al Gore had actually won Florida—if the votes had been properly counted. The national popular vote margin of victory—approximately 500,000—was impressive in its own right and probably reflected the intensive union effort to mobilize the Democratic base. Despite all this, Al Gore lost, for reasons that by now have been seared into the national consciousness and the history books. This was a bitter defeat for organized labor, but spirits were lifted by one other statistic. When the votes for Gore and Nader were combined, the result was a nearly 52 percent majority for the center-left in American politics—the highest such percentage recorded since Lyndon Johnson's historic landslide victory in 1964. With an election result like this, the basis for GOP triumphalism would seem shallow indeed.

The outcomes in the congressional races were also largely disappointing for union activists, although the results did reveal a few pleasant surprises. Most union strategists had anticipated that the 2000 election could lead to a Democratic majority in the House and perhaps in the Senate as well if the Democrats were very lucky. That ideal outcome did not occur, of course, as the Democrats found it ever harder to claw back those last few seats needed to attain a House majority: they ended the election with an unimpressive two seat gain. But the Democrats surprised everyone by fighting to a 50–50 tie in the Senate—a crucial achievement if labor is to block the anti-union legislation that might now be supported by President Bush and the House GOP majority. A final consolation can also be found in the very real possibility that the Democrats could take control over both houses of Congress in the midterm elections of 2002, although redistricting and the strength of the GOP in southern congressional districts make this outcome far from certain.

Conclusion

In historical perspective, what is most striking about the 2000 election is the way in which organized labor was once again trapped by the peculiarities of the American political system. This system is one marked by numerous provisions intended to weaken or limit majority rule by dividing and fragmenting power, frequently through procedures that give regional interests a de facto form of veto power. One such anti-majoritarian provision—the filibuster rule in the Senate—is identified in this book as a major factor blocking labor law reform (and other progressive legislation) for the past half century. In the 2000 election it was the electoral college that finally came into its own as an anti-majoritarian institution—one quite capable of effectively undermining labor's political aspirations. Designed in a predemocratic era and based on a truly outmoded fetishization of the federal principle, the electoral college has joined the filibuster as a prime spoiler of union strategy. While it is true that labor has sometimes benefited from anti-majoritarian features of the U.S. political system (and will no doubt do so again), it is hard not to draw the conclusion that ultimately it would be better served by a political system that allowed a national majority to rule more directly.

The election of a Republican president—even one as weak and partially delegitimized as George W. Bush—will, of course, have some adverse consequences for the labor movement. The Department of Labor and the National Labor Relations Board will no longer be composed of liberal academics, former unionists, and other pro-labor allies. The president will no longer be counted on to veto anti-labor bills (although the stronger Democratic position in the Senate should, especially using the filibuster, fulfill much the same function). The federal judiciary will no longer see an influx of liberal and moderate judges but will instead recommence the conservative shift that began during the Reagan and Bush years. And, of course, union presidents will no longer have their rides on Air Force One and invitations to state dinners at the White House. But it seems unlikely that the Republicans will be in a position to implement a vigorously anti-labor program; their weakness in Congress and in public opinion make such a move far too difficult. In this respect, the situation is actually less threatening than that faced by labor after the 1980 election, despite the friendly congressional majorities awaiting the new Republican president. George W. Bush is no Ronald Reagan, and for that union leaders can truly be thankful.

There is, finally, a certain advantage in the novel situation facing labor as of January 20, 2001. With the presidency back in the hands of the Republicans until at least 2005, the tension, mainly trade-related, that has emerged between the unions and the presidential wing of the Democratic party can at last subside. Now, with Democratic political leadership defaulting to the congressional wing of the party, unions can simply stick to the cozy Capitol Hill relationships they know best. At the same time, another truth will soon be recognized: that in Washington it is far easier for interests to unite in defense of the status quo and against partisan enemies than to join together in support of a program of reform that may threaten entrenched power. Bill Clinton rediscovered this truth, and it will soon be George W. Bush's turn. It is this truth that will also ensure that the labor-Democrat alliance in Congress will persist in very good shape—perhaps its best shape ever—as the new Bush presidency unfolds.

Notes

Introduction

[1] Indeed, the need to incorporate the rise of such powerful organizations into the American legal order has been interpreted by at least one author as the force that finally dissolved the feudalistic remnants of an older master-servant relationship and replaced them with the contractual ties of modern liberalism. See Karen Orren, *Belated Feudalism: Labor, the Law, and Liberal Development in the United States* (Cambridge: Cambridge University Press, 1991).

[2] James B. Parks, "Job, Income Security at Top of UAW Agenda," *AFL-CIO News*, April 22, 1996. Ironically, the effects of the strike were heightened by the corporation's commitment to "just-in-time" lean production, which reduced the supply of back parts maintained in any one plant.

[3] See the essays in John H. Goldthorpe, ed., *Order and Conflict in Contemporary Capitalism* (Oxford: Oxford University Press, 1984), and Harold Wilensky and Lowell Turner, *Democratic Corporatism and Policy Linkages: The Interdependence of Industrial, Labor-Market, Incomes, and Social Policies in Eight Countries*, Research Series No. 9 (Berkeley: University of California, Berkeley, Institute of International Studies, 1987).

[4] For some of this discussion, see Samuel Kernell, *Going Public: New Strategies of Presidential Leadership*, 3rd ed. (Washington, D.C.: Congressional Quarterly, 1997); Anthony King, ed., *The New American Political System* (Washington, D.C.: American Enterprise Institute, 1979); William M. Lunch, *The Nationalization of American Politics* (Berkeley: University of California Press, 1987); and Nelson Polsby, *The Consequences of Party Reform* (New York: Oxford University Press, 1983).

[5] Joyce is quoted in "Discussion" of Richard B. Freeman, "Why Are Unions Faring Poorly in NLRB Representation Elections?" in *Challenges and Choices Facing American Labor*, ed. Thomas A. Kochan (Cambridge, Mass.: Massachusetts Institute of Technology Press, 1986), 71.

[6] Meany is quoted in Archie Robinson, *George Meany and His Times: A Biography* (New York: Simon and Schuster, 1981), 241.

[7] Lane Kirkland, "Report on Congress," *AFL-CIO News*, October 20, 1984.

1 *The Debate about Decline*

[1] Thomas Byrne Edsall, *The New Politics of Inequality* (New York: W. W. Norton, 1984), 174; David Vogel, *Fluctuating Fortunes: The Political Power of Business in America* (New York: Basic Books, 1989), 293; Mike Davis, *Prisoners of the American Dream: Politics and Economy in the History of the US Working Class* (London: Verso, 1986), 289, 292. Ironically, Davis cited Missouri Representative Richard Gephardt—who in the 1990s would come to be seen by many

commentators as an "Old Democrat" with deep ties to labor—as among the worst offenders in the Democrats' betrayal of the unions.

[2] For more examples, see William C. Berman, *America's Right Turn: From Nixon to Bush* (Baltimore: Johns Hopkins University Press, 1994), 117, and Thomas Ferguson and Joel Rogers, *Right Turn: The Decline of the Democrats and the Future of American Politics* (New York: Hill and Wang, 1986), 61.

[3] Ronald Radosh, *Divided They Fell: The Demise of the Democratic Party, 1964–1996* (New York: Free Press, 1996), 235, 236.

[4] William Form, *Segmented Labor, Fractured Politics: Labor Politics in American Life* (New York: Plenum Press, 1995), 259.

[5] Marick F. Masters, Robert S. Atkin, and John Thomas Delaney, "Unions, Political Action, and Public Policies: A Review of the Past Decade," *Policy Studies Journal* 18 (1989–90): 479. See also James T. Bennett, "Private Sector Unions: The Myth of Decline," *Journal of Labor Research* 12 (1991): 1–12; John Thomas Delaney and Marick F. Masters, "Unions and Political Action," in *The State of the Unions*, ed. George Strauss, Daniel G. Gallagher, and Jack Fiorito (Madison, Wis.: Industrial Relations Research Association, 1991), 277–312; and Arthur Shostak, *Robust Unionism: Innovations in the Labor Movement* (Ithaca: ILR Press, 1991), 190–202.

[6] News release, Bureau of Labor Statistics, Department of Labor, January 30, 1998 (website: http://stats.bls.gov/news.release/union2.nws.htm).

[7] Ibid.; Michael Goldfield, *The Decline of Organized Labor in the United States* (Chicago: University of Chicago Press, 1987), 10.

[8] Data on the membership peaks for the Steelworkers and Autoworkers can be found in Leo Troy, "The Rise and Fall of American Trade Unions: The Labor Movement from FDR to RR," in *Unions in Transition: Entering the Second Century*, ed. Seymour Martin Lipset (San Francisco: Institute for Contemporary Studies, 1986), 92.

[9] News release, Bureau of Labor Statistics, Department of Labor, January 30, 1998 (http://stats.bls.gov/news.release/union2.nws.htm).

[10] Bennett, "Private Sector Unions," 3. See also Marick F. Masters, *Unions at the Crossroads: Strategic Membership, Financial, and Political Perspectives* (Westport, Conn.: Quorum Books, 1997), chaps. 4–5.

[11] AFL-CIO press release, February 22, 1996 (website: http://www.aflcio.org/publ/press96/pr0222.html).

[12] Bennett, "Private Sector Unions," 5; see also James T. Bennett and Thomas J. DiLorenzo, "Tax-Funded Unionism: The Unemployment Connection," *Journal of Labor Research* 7 (1986): 363–86; James T. Bennett and Thomas J. DiLorenzo, "Tax-Funded Unionism II: The Facade of Culture and Democracy," *Journal of Labor Research* 8 (1987): 31–46; and James T. Bennett and Thomas J. DiLorenzo, "Tax-Funded Unionism III: Front Organizations," *Journal of Labor Research* 8 (1987): 179–90.

[13] Goldfield, *The Decline of Organized Labor*, 8.

[14] Irving Bernstein, *The Lean Years: A History of the American Worker, 1920–1933* (Boston: Houghton Mifflin, 1960), 84.

[15] Gary N. Chaison and Dileep G. Dhavale, "A Note on the Severity of the Decline in Union Organizing Activity," *Industrial and Labor Relations Review* 11 (1990): 307–22, and Masters, *Unions at the Crossroads*, 55.

[16] Kevin Galvin, "AFL-CIO Outlines Membership Strategy," Associated Press Wire Services, February 17, 1997.

[17] News release, Bureau of Labor Statistics, "Major Work Stoppages, 1996," Department of Labor, February 12, 1997 (website: http://stats.bls.gov/news.release/wkstp.nws.htm).

[18] Compare, for example, Richard Freeman, "What Does the Future Hold for U.S. Unionism?" in *The Challenge of Restructuring: North American Labor Movements Respond*, ed. Jane Jenson and Rianne Mahon (Philadelphia: Temple University Press, 1993), to Leo Troy, "The End of Unionism: A Reappraisal," *Society*, March/April 1995, 26–33.

[19] A useful summary of the contending explanations can be found in Gary N. Chaison and Joseph B. Rose, "Continental Divide: The Direction and Fate of North American Unions," in *Advances in Industrial and Labor Relations*, ed. David Lewin, David Lipsky, and Donna Sockell, 5 (1991): 169–205. See also Masters, *Unions at the Crossroads*, 51–59, and Bruce

Western, *Between Class and Market: Postwar Unionization in the Capitalist Democracies* (Princeton: Princeton University Press, 1997).

[20] For a more detailed description, see Christopher L. Tomlins, *The State and the Unions: Labor Relations, Law, and the Organized Labor Movement in America, 1880–1960* (Cambridge: Cambridge University Press, 1985), and, from a rather different perspective, Melvyn Dubofsky, *The State and Labor in Modern America* (Chapel Hill: University of North Carolina, 1994), 201–23.

[21] William B. Gould IV, *Agenda for Reform: The Future of Employment Relationships and the Law* (Cambridge, Mass.: MIT Press, 1993), 22; James A. Gross, *Broken Promise: The Subversion of U.S. Labor Relations Policy, 1947–1994* (Philadelphia: Temple University Press, 1995), 246–71.

[22] What follows is, I hope, a fair summation and synthesis of the complementary and mutually reinforcing analyses found in the following works: Berman, *America's Right Turn*; Davis, *Prisoners of the American Dream*; Edsall, *The New Politics of Inequality*; Thomas Edsall and Mary Edsall, *Chain Reaction: The Impact of Race, Rights, and Taxes on American Politics* (New York: W. W. Norton, 1991); Ferguson and Rogers, *Right Turn*; Goldfield, *The Decline of Organized Labor*; Jerome Himmelstein, *To the Right: The Transformation of American Conservatism* (Berkeley: University of California Press, 1990); Kim Moody, *An Injury to All: The Decline of American Unionism* (New York: Verso, 1988); Frances Fox Piven and Richard Cloward, *The New Class War: Reagan's Attack on the Welfare State and Its Consequences* (New York: Pantheon Books, 1982); Patricia Cayo Sexton, *The War on Labor and the Left: Understanding America's Unique Conservatism* (Boulder, Colo.: Westview Press, 1991); and Vogel, *Fluctuating Fortunes*.

[23] This view is defended most plausibly, of course, in J. David Greenstone's *Labor in American Politics*, 2nd ed. (Chicago: University of Chicago Press, 1977).

[24] Bob Woodward, *The Agenda: Inside the Clinton White House* (New York: Simon and Schuster, 1994), 60–69, 148–49, 377–78.

[25] See Graham Wilson, "The Clinton Administration and Interest Groups," in *The Clinton Presidency: First Appraisals*, ed. Colin Campbell and Bert A. Rockman (Chatham, N.J.: Chatham House, 1996), 218–19, 224.

[26] See, for example, Edsall, *New Politics of Inequality*; Samuel Kernell, *Going Public: New Strategies of Presidential Leadership*, 3rd ed. (Washington, D.C.: Congressional Quarterly, 1997); William M. Lunch, *The Nationalization of American Politics* (Berkeley: University of California Press, 1987); Nelson Polsby, *The Consequences of Party Reform* (New York: Oxford University Press, 1983); and Byron Shafer, *Quiet Revolution: The Struggle for the Democratic Party and the Shaping of Post-Reform Politics* (New York: Russell Sage Foundation, 1983).

[27] The term is used by Mike Davis in *Prisoners of the American Dream*, 52.

[28] For penetrating discussions of unions as organizations, see James Q. Wilson, *Political Organizations* (Princeton: Princeton University Press, 1995), chap. 7, and Richard A. Lester, *As Unions Mature: An Analysis of the Evolution of American Unionism* (Princeton: Princeton University Press, 1958).

[29] Nelson Polsby, *Community Power and Political Theory* (New Haven: Yale University Press, 1980).

2 *Labor Unions and Political Bargaining*

[1] Few would dispute that union presidents like being in office and want to stay in power. For useful discussions, see Jack Barbash, *The Practice of Unionism* (New York: Harper and Brother, 1956), 368–72; Jack Barbash, *American Unions: Structure, Government, and Politics* (New York: Random House, 1967), 80–85; Herman Benson, "The Fight for Union Democracy," in *Unions in Transition: Entering the Second Century*, ed. Seymour Martin Lipset (San Francisco: Institute for Contemporary Studies, 1986); Gordon L. Clark, *Unions and Communities under Siege: American Communities and the Crisis of Organized Labor* (Cambridge: Cambridge University Press, 1989), 34–39; and Glenn Perusek, "Classical Political Sociology and Union Behavior," in *Trade Union Politics: American Unions and Economic Change, 1960s–1990s*, ed. Glenn Perusek and Kent Worcester (Atlantic Highlands, N.J.: Humanities Press, 1995). Of course, the classic source for such reasoning is Robert Michels, *Political Parties: A Sociological*

Study of the Oligarchical Tendencies of Modern Democracy, trans. Eden and Cedar Paul (1915; reprint, New York: Dover, [1959]).

[2] The fact that most union presidents, as well as other elected union officials, are regularly reelected no more vitiates the value of assuming that their actions are guided by this goal than does the similarly high reelection rates for members of the U.S. Congress. Both are reelected in large part because of the efforts they make to ensure this outcome. See Morris P. Fiorina, *Congress: Keystone of the Washington Establishment*, 2nd ed. (New Haven: Yale University Press, 1989), and David Mayhew, *Congress: The Electoral Connection* (New Haven: Yale University Press, 1974), 1–9.

[3] Richard A. Lester, *As Unions Mature: An Analysis of the Evolution of American Unionism* (Princeton: Princeton University Press, 1958), 17.

[4] See William M. Leiserson, *American Trade Union Democracy* (New York: Columbia University Press, 1959); Joel Seidman, "Some Requirements for Union Democracy," in *Labor: Readings on Major Issues*, ed. Richard A. Lester (New York: Random House, 1965); Derek C. Bok and John T. Dunlop, *Labor and the American Community* (New York: Simon and Schuster, 1970), chap. 3; and, more recently, John T. Dunlop, *The Management of Labor Unions: Decision Making with Historical Constraints* (Lexington, Mass.: Lexington Books, 1990), 103.

[5] For a discussion of how group leaders use their relationships with government officials to procure benefits for internal use, see Terry M. Moe, *The Organization of Interests: Incentives and the Internal Dynamics of Political Interest Groups* (Chicago: University of Chicago Press, 1980), 59–61. For an analysis of this phenomenon in terms of "rent seeking in the political marketplace," see Barry T. Hirsch and John T. Addison, *The Economic Analysis of Unions: New Approaches and Evidence* (Boston: Allen and Unwin, 1986), 274–75, and Roger L. Faith and Joseph D. Reid, Jr., "The Labor Union as Its Members' Agent," *Research in Labor Economics* 6 (1983): 3–25.

[6] The logic of "credit-claiming" is well-described in a different context in Mayhew, *Congress*, 52–61.

[7] Good summaries of the debates on interest group power are found in Michael Hayes, *Lobbyists and Legislators: A Theory of Political Markets* (New Brunswick, N.J.: Rutgers University Press, 1981); James Q. Wilson, *Political Organizations* (Princeton: Princeton University Press, 1995); and John R. Wright, *Interest Groups and Congress: Lobbying, Contributions, and Influence* (Boston: Allyn and Bacon, 1996). My claim that politicians (members of Congress, most notably) are motivated by reelection has, of course, a long lineage. See Mayhew, *Congress*, and the recent synthesis in R. Douglas Arnold, *The Logic of Congressional Action* (New Haven: Yale University Press, 1990).

[8] Alessandro Pizzorno, "Political Exchange and Collective Identity in Industrial Conflict," in *The Resurgence of Class Conflict in Western Europe Since 1968*, ed. Colin Crouch and Alessandro Pizzorno (London: Macmillan, 1978), 280.

[9] Such an outcome was clearly the goal of union leaders in the famous strike by air traffic controllers in 1981. See Marick F. Masters, *Unions at the Crossroads: Strategic Membership, Financial, and Political Perspectives* (Westport, Conn.: Quorum Books, 1997), 25.

[10] Commentary on the idea of structural power is found in Charles Lindblom, *Politics and Markets: The World's Political Economic Systems* (New York: Basic Books, 1977); G. William Domhoff, *The Power Elite and the State* (Hawthorne, N.Y.: Aldine de Gruyter, 1990), chap. 7; and Martin Carnoy, *The State and Political Theory* (Princeton: Princeton University Press, 1984). See also Karen Orren, "Union Politics and Postwar Liberalism in the United States, 1946–1979," *Studies in American Political Development* 1 (1986): 215–52.

[11] David Truman, *The Governmental Process*, 2nd ed. (New York: Alfred A. Knopf, 1971); Kay Schlozman and John Tierney, *Organized Interests and American Democracy* (New York: Harper and Row, 1986); Jack Walker, *Mobilizing Interest Groups in America: Patrons, Professions, and Social Movements* (Ann Arbor: University of Michigan Press, 1991); John P. Heinz, Edward O. Laumann, Robert L. Nelson, and Robert H. Salisbury, *The Hollow Core: Private Interests in National Policy Making* (Cambridge, Mass.: Harvard University Press, 1993); and Wright, *Interest Groups and Congress*.

[12] On the importance of a group's "comparative advantage" vis-à-vis other interest groups, as well as the effects of a group's "recurrent" dealings with members of Congress, see John Mark Hansen, *Gaining Access: Congress and the Farm Lobby, 1919–1981* (Chicago: University of Chicago Press, 1991), 13–19.

[13] Joseph C. Goulden, *Meany: Unchallenged Strong Man of American Labor* (New York: Atheneum, 1972), 403–58.

[14] What follows is influenced by the literature on "political exchange" between labor unions and the state in Western Europe. See Martin J. Bull, "The Corporatist Ideal Type and Political Exchange," *Political Studies* 40 (1992): 255–72; Pizzorno, "Political Exchange and Collective Identity"; and Marino Regini, "The Conditions for Political Exchange: How Concertation Emerged and Collapsed in Italy and Great Britain," in *Order and Conflict in Contemporary Capitalism*, ed. John H. Goldthorpe (Oxford: Oxford University Press, 1984). The idea of a "bargaining regime" is also influenced by work in international relations, which defines "regime" as a set of "implicit or explicit principles, norms, rules, and decision-making procedures around which actors' expectations converge." See Stephen D. Krasner, "Structural Causes and Regime Consequences: Regimes as Intervening Variables," in *International Regimes*, ed. Krasner (Ithaca: Cornell University Press, 1983), 2.

[15] My emphasis on the importance of the centralization or fragmentation of bargaining capacity fits well with the analytical emphases of the literature on the development of democratic corporatism in Western Europe. While I accept the conclusion of scholars in this tradition that the United States is an example of "low" corporatism, their identification of the causal importance of the degree of centralization remains relevant for understanding the evolution of state/union relationships in the United States. See Alan Cawson, *Corporatism and Political Theory* (Oxford: Blackwell, 1986); Goldthorpe, ed., *Order and Conflict in Contemporary Capitalism*; Peter Hall, *Governing the Economy: The Politics of State Intervention in Britain and France* (Oxford: Oxford University Press, 1984); Peter J. Katzenstein, *Corporatism and Change: Austria, Switzerland, and the Politics of Industry* (Ithaca: Cornell University Press, 1984); and Philippe C. Schmitter and Gerhard Lehmbruch, eds., *Trends toward Corporatist Intermediation* (Beverly Hills, Calif.: Sage, 1979).

[16] If Republicans are in office, cooperation is possible but far less likely, and it is more probable that the centralization of power on each side will actually stimulate greater conflict.

[17] I am using the term "pluralism" here in the manner of scholars of comparative politics, who view it as a bargaining regime composed of fragmented and competing interesting groups engaged in "pressure-group" lobbying. Such a regime stands in contrast to the centralized, monopolistic, and well-integrated interest groups characteristic of "neo-corporatism." See Gerhard Lehmbruch, "Concertation and the Structure of Corporatist Networks," in Goldthorpe, ed., *Order and Conflict in Contemporary Capitalism*. Although my interpretation of the term differs, I have also been influenced by Samuel Kernell's concept of "institutionalized pluralism," by which he means the relatively stable and hierarchical bargaining regime that prevailed in American politics before the 1970s. See Samuel Kernell, *Going Public: New Strategies of Presidential Leadership*, 3rd ed. (Washington, D.C.: Congressional Quarterly, 1997), chap. 2.

[18] Douglass C. North, *Institutions, Institutional Change, and Economic Performance* (Cambridge: Cambridge University Press, 1990), 12.

[19] This is the point that J. David Greenstone made so clearly in *Labor in American Politics*, 2nd ed. (Chicago: University of Chicago Press, 1977).

[20] Although I use "crisis of representation" somewhat differently, I am influenced by Regini's development of this concept. See Regini, "The Conditions for Political Exchange," 133.

[21] Some claim that structure alone counts, but I argue that strong leadership can in some cases substitute for formal institutions. For similar ideas, see Bull, "The Corporatist Ideal Type and Political Exchange," 270, and Regini, "The Conditions for Political Exchange," 132.

[22] Goulden, *Meany*. See also Robert H. Zieger, "George Meany: Labor's Organization Man," in *Labor Leaders in America*, ed. Melvyn Dubofsky and Warren Van Tine (Urbana: University of Illinois Press, 1987).

[23] The classic work is still E. E. Schattschneider, *Party Government* (New York: Holt, Rinehart, and Winston, 1942).

3 Labor and the Johnson Administration: The Limits of Cooperation

[1] George Meany to President Lyndon Johnson, December 29, 1967, Legislative Reference Files, 1/29/28, "LBJ," George Meany Memorial Archives, Silver Spring, Maryland.

[2] Press conference with Walter Reuther, March 12, 1968, Walter Reuther Papers, box

564, folder 20, Archives of Labor History and Urban Affairs, Wayne State University, Detroit, Michigan.

[3] The interpretation that follows is influenced by the accounts in Samuel Kernell, *Going Public: New Strategies of Presidential Leadership*, 3rd ed. (Washington, D.C.: Congressional Quarterly, 1997), esp. 12–20; Anthony King, ed., *The New American Political System* (Washington, D.C.: American Enterprise Institute, 1979); and William M. Lunch, *The Nationalization of American Politics* (Berkeley: University of California Press, 1987), esp. chap. 1.

[4] Charles C. Heckscher, *The New Unionism: Employee Involvement in the Changing Corporation* (1988; reprint, Ithaca: ILR Press, 1996), esp. chap. 3; Thomas Kochan, Harry Katz, and Robert McKersie, *The Transformation of American Industrial Relations* (1987; reprint, Ithaca: ILR Press, 1994); Christopher L. Tomlins, *The State and the Unions: Labor Relations, Law, and the Organized Labor Movement in America, 1880–1960* (Cambridge: Cambridge University Press, 1985), 252–53; and Arnold S. Tannenbaum, "Unions," in *Handbook of Organizations*, ed. James G. March (Chicago: Rand McNally, 1965).

[5] J. David Greenstone, *Labor in American Politics*, 2nd ed. (Chicago: University of Chicago Press, 1977), chap. 2; Richard A. Lester, *As Unions Mature: An Analysis of the Evolution of American Unionism* (Princeton: Princeton University Press, 1958), esp. chap. 3; Seymour Martin Lipset, "The Political Process in Trade Unions: A Theoretical Statement," in *Labor and Trade Unionism: An Interdisciplinary Reader*, ed. Walter Galenson and Seymour Martin Lipset (New York: John Wiley and Sons, 1960).

[6] See Nelson Lichtenstein, *The Most Dangerous Man in Detroit* (New York: Basic Books, 1995), 322–23.

[7] Meany is quoted in Archie Robinson, *George Meany and His Times: A Biography* (New York: Simon and Schuster, 1981), 234.

[8] The quotes are from John McMullan, "How Johnson Won Plaudits of Labor," *Detroit Free Press*, December 8, 1963. See also "Johnson's Talk to Labor and Business," *New York Times*, December 5, 1963, and Joseph C. Goulden, *Meany: Unchallenged Strong Man of American Labor* (New York: Atheneum, 1972), 337.

[9] Kim McQuaid, *Big Business and Presidential Power: From FDR to Reagan* (New York: Morrow, 1982), 223–28.

[10] For good descriptions of how the old nominating system worked, see Lunch, *The Nationalization of American Politics*, and Nelson Polsby, *The Consequences of Party Reform* (New York: Oxford University Press, 1983).

[11] See Kenneth A. Bode and Carol F. Casey, "Party Reform: Revisionism Revised," in *Political Parties in the Eighties*, ed. Robert A. Goldwin (Washington, D.C.: American Enterprise Institute, 1980).

[12] Theodore K. White, *The Making of the President, 1972* (New York: Atheneum, 1973), 236.

[13] Lane Kirkland to International Union Presidents et al., memo, November 12, 1982, "Politics and Labor" file, AFL-CIO Library, Washington, D.C.

[14] Lane Kirkland, "Politics and Labor After 1980," *AFL-CIO Federationist*, January 1981, 20.

[15] Discussions of the MFDP challenge can be found in Lichtenstein, *Most Dangerous Man*, 392–95, and Kevin Boyle, *The UAW and the Heyday of American Liberalism, 1945–1968* (Ithaca: Cornell University Press, 1995), 193–96.

[16] Goldberg is quoted in James L. Cochrane, "Moral Suasion Goes to War," in *Exhortation and Controls: The Search for a Wage-Price Policy, 1945–1971*, ed. Craufurd D. Goodwin (Washington, D.C.: Brookings Institution, 1975), 212.

[17] Willard Wirtz to President Johnson, September 24, 1964, Name File, Walter Reuther, folder "Walter Reuther, 11/22/63–12/31/64," Lyndon Baines Johnson Library, Austin, Texas.

[18] Reuther is quoted in Lichtenstein, *Most Dangerous Man*, 400.

[19] Willard Wirtz to President Johnson, May 20, 1964, Name File, George Meany, folder "Meany, 1/1/63–12/31/64," LBJ Library.

[20] See Irving Bernstein, *Promises Kept: John F. Kennedy's New Frontier* (New York: Oxford University Press, 1991), 38–43, 106. For further discussion of the effects of the conservative coalition, see Robert H. Zieger, *American Workers, American Unions*, 2nd ed. (Baltimore: Johns Hopkins University Press, 1994), 119.

[21] Kenneth Shepsle, "The Changing Textbook Congress," in *Can the Government Govern?*, ed. John Chubb and Paul Peterson (Washington, D.C.: Brookings Institution, 1989), 247–48;

Margaret Weir, Ann Shola Orloff, and Theda Skocpol, "Introduction: Understanding American Social Politics," in *The Politics of Social Policy in the United States*, ed. Weir, Orloff, and Skocpol (Princeton: Princeton University Press, 1988), 22–24.

[22] For a rich description of the congressional barriers during the 1960s, see Bernstein, *Promises Kept*, and Irving Bernstein, *Guns or Butter: The Presidency of Lyndon Johnson* (New York: Oxford University Press, 1996), esp. chaps. 2–11.

[23] Shepsle, "The Changing Textbook Congress," 246.

[24] Quoted in Nelson Polsby, *Congress and the Presidency*, 4th ed. (Englewood Cliffs, N.J.: Prentice-Hall, 1986), 114.

[25] Oral history interview of George Meany by Paige E. Mulhollan, August 4, 1969. LBJ Library.

[26] Goulden, *Meany*, 338.

[27] Lichtenstein, *Most Dangerous Man*, 389.

[28] Boyle, *UAW and American Liberalism*, 205.

[29] A. H. Raskin, "AFL-CIO: A Confederation or Federation? Which Road for the Future?" *Annals of the American Academy of Political and Social Sciences* 350 (November 1963): 214.

[30] Greenstone, *Labor in American Politics*, chap. 10.

[31] Ibid., 357.

[32] AFL-CIO, *Labor Looks at Congress, 1965* (Washington, D.C.: AFL-CIO Department of Legislation, 1965).

[33] Congressional Quarterly, *Congress and the Nation*, vol. 2, *1965–1968* (Washington, D.C.: Congressional Quarterly, 1969), 601.

[34] Speech by Andrew Biemiller, no date, Andrew Biemiller Papers, folder 1/85/54, Meany Archives.

[35] Andrew Biemiller to Harry Barnes, September 8, 1964, Biemiller Papers, box 1/85/48, Meany Archives; Biemeiller is quoted in Robinson, *George Meany*, 244.

[36] Congressional Quarterly, *Congress and the Nation*, vol. 2, *1965–1968*, 601.

[37] Speech by Andrew Biemiller, no date, Biemiller Papers, box 1/85/54, Meany Archives.

[38] AFL-CIO news release, January 6, 1964, "Congress, 88th" folder, AFL-CIO Library.

[39] Greenstone, *Labor in American Politics*, 340–41. For broader discussion of the AFL-CIO's support for civil rights, see Alan Draper, *A Rope of Sand: The AFL-CIO Committee on Political Education, 1955–1967* (New York: Praeger, 1989), chap. 5, and Joseph L. Rauh, Jr., "The Role of the Leadership Conference on Civil Rights in the Civil Rights Struggle of 1963–64," in *The Civil Rights Act of 1964: The Passage of the Law That Ended Racial Segregation*, ed. Robert Loevy (Albany: State University of New York Press, 1997), 52–53.

[40] Bolling is quoted in Goulden, *Meany*, 322.

[41] Martha Derthick, *Policymaking for Social Security* (Washington, D.C.: Brookings Institution, 1979), 110–31.

[42] Greenstone, *Labor in American Politics*, 338; Derthick, *Policymaking for Social Security*, chap. 5.

[43] James R. Sundquist, *Politics and Policy: The Eisenhower, Kennedy, and Johnson Years* (Washington, D.C.: Brookings Institution, 1968), 392.

[44] Greenstone, *Labor in American Politics*, 337–38; Bernstein, *Guns or Butter*, 163, 182.

[45] Boyle, *UAW and American Liberalism*, 183.

[46] Joseph Califano, *The Triumph and Tragedy of Lyndon Johnson: The White House Years* (New York: Simon and Schuster, 1991), 130; Lichtenstein, *Most Dangerous Man*, 402–3.

[47] AFL-CIO, *Labor Looks at Congress, 1965*, 1.

[48] Gordon L. Clark, *Unions and Communities under Siege: American Communities and the Crisis of Organized Labor* (Cambridge: Cambridge University Press, 1989), 201.

[49] Bernstein, *Guns or Butter*, 309.

[50] Wirtz is quoted in ibid., 312.

[51] Mike Davis, *Prisoners of the American Dream: Politics and Economy in the History of the US Working Class* (London: Verso, 1986), chap. 2; Kim Moody, *An Injury to All: The Decline of American Unionism* (London: Verso, 1988), 38–39.

[52] Gilbert Gall, *The Politics of Right-to-Work: The Labor Federation as a Special Interest, 1943–1979* (New York: Greenwood Press, 1988), 155. See also Goulden, *Meany*, 348.

[53] Willard Wirtz to President Johnson, December 1, 1964, WHCF FG 133, "11/19/64–12/31/64," LBJ Library.

[54] Willard Wirtz to President Johnson, February 5, 1964, WHCF, box 1, "LA—Labor Management Relations," LBJ Library.

[55] Meany is quoted in Robinson, *George Meany*, 247.

[56] "Why Labor Didn't Get All It Wanted From Congress," *U.S. News and World Report*, October 25, 1965, 93–96.

[57] Interview of George Meany, LBJ Library.

[58] Califano, *Triumph and Tragedy*, 44.

[59] David Plotke, *Building a Democratic Political Order: Reshaping American Liberalism in the 1930s and 1940s* (Cambridge: Cambridge University Press, 1996), 247.

[60] Selig Perlman, "The Basic Philosophy of the American Labor Movement," in *Labor in the American Economy*, ed. Gordon S. Watkins, Annals of the American Academy of Political and Social Science, vol. 274 (Philadelphia: American Academy of Political and Social Science, 1951), 60. The point has been reiterated by William Forbath, *Law and the Shaping of the American Labor Movement* (Cambridge, Mass.: Harvard University Press, 1991), and Victoria Hattam, *Labor Visions and State Power: The Origins of Business Unionism in the United States* (Princeton: Princeton University Press, 1993). And for a similar emphasis on the unique importance of regional factors and a powerful legislature in American policymaking, see Elizabeth Sanders, "Industrial Concentration, Sectional Competition, and Antitrust Politics in America, 1880–1980," *Studies in American Political Development* 1 (1986): 142–214.

[61] Richard Neustadt, *Presidential Power and the Modern Presidents: The Politics of Leadership from Roosevelt to Reagan* (New York: Free Press, 1990), 201.

[62] Lichtenstein, *Most Dangerous Man*, chaps. 11, 16.

[63] See Cathie Jo Martin, *Shifting the Burden: The Struggle Over Growth and Taxation* (Chicago: University of Chicago Press, 1991), chap. 3; Margaret Weir, "The Federal Government and Unemployment: The Frustration of Policy Innovation from the New Deal to the Great Society," in Weir, Orloff, and Skocpol, *Politics of Social Policy*, 171.

[64] Califano, *Triumph and Tragedy*, 144.

[65] Herbert Stein, *Presidential Economics: The Making of Economic Policy from Roosevelt to Reagan* (Washington, D.C.: American Enterprise Institute, 1988), 107.

[66] The AFL-CIO's analysis can be found in a memo from Walter Heller to President Johnson, May 19, 1964, WHCF LA 32, "LA 8, Wages-Hours 11/22/63–4/4/66," LBJ Library.

[67] Ibid.

[68] Bernstein, *Guns or Butter*, 359, 365.

[69] Califano, *Triumph and Tragedy*, 111–12.

[70] Ibid., 189.

[71] Walter W. Rostow, *The Diffusion of Power: An Essay in Recent History* (New York: Macmillan, 1972), 324.

[72] Califano, *Triumph and Tragedy*, 105.

[73] Arnold Weber, "The Continuing Courtship: Wage-Price Policy through Five Administrations," in Goodwin, *Exhortation and Controls*, 365.

[74] Califano, *Triumph and Tragedy*, 91.

[75] See Heckscher, *New Unionism*, 50–51; John Goldthorpe, ed., *Order and Conflict in Contemporary Capitalism* (New York: Oxford University Press, 1984); Lichtenstein, *Most Dangerous Man*, 361–62; and Leo Panitch, "The Development of Corporatism in Liberal Democracies," *Comparative Political Studies* 10 (1977): 61–90.

[76] Stein, *Presidential Economics*, 121.

[77] Califano, *Triumph and Tragedy*, 144.

[78] Cochrane, "Moral Suasion Goes to War," 280.

[79] Califano, *Triumph and Tragedy*, 144–46; Lichtenstein, *Most Dangerous Man*, 417.

[80] Bernstein, *Guns or Butter*, 376–77.

[81] Gardner Ackley to the President, memo, July 27, 1966, EX BE 5, 7/15/66–8/24/66, LBJ Library.

[82] Goulden, *Meany*, 339.

[83] Lichtenstein, *Most Dangerous Man*, 334.

[84] Interview of George Meany, LBJ Library.

[85] Doris Kearns [Goodwin], *Lyndon Johnson and the American Dream* (New York: Signet, 1976), 189.

[86] A number of memos from Joseph Califano to the president detail the intensity of Meany's

opposition to any appointments that served the interests of Walter Reuther. Califano noted in one instance: "Kirkland said that the AFL-CIO was opposed to sitting on any Committee that had Walter Reuther on it. . . . Kirkland said, 'How would you like it if the AFL-CIO started inviting Bobby Kennedy to speak at all their conventions?'" See Joe Califano to the President, June 6, 1967, "Reuther 1/167–1/31/67," White House Name File, LBJ Library.

[87] Kearns, *Lyndon Johnson*, 166.

[88] Boyle, *UAW and American Liberalism*, 237.

[89] On the growing business disaffection, see Kim McQuaid, *Uneasy Partners: Big Business in American Politics, 1945–1990* (Baltimore: Johns Hopkins University Press, 1994), 131; and David Vogel, *Fluctuating Fortunes: The Political Power of Business in America* (New York: Basic Books, 1989), chap. 3.

[90] Marvin Watson to President Johnson, memo, September 13, 1967, Name File, George Meany, Folder "1/1/66," LBJ Library.

4 *Crises of Representation, 1968–1976*

[1] Johnson is quoted in Joseph Califano, *The Triumph and Tragedy of Lyndon Johnson: The White House Years* (New York: Simon and Schuster, 1991), 141.

[2] James Ceaser, *Reforming the Reforms: A Critical Analysis of the Presidential Selection Process* (Cambridge, Mass.: Ballinger, 1982), 2.

[3] Arthur Schlesinger, Jr., "The Future of the Democratic Party," speech delivered at the Chicago Democratic Dinner, September 29, 1968, Archives of Labor History and Urban Affairs, Wayne State University, Detroit, Michigan.

[4] Oral history interview of George Meany by Arthur J. Goldberg, July 16 and August 18, 1964, John F. Kennedy Library, Boston, Mass.

[5] Oral history interview of David McDonald by Charles T. Morrissey, February 15, 1966, JFK Library.

[6] David McDonald, *Union Man* (New York: E. P Dutton, 1969), 283.

[7] Ibid., 285.

[8] For discussion of the roles of Reuther and Meany in 1960, see Roscoe Born, "Unions Drive to Recast Democratic Party in a More Liberal Mold," *Wall Street Journal*, July 12, 1960; William J. Eaton, "Labor Hails Kennedy Victory," *Washington Post*, July 15, 1960; and Joseph Loftus, "Labor Chiefs Act to Bar Johnson from the Ticket," *New York Times*, July 9, 1960.

[9] Reuther is quoted in Frank Cormier and William J. Eaton, *Reuther* (Englewood Cliffs, N.J.: Prentice-Hall, 1970), 369.

[10] Michael Paul Rogin, "Nonpartisanship and the Group Interest," in *Ronald Reagan, the Movie, and Other Episodes in Political Demonology* (Berkeley: University of California Press, 1987).

[11] Meany is quoted in Archie Robinson, *George Meany and His Times: A Biography* (New York: Simon and Schuster, 1981), 19, 91.

[12] Rogin, "Nonpartisanship and the Group Interest," 122.

[13] Joseph C. Goulden, *Meany: Unchallenged Strong Man of American Labor* (New York: Atheneum, 1971), 360–65.

[14] Meany is quoted in Robinson, *George Meany*, 276.

[15] AFL-CIO press release, April 3, 1968.

[16] For discussion, see James P. Gannon, "Labor in the 1968 Campaign," *Issues in Industrial Society* 1 (1969): 32.

[17] Jean Gould and Lorena Hickok, *Walter Reuther: Labor's Rugged Individualist* (New York: Dodd and Mead, 1972), 352.

[18] Arthur M. Schlesinger, Jr., *Robert Kennedy and His Times* (New York: Ballantine Books, 1978), 205.

[19] Nelson Lichtenstein, *The Most Dangerous Man in Detroit: Walter Reuther and the Fate of American Labor* (New York: Basic Books, 1995), 360–61.

[20] Lane Kirkland to International Union Presidents et al., memo, November 12, 1982, "Politics and Labor" file, AFL-CIO Library, Washington, D.C. The UAW, which did not endorse Humphrey, was no longer a member of the federation, allowing Kirkland to proclaim a degree of labor unity that was somewhat misleading.

[21] Theodore K. White, *The Making of the President, 1968* (New York: Atheneum, 1969), 336.

[22] Numerous Gallup polls, as well as election results in several primaries, demonstrated considerable rank-and-file support for Senator Kennedy. See "Why Unions Are Running Scared in 1968," *Nation's Business*, June 1968, 36–39.

[23] Kevin Boyle, *UAW and the Heyday of American Liberalism, 1945–1968* (Ithaca: Cornell University Press, 1995), 244.

[24] David Broder, "COPE Director Al Barkan Flexing Labor's Big Muscle," *Washington Post*, May 7, 1968.

[25] James P. Gannon, "Unions Strive Mightily to Win the Nomination for the Vice-President," *Wall Street Journal*, August 26, 1968.

[26] See Penn Kemble, "The Democrats after 1968," *Commentary*, February 1969, 35–42.

[27] Kirkland is quoted in White, *Making of the President, 1968*, 453.

[28] Ibid.

[29] Especially useful accounts include Nelson Polsby, *The Consequences of Party Reform* (Oxford: Oxford University Press, 1983); Austin Ranney, *Curing the Mischiefs of Faction: Party Reform in America* (Berkeley: University of California Press, 1975); Howard Reiter, *Selecting the President: The Nominating Process in Transition* (Philadelphia: University of Pennsylvania Press, 1985); and Andrew E. Busch, *Outsiders and Openness in the Presidential Nominating Process* (Pittsburgh: University of Pittsburgh Press, 1997).

[30] Byron Shafer, *Quiet Revolution: The Struggle for the Democratic Party and Shaping of Post-Reform Politics* (New York: Russell Sage Foundation, 1983), 231.

[31] Stephen Schlesinger, *The New Reformers: Forces for Change in American Politics* (Boston: Houghton Mifflin, 1975), 84.

[32] See Thomas Byrne Edsall, *The New Politics of Inequality* (New York: W. W. Norton, 1984); Thomas Edsall and Mary Edsall, *Chain Reaction: The Impact of Race, Rights, and Taxes on American Politics* (New York: W. W. Norton, 1991); and Shafer, *Quiet Revolution*. For a more nuanced interpretation that breaks with conventional account of party reform, see David Plotke, "Party Reform as Failed Democratic Renewal," *Studies in American Political Development* 10 (1996): 223–88.

[33] See the discussion in G. William Domhoff, *Who Rules America Now?* (New York: Simon and Schuster, 1983), 166–80.

[34] Meany is quoted in a memo from Paul Schrade to Walter P. Reuther, September 12, 1969, Walter Reuther Papers, box 437, folder 9, Reuther Library.

[35] Ibid.

[36] Shafer, *Quiet Revolution*, 97.

[37] Transcript of AFL-CIO President George Meany's press conference, September 18, 1968, New York City, George Meany Memorial Archives, Silver Spring, Maryland.

[38] George Meany, "Meany Spells Out Reasons for Policy on 1972 Election," *AFL-CIO News*, August 12, 1972.

[39] George Meany, interview by Mike Wallace, *Sixty Minutes*, CBS, February 13, 1972.

[40] Meany is quoted in Robinson, *George Meany*, 322–23.

[41] J. David Greenstone, *Labor in American Politics*, 2nd ed. (Chicago: University of Chicago Press, 1977), xxv.

[42] William Form, *Segmented Labor, Fractured Politics: Labor Politics in American Life* (New York: Plenum Press, 1995), 275.

[43] Graham Wilson, *Unions in American National Politics* (London: Macmillan, 1979), 44.

[44] Jerry Wurf, "What Labor Has against McGovern," *New Republic*, August 5 and 12, 1972, 21–23.

[45] The operative is quoted in Norman Miller, "As Convention Opening Nears, All-Out Warfare Threatens to Rip Party," *Wall Street Journal*, July 5, 1972. See also Peter B. Levy, *The New Left and Labor in the 1960s* (Urbana: University of Illinois Press, 1994), 180–81.

[46] Barkan is quoted in William Crotty, *Decision for the Democrats: Reforming the Party Structure* (Baltimore: Johns Hopkins University Press, 1978), 111.

[47] Wilson Carey McWilliams, "Meany," *New York Times*, October 22, 1972.

[48] Wurf is quoted in Schlesinger, *The New Reformers*, 95.

[49] Beirne is quoted in ibid.

[50] Quoted in ibid., 93.

[51] Jeffrey L. Pressman, Denis G. Sullivan, and F. Christopher Arterton, "Cleavages, Decisions, and Legitimation: The Democrats' Mid-Term Conference, 1974," *Political Science Quar-*

terly 91 (1976): 89–107. The convention is also described well in Crotty, *Decision for the Democrats*, 244–59.

[52] Christopher Lydon, "Labor's Power Broker Frustrated by Democrats," *New York Times*, December 6, 1974.

[53] "Meany's Neutrality Fails to Catch On," *Business Week*, July 29, 1972, 14–15.

[54] A. H. Raskin, "Mr. Labor: 'Ideology Is Baloney,'" *New York Times*, October 23, 1972.

[55] McDonald, *Union Man*, 285.

[56] Particularly useful discussions of these changes can be found in James Sundquist, *The Decline and Resurgence of Congress* (Washington, D.C.: Brookings Institution, 1981), and David Rohde, *Parties and Leaders in the Postreform House* (Chicago: University of Chicago Press, 1991).

[57] Terry Catchpole, *How to Cope with COPE: The Political Operations of Organized Labor* (New Rochelle, N.Y.: Arlington House, 1968), 310–15.

[58] Al Barkan to President Meany, memo, April 6, 1967, LRF 1/34/16, and transcript, "House Out of Order," Georgetown University Radio Forum, LRF, Meany Archives.

[59] Meany is quoted in Goulden, *Meany*, 218.

[60] Transcript, Biemiller Files, Folder 1/85/44, Meany Archives.

[61] Kenneth A. Shepsle, "The Changing Textbook Congress," in *Can the Government Govern?*, ed. John E. Chubb and Paul Peterson (Washington, D.C.: Brookings Institution, 1989), 251.

[62] Rohde, *Parties and Leaders*, 31.

[63] AFL-CIO, *Labor Looks at Congress, 1975* (Washington, D.C.: AFL-CIO Department of Legislation, 1975), 105.

[64] Jack Beidler to Members of U.S. House of Representatives, November 12, 1974, Biemiller Staff Files, 1/85/75, Meany Archives.

[65] Young is quoted in Alan Ehrenhalt, "The AFL-CIO: How Much Clout in Congress?" *Congressional Quarterly*, July 19, 1975, 1532.

[66] All quotes are in ibid.

[67] Sundquist, *Decline and Resurgence of Congress*, 371.

[68] William M. Lunch, *The Nationalization of American Politics* (Berkeley: University of California Press, 1987), 100.

[69] Gregg Easterbrook, "What's Wrong with Congress," *Atlantic*, December 1984, 58.

[70] Sundquist, *Decline and Resurgence of Congress*, 395.

5 *Labor and the Carter Administration: The Origins of Conflict*

[1] Meany is quoted in Archie Robinson, *George Meany and His Times: A Biography* (New York: Simon and Schuster, 1981), 374, 369, 379.

[2] Quoted in Charles O. Jones, *The Trusteeship Presidency: Jimmy Carter and the United States Congress* (Baton Rouge: Louisiana State University Press, 1988), 41.

[3] Alan Ehrenhalt, "The Labor Coalition and the Democrat: A Tenuous Romance," in *Labor and American Politics*, ed. Charles Rehmus, Doris McLaughlin, and Frederick Nesbitt (Ann Arbor: University of Michigan Press, 1978), 215.

[4] Laurence H. Shoup, *The Carter Presidency and Beyond: Power and Politics in the 1980s* (Palo Alto, Calif.: Ramparts Press, 1980), 61.

[5] Eizenstat is quoted in Erwin Hargrove, *Jimmy Carter as President* (Baton Rouge: Louisiana State University Press, 1988), 34–35.

[6] See Martin Halpern, "Jimmy Carter and the UAW: Failure of an Alliance," *Presidential Studies Quarterly* 16 (1996): 755–77.

[7] Quoted in Joseph C. Goulden, *Jerry Wurf: Labor's Last Angry Man* (New York: Atheneum, 1982), 259.

[8] "How Jimmy Carter Rates with Union Leaders," *U.S. News and World Report*, July 5, 1976, 110–11.

[9] Barkan is quoted in James Singer, "Election Victories Mean Labor Can Come In from the Cold," *National Journal*, November 20, 1976, 1656.

[10] Elizabeth Drew, *American Journal: The Events of 1976* (New York: Random House, 1977), 165.

[11] Ibid., 67

[12] Baron is quoted in Ehrenhalt, "The Labor Coalition," 220.

[13] Ibid.

[14] Drew, *American Journal*, 302.

[15] Nelson Polsby, *The Consequences of Party Reform* (New York: Oxford University Press, 1983), 129.

[16] See "Profile: F. Ray Marshall," *Congressional Quarterly*, December 25, 1976, 3359, and Gary M. Fink, "F. Ray Marshall: Secretary of Labor and Jimmy Carter's Ambassador to Organized Labor," *Labor History* 37 (1996): 463–79.

[17] Wurf is quoted in Goulden, *Jerry Wurf*, 264.

[18] See Jones, *Trusteeship Presidency*, and Hargrove, *Jimmy Carter*.

[19] Quoted in James W. Singer, "Already Crying the Blues," *National Journal*, February 19, 1977, 293.

[20] Meany is quoted in Robinson, *George Meany*, 363.

[21] Hargrove, *Jimmy Carter*, 83.

[22] Joseph Califano, *Governing America: An Insider's Report from the White House and the Cabinet* (New York: Simon and Schuster, 1981), 102–5.

[23] David Stephens, "President Carter, the Congress, and the NEA: Creating the Department of Education," *Political Science Quarterly* 98 (1983–84): 641–63.

[24] Useful discussions of labor's views on Humphrey-Hawkins can be found in Gary M. Fink, "Fragile Alliance: Jimmy Carter and the American Labor Movement," in *The Presidency and Domestic Policies of Jimmy Carter*, ed. Herbert Rosenbaum and Alexej Ugrinsky (Westport, Conn.: Greenwood Press, 1994), and David Vogel, *Fluctuating Fortunes: The Political Power of Business in America* (New York: Basic Books, 1988), 141–43, 157.

[25] See Arnold R. Weber, "What Labor Expected of Jimmy Carter," *Across the Board*, May 1978, 56–61.

[26] Victor Kamber, former AFL-CIO lobbyist, interview by author, December 12, 1989, and Kenneth Young, former AFL-CIO director of legislation, interview by author, December 8, 1989.

[27] Young is quoted in James W. Singer, "The AFL-CIO's Ken Young Looks for Better Times on the Hill," *National Journal*, February 10, 1979, 224.

[28] Ford and Thompson are quoted in Barry M. Hager and Mary Eisner Eccles, "Labor Lowers Its Sights, Redoubles Its Efforts," *Congressional Quarterly*, July 30, 1977, 1602.

[29] Good accounts of the legislative battle can be found in Gilbert Gall, *The Politics of Right-to-Work: The Labor Federations as Special Interests, 1943–1979* (New York: Greenwood Press, 1988); Sar A. Levitan and Martha R. Cooper, *Business Lobbies: The Public Good and the Bottom Line* (Baltimore: Johns Hopkins University Press, 1984); and Barbara Townley, *Labor Law Reform in U.S. Industrial Relations* (Brookfield, Vt.: Gower Publishing, 1986).

[30] "Remarks of the President Upon Addressing United Steelworkers of America," September 20, 1978, transcript in "W.H., President, September 1978," box 122, RG 174, files of Ray Marshall, National Archives, Washington, D.C..

[31] James I. Kaplan, "Labor Law: The Politics of Minority Rule," *AFL-CIO American Federationist*, December 1978, 21.

[32] For discussion, see Levitan and Cooper, *Business Lobbies*, 134.

[33] Townley, *Labor Law Reform*, 174; Levitan and Cooper, *Business Lobbies*, 128–32.

[34] Gall, *The Politics of Right-to-Work*, 201.

[35] Thomas Ferguson and Joel Rogers, "Labor Law Reform and Its Enemies," *Nation*, January 6–13, 1979, 19. See also Mike Davis, *Prisoners of the American Dream: Politics and Economy in the History of the US Working Class* (London: Verso, 1986), 135.

[36] Memo, Stuart Eizenstat to President Carter, June 19, 1978, "Labor Law Reform [O/A 6342] [4]," box 232, DPS-Eizenstat, Jimmy Carter Library, Atlanta, Georgia.

[37] See Carter's handwritten comments on ibid.

[38] Quoted in Helene Dewar and Fred Barbash, "Carter 'Livid' at Meany, Aide Reports," *Washington Post*, August 11, 1978.

[39] Thomas Donahue, interview by author, January 29, 1990.

[40] Halpern, "Jimmy Carter and the UAW," 760.

[41] Ibid., 763.

[42] Harrison Donnelly, "Organized Labor Found 1978 a Frustrating Year, Had Few Victories in Congress," *Congressional Quarterly*, December 30, 1978, 3540.

[43] Paster is quoted in ibid.

[44] AFL-CIO, *Labor Looks at Congress, 1978* (Washington, D.C.: AFL-CIO Department of Legislation, 1979), 6.

[45] For similar conclusions, see Peter G. Bruce, "Political Parties and Labor Legislation in Canada and the U.S.," *Industrial Relations* 28 (1989): 115–41.

[46] For a summary of the extensive literature on this topic, see David Plotke, "The Political Mobilization of Business," in *The Politics of Interests: Interest Groups Transformed*, ed. Mark Petracca (Colorado, Colo.: Westview Press, 1992), and Jerome L. Himmelstein, *To the Right: The Transformation of American Conservatism* (Berkeley: University of California Press, 1990).

[47] Andrew Biemiller in AFL-CIO, *Labor Looks at Congress, 1978*, i–ii.

[48] Thomas Byrne Edsall, *The New Politics of Inequality* (New York: W. W. Norton, 1984), 131.

[49] David Montgomery, *Workers' Control in America: Studies in the History of Work, Technology, and Labor Struggles* (Cambridge: Cambridge University Press, 1979), 170; Joel Rogers, "Don't Worry, Be Happy: The Postwar Decline of Private-Sector Unionism in the United States," in *The Challenge of Restructuring: North American Labor Movements Respond*, ed. Jane Jenson and Rianne Mahon (Philadelphia: Temple University Press, 1993), 65; Davis, *Prisoners of the American Dream*, 135.

[50] Even Melvyn Dubofsky writes in reference to the labor law reform battle: "the congressional majority dealt the AFL-CIO's cause a fatal blow"; Dubofsky, *The State and Labor in Modern America* (Chapel Hill: University of North Carolina Press, 1994), 227. Of course, it was only a minority in the Senate that opposed labor. The unions clearly had majority support in both bodies—but a majority is not always enough in American politics.

[51] See A. H. Raskin, "Big Labor Tries to Break Out of Its Rut," *Fortune*, August 27, 1979, 33.

[52] Fraser is quoted in Kim Moody, *An Injury to All: The Decline of American Unionism* (London: Verso, 1988), 148–49.

[53] Compare Douglas Fraser to President Carter, letter, August 11, 1978, "Labor Law Reform [O/A 6342] [3]," box 232, files of Stuart Eizenstat, Carter Library, with comments by Fraser in Vogel, *Fluctuating Fortunes*, 157.

[54] Landon Butler to President Carter, memo, December 22, 1980 (copy in personal possession of author).

[55] One useful discussion is Fred Hirsch and John H. Goldthorpe, eds., *The Political Economy of Inflation* (Cambridge, Mass.: Harvard University Press, 1978).

[56] President Carter to George Meany, June 5, 1978, "Anti-Inflation Policy, [O/A 6338] [2]," box 143, files of Stuart Eizenstat, Carter Library.

[57] Ray Marshall to President Carter, memo, May 8, 1978, "Labor General [O/A 6245]," box 231, DPS-Eizenstat, Carter Library (emphasis in the original).

[58] "Carter Imposes Voluntary Anti-Inflation Plan," *Congressional Quarterly*, October 28, 1978, 3118.

[59] Meany is quoted in Robinson, *George Meany*, 381.

[60] Meany is quoted in Susan Fraker, "Living with Phase Two," *Newsweek*, November 13, 1978, 18.

[61] See A. H. Raskin, "It Isn't Labor Day," *Nation*, September 9, 1978, 197–201.

[62] Helene Dewar and Fred Barbash, "Carter 'Livid' at Meany, Aide Reports," *Washington Post*, August 11, 1978.

[63] Landon Butler, Stuart Eizenstat, and Ray Marshall to President Carter, draft memo, January 1979, folder "WH—President's Anti-Inflation Program," box 92, RG 174, files of Ray Marshall, National Archives.

[64] Butler to Carter, memo, December 22, 1980.

[65] Watts is quoted in Robert W. Merry, "Communications Workers' Head Attacks Meany for Opposing Carter's Wage Plan," *Wall Street Journal*, December 12, 1978. .

[66] Stuart Eizenstat, Charles Schultze, and Alfred Kahn to President Carter, memo, December 6, 1978, "Anti-Inflation Policy [O/A 6338] [1]," box 143, files of Stuart Eizenstat, Carter Library.

[67] Kirkland is quoted in Robinson, *George Meany*, 385.

[68] Butler to Carter, memo, December 22, 1980.

[69] The entire text of the accord can be found as an appendix to Robert J. Flanagan, "The National Accord as a Social Contract," *Industrial and Labor Relations Review* 34 (1980): 35–50.

[70] Zack is quoted in David Moberg, "Rumblings Underlie AFL-CIO Surface," *In These Times*, December 5–11, 1979, 8.

[71] Ray Marshall, interview by Labor Department, February 26, 1981, Labor Department Archives, Washington, D.C.

[72] Flanagan, "National Accord," 46.

[73] See "Acting under National Accord, Administration Gives Labor Detailed Participatory Briefing on Its Upcoming Budget," *Daily Labor Report*, no. 11, June 16, 1980.

[74] For discussion of Federal Reserve Board policy at this time, see Gerald Epstein, "Domestic Stagflation and Monetary Policy: The Federal Reserve and the Hidden Election," in *The Hidden Election: Politics and Economics in the 1980 Presidential Campaign*, ed. Thomas Ferguson and Joel Rogers (New York: Pantheon, 1981), and William Greider, *Secrets of the Temple: How the Federal Reserve Board Runs the Country* (New York: Simon and Schuster, 1987).

[75] Butler to Carter, memo, December 22, 1980.

[76] See, for example, Peter Gourevitch, *Politics in Hard Times: Comparative Responses to International Economic Crises* (Ithaca: Cornell University Press, 1986), and Joel Krieger, *Reagan, Thatcher, and the Politics of Decline* (Oxford: Oxford University Press, 1986).

[77] Butler to Carter, memo, December 22, 1980.

[78] Quoted in Elizabeth Drew, "A Reporter at Large: Constituencies," *New Yorker*, January 15, 1979, 50.

[79] The role of unions in the 1980 primaries is described in greater depth in James W. Singer, "Choosing Sides—Labor Unions Work for Kennedy and Carter in Pennsylvania," *National Journal*, April 19, 1980, 640–44.

[80] Elizabeth Drew, *Portrait of an Election: The 1980 Presidential Campaign* (New York: Simon and Schuster, 1981), 224.

[81] Hamilton Jordan to President Carter, memo, June 29, 1977, "Labor Law Reform [O/A 6342] [4]," box 232, files of Stuart Eizenstat, Carter Library.

[82] See James W. Singer, "Unions Hard at Work for Carter's Reelection," *National Journal*, November 1, 1980, 1836–39; Philip Shabecoff, "Unions Back Carter for Fear of Reagan," *New York Times*, October 29, 1980; and Laura Weiss, "Labor Unions, Split by Battle for Democratic Nomination, Worry about Reagan Inroads," *Congressional Quarterly*, June 21, 1980, 1733–37.

[83] Butler to Carter, memo, December 22, 1980. See also James W. Singer, "Closing Ranks behind Carter," *National Journal*, July 5, 1980, 1108, and Singer, "Unions Hard at Work."

[84] See William Schneider, "The November 6 Vote for President: What Did It Mean?" in *The American Elections of 1984*, ed. Austin Ranney (Durham, N.C.: Duke University Press, 1985), 233.

6 The Union Strategy to Regain the Presidency

[1] See Adam Clymer, "Labor and the Democrats: Mutual Sense of Reliance Grows as Unions Become Key Source of Financing for Party," *New York Times*, November 20, 1981.

[2] Thomas Byrne Edsall, *The New Politics of Inequality* (New York: W. W. Norton, 1984), 164.

[3] Robert S. Greenberger, "Labor and Democrats: Can the Marriage Be Saved?" *Wall Street Journal*, August 25, 1982.

[4] See Arthur B. Shostak, *Robust Unionism: Innovations in the Labor Movement* (Ithaca: ILR Press, 1991), chaps. 7, 10, 11; William J. Lanouette, "Labor Beginning Earlier to Press for Democratic Victories in November," *National Journal*, May 8, 1982, 817–19; and Maxwell Glen, "Labor Trying to Bring Its Rebellious Members Back to the Democratic Fold," *National Journal*, October 30, 1982, 1837–40.

[5] See James T. Bennett, "Private Sector Unions: The Myth of Decline," *Journal of Labor Research* 12 (1991): 1–12, and Marick F. Masters and Robert S. Atkin, "Financial and Political Resources of Nine Major Public Sector Unions in the 1980s," *Journal of Labor Research* 17 (1996): 183–98.

[6] Kirkland is quoted in Joseph Clark, "Labor Remains in Politics," *Dissent*, Winter 1985, 155–56.

[7] Kirkland and McBride are quoted in Martin Schram, "The Man Who Would Be King-

maker: 'Boss' Kirkland and the AFL-CIO's Gamble on Electing the Next President," *Washington Post*, December 15, 1982.

[8] Jensen is quoted in Dom Bonafede, "Labor's Early Endorsement Will Prove a Psychological Boost and Then Some," *National Journal*, September 24, 1983, 1941.

[9] Jackson is quoted in Howell Raines, "Jackson Assails Labor's Support for Mondale as Move by 'Bosses,'" *New York Times*, November 28, 1983.

[10] Quoted in Greenberger, "Labor and Democrats."

[11] See the discussions of union demobilization in Thomas Geoghegan, *Which Side Are You On? Trying to Be for Labor When It's Flat on Its Back* (New York: Penguin Books, 1992), chaps. 2, 9, and Glenn Perusek, "Classical Political Sociology and Union Behavior," in *Trade Union Politics: American Unions and Economic Change, 1960s–1990s*, ed. Perusek and Ken Worcester (Atlantic Highlands, N.J.: Humanities Press, 1995).

[12] Pierce is quoted in Harold Meyerson, "Labor's Lessons: An Experiment That Worked, Sort Of," *New Republic*, July 9, 1984, 11.

[13] William Winpisinger, interview by author, October 18, 1989.

[14] Quoted in Harold Meyerson, "Labor Rebuilds for Grassroots Clout," *In These Times*, August 8–21, 1984, 2.

[15] John Perkins, speech on file in the AFL-CIO Library, Washington, D.C. (no date).

[16] Herbert Alexander and Brian Haggerty, *Financing the 1984 Election* (Lexington, Mass.: D. C. Heath, 1987), 183.

[17] Jack W. Germond and Jules Witcover, "Labor Unmoved by Kirk's No-Endorsement Plea," *National Journal*, March 30, 1985, 708. See also A. H. Raskin, "Labor: A Movement in Search of a Mission," in *Unions in Transition: Entering the Second Century*, ed. Seymour Martin Lipset (San Francisco: Institute for Contemporary Studies, 1986), 30.

[18] Many of the expenditures did not have to be reported to the FEC. For example, partisan communications that appeared in regularly published unions newsletters or magazines devoted primarily to subjects other than campaign advocacy did not have to be reported as campaign expenditures. See Alexander and Haggerty, *Financing the 1984 Election*, 181.

[19] Ibid.

[20] Ibid., 379.

[21] The figures that follow are from David J. Sousa, "Union Politics in an Era of Decline" (Ph.D. diss., University of Minnesota, 1991), 263–69, and David J. Sousa, "Organized Labor in the Electorate, 1960–1988," *Political Research Quarterly* 46 (1993), 741–58.

[22] See Clark, "Labor Remains in Politics," 154.

[23] For further evidence on the extent to which unionized workers are more Democratic than other blue-collar workers, see David Halle and Frank Romo, "The Blue Collar Working Class," in *America at Century's End*, ed. Alan Wolfe (Berkeley: University of California Press, 1991), 157.

[24] Lane Kirkland, speech, December 5, 1984, AFL-CIO Library.

[25] See Andrew Rosenthal, "Videotape Is Labor's Way to Shun '84 Mistake," *New York Times*, September 7, 1987.

[26] Quoted in David Broder, "Renaissance of Labor's Power," *Washington Post*, August 19, 1988.

[27] This view was expressed by Paul Jensen, the labor liaison for the Dukakis campaign (interview by author, February 22, 1990), and by Sam Dawson, political director for the Steelworkers (interview by author, June 21, 1990).

[28] Quoted in David Shribman, "Divided and Dispirited as Iowa Caucuses Near, Organized Labor Just Isn't Organized Politically," *Wall Street Journal*, January 19, 1988.

[29] Ibid.

[30] Perkins is quoted in ibid.

[31] A. H. Raskin, "After Meany," *New Yorker*, August 25, 1980, 38; Raskin quotes Donahue, 38. See also James W. Singer, "A Man for All Unions," *National Journal*, September 27, 1980, 1623.

[32] Byron Shafer, *Bifurcated Politics: Evolution and Reform in the National Party Convention* (Cambridge, Mass.: Harvard University Press, 1988), 128.

[33] Reuther is quoted in B. J. Widick, *Labor Today: The Triumphs and Failures of Unionism in the United States* (Boston: Houghton Mifflin, 1964), 116.

[34] Graham Wilson, *Unions in American National Politics* (London: Macmillan, 1979), 55.

[35] Kim Moody, *An Injury to All: The Decline of American Unionism* (New York: Verso, 1988), 38.

[36] Keating in Morris Hillquit, *Shall a Labor Party Be Formed?*, debated by Morris Hillquit, affirmative, Edward Keating, negative; Howard Melish, presiding (New York: Academy Press, 1923), 13. This debate from the 1920s frames the relevant issues far more precisely—on both sides—than do many current discussions.

7 *Labor and the Congressional Democrats*

[1] See, for example, Thomas Byrne Edsall, *The New Politics of Inequality* (New York: W. W. Norton, 1984); Thomas Ferguson and Joel Rogers, *Right Turn: The Decline of the Democrats and the Future of American Politics* (New York: Hill and Wang, 1986); Benjamin Ginsberg, "Money and Power: The New Political Economy of American Elections," in *The Political Economy: Readings in the Politics and Economics of American Public Policy*, ed. Thomas Ferguson and Joel Rogers (Armonk, N.Y.: M. E. Sharpe, 1984); William Greider, *Who Will Tell the People? The Betrayal of American Democracy* (New York: Simon and Schuster, 1992); and Robert Kuttner, *The Life of the Party: Democratic Prospects in 1988 and Beyond* (New York: Viking Penguin, 1987).

[2] For examples of such claims, see David Brody, *Workers in Industrial America: Essays on the Twentieth Century Struggles* (New York: Oxford University Press, 1980), 240; Edsall, *New Politics of Inequality*, 171; and Kim Moody, *An Injury to All: The Decline of American Unionism* (London: Verso, 1988), 161.

[3] Hatch is quoted in Bill Keller, "Organized Labor's Vital Signs Show Waning Political Clout; But Numbers Don't Tell All," *Congressional Quarterly*, August 28, 1982, 2113.

[4] Andrew Biemiller, "A Report on Congress, 1978," *AFL-CIO News*, September 9, 1978, insert.

[5] David Rohde, *Parties and Leaders in the Postreform House* (Chicago: University of Chicago Press, 1991), 34–39.

[6] Ibid., 105–19.

[7] Wright is quoted in John M. Barry, *The Ambition and the Power* (New York: Viking, 1989), 656.

[8] Wright is quoted in Janet Hook, "Speaker Jim Wright Takes Charge in the House," *Congressional Quarterly*, July 11, 1987, 1487.

[9] Richard E. Cohen, "Labor Comes Alive," *National Journal*, July 16, 1988, 1864–68. For earlier ties, see Barbara Sinclair, *Majority Leadership in the U.S. House* (Baltimore: Johns Hopkins University Press, 1983), 122–26.

[10] Williams is quoted in Cohen, "Labor Comes Alive," 1864.

[11] Tom Nides, House Speaker's leadership staff, interview by author, May 17, 1990.

[12] The information that follows is based on interviews by the author with Peggy Taylor, associate director of the AFL-CIO Department of Legislation, November 30, 1989; Robert McGlotten, director of the AFL-CIO Department of Legislation, January 19, 1990; and Geri Palast, director of politics and legislation, Service Employees International Union, March 21, 1990.

[13] Barry, *Ambition and the Power*, 280.

[14] Penny is quoted in Cohen, "Labor Comes Alive," 1864.

[15] Quoted in Barry, *Ambition and the Power*, 409.

[16] This section is based on interviews by the author with Tom Nides and with Jon Weintraub, administrative assistant to Representative Pat Williams, January 30, 1990.

[17] Barry, *Ambition and the Power*, 273.

[18] Ibid., 397.

[19] Marick F. Masters and Asghar Zardkoohi, "Labor Unions and the U.S. Congress: PAC Allocations and Legislative Voting," *Advances in Industrial and Labor Relations* 4 (1987): 80–83.

[20] For a discussion of the information-providing functions of interest groups, see John R. Wright, *Interest Groups and Congress: Lobbying, Contributions, and Influence* (Boston: Allyn and Bacon, 1996).

[21] See Paul Starobin, "Unions Turn to Grass Roots to Rebuild Hill Clout," *Congressional Quarterly*, September 2, 1989, 2249–54.

[22] Lane Kirkland, *Report on Congress, 1987* (Washington, DC: AFL-CIO Department of Legislation, 1988), 2; Mike Gildea, AFL-CIO Department of Legislation, interview by author, September 28, 1989.

[23] William Form, *Segmented Labor, Fractured Politics: Labor Politics in American Life* (New York: Plenum Press, 1995), 303.

[24] J. David Greenstone, *Labor in American Politics*, 2nd ed. (Chicago: University of Chicago Press, 1977), 357.

[25] Andrew J. Biemiller, "Reflections on the People's Lobby," *AFL-CIO American Federationist*, January 1979, 17.

[26] The following figures are drawn from Marick F. Masters, Robert S. Atkin, and John Thomas Delaney, "Unions, Political Action, and Public Policies: A Review of the Past Decade," *Policy Studies Journal* 18 (1989–90), 471–80.

[27] David J. Sousa, "Union Politics in an Era of Decline" (Ph.D. diss., University of Minnesota, 1991), 107, 108.

[28] For a detailed quantitative analysis, see Gregory M. Saltzman, "Congressional Voting on Labor Issues: The Role of PACs," *Industrial and Labor Relations Review* 40 (1987), 163–69.

[29] This conclusion is based on numerous interviews with union lobbyists, members of Congress, and congressional staffers in fall 1990. See also Julie Kosterlitz, "Laboring Uphill," *National Journal*, March 2, 1996, 475.

[30] John T. Delaney and Marick F. Masters, "Unions and Political Action," in *The State of the Unions*, ed. George Strauss, Daniel G. Gallagher, and Jack Fiorito (Madison, Wis.: Industrial Relations Research Association, 1991), 320.

[31] Sousa, "Union Politics in an Era of Decline," 97.

[32] See Charles R. Babcock, "Pumping Up PACs with Payroll Deductions," *Washington Post*, November 7, 1989.

[33] See Chuck Alston, "Republicans Seek to Reduce Labor's Clout at the Polls," *Congressional Quarterly*, March 31, 1990, 961–63; James T. Bennett, "Private Sector Unions: The Myth of Decline," *Journal of Labor Research* 12 (1991): 1–12; and Larry Sabato, *PAC Power: Inside the World of Political Action Committees* (New York: W. W. Norton, 1985), 14–15.

[34] Saltzman, "Congressional Voting on Labor Issues," 175.

[35] Masters, Atkin, and Delaney, "Unions, Political Action, and Public Policies," 475. On tendency of unions to favor junior members of Congress with their PAC contributions, see also James W. Endersby and Michael C. Munger, "The Impact of Legislator Attitudes on Union PAC Campaign Contributions," *Journal of Labor Research* 13 (1992): 79–98.

[36] M. Margaret Conway, "PACs in the Political Process," in *Interest Group Politics*, ed. Allan Cigler and Burdett Loomis, 3rd ed. (Washington, D.C.: Congressional Quarterly, 1991), 208–9.

[37] Rhodes Cook, "PACs Invest in 1989 Races amid Moves to Curb Role," *Congressional Quarterly*, October 21, 1989, 1822–25.

[38] David B. Magleby and Candice J. Nelson, *The Money Chase: Congressional Campaign Finance Reform* (Washington, D.C.: Brookings Institution, 1990), 85.

[39] Brooks Jackson, *Honest Graft* (Washington, D.C.: Farragut, 1990), 156–59.

[40] See John Thomas Delaney, Marick F. Masters, and Susan Schwochau, "Union Membership and Voting for COPE-Endorsed Candidates," *Industrial and Labor Relations Review* 43 (1990): 621–35, and Michael H. LeRoy, "The 1988 Elections: Re-emergence of the Bloc Vote?" *Labor Studies Journal* 15 (1990): 5–32.

[41] Sousa, "Union Politics in an Era of Decline," 283, and David J. Sousa, "Organized Labor in the Electorate, 1960–1988," *Political Research Quarterly* 46 (1993): 744–45.

[42] Barry, *Ambition and the Power*, 280 (emphasis in the original).

[43] Macon Morehouse, "Conservative Coalition: Still Alive, but Barely," *Congressional Quarterly*, November 19, 1988, 3343–52; William J. Keefe, *Parties, Politics, and Public Policy in America* (Washington, D.C.: Congressional Quarterly, 1991), 258–63.

[44] Quoted in Jonathan Rauch, "Plant Closing Law's Political Dynamics," *National Journal*, August 15, 1987, 2097.

[45] Peter A. Susser, "Election-Year Politics and the Enactment of Federal 'Plant-Closing' Legislation," *Employee Relations Law Journal* 14 (1988): 356.

[46] Barry, *Ambition and the Power*, 190.

[47] Ibid.

[48] Lane Kirkland, *Report on Congress, 1988* (Washington, D.C.: AFL-CIO Department of Legislation, 1989).

[49] Ethan A. Bronner, *Battle for Justice: How the Bork Nomination Shook America* (New York: W. W. Norton, 1989), 145–47, 158.

[50] See Masters, Atkin, and Delaney, "Unions, Political Action, and Public Policies," 478.

[51] David Price, *The Congressional Experience: A View from the Hill* (Boulder, Colo.: Westview Press, 1992), 77–78; Kirkland, *Report on Congress, 1987*, p. 2.

[52] Quoted in Frank Swoboda, "Expecting Change of Fortune, Labor Recasts Agenda," *Washington Post*, November 10, 1987.

[53] Herbert R. Northrup, "'New' Union Approaches to Membership Decline: Reviving the Policies of the 1920s?" *Journal of Labor Research* 12 (1991): 333–47.

[54] An interesting if polemical discussion can be found in Max Green, *Epitaph for American Labor: How Union Leaders Lost Touch with America* (Washington, D.C.: AEI Press, 1996), chap. 9 and appendix 10-A.

[55] My terminology here is derived from Wilson's classification of policies and their effects. See James Q. Wilson, *Political Organizations* (Princeton: Princeton University Press, 1995), chap. 16.

[56] Greenstone, *Labor in American Politics*, 357, and chap. 10 in general. Though I cite the second edition, this work was first published in 1969.

[57] For a cogent critique of the truly antediluvian filibuster rule, see Sarah A. Binder and Steven S. Smith, *Politics or Principle? Filibustering in the U.S. Senate* (Washington, D.C.: Brookings Institution, 1997). For an earlier discussion of the role of the filibuster in blocking "basic social and economic reforms," see Gary Orfield, *Congressional Power: Congress and Social Change* (New York: Harcourt Brace Jovanovich, 1975, 44.

8 The Clinton Administration: The Legacy of the Past

[1] Gwen Ifill, "Clinton Promises to Trim 100,000 Jobs," *New York Times*, June 18, 1992. For more discussion of AFSCME's role, see Julie Kosterlitz, "Labor's Pit Bull," *National Journal*, August 2, 1997, 1550.

[2] Sam Roberts, "Brown and Clinton Trade Blows in New York Contest," *New York Times*, March 26, 1992; Todd S. Purdum, "Union Members Do Footwork of Candidates," *New York Times*, April 4, 1992.

[3] Quoted in Richard L. Berke, "Unions, Changing Strategy, Try Local Approach on Candidate," *New York Times*, January 14, 1992.

[4] See Ross K. Baker, "Sorting Out and Suiting Up: The Presidential Nominations," in *The Election of 1992: Reports and Interpretations*, ed. Gerald M. Pomper (Chatham, N.J.: Chatham House, 1993), 66.

[5] AFL-CIO, *Report to the 1993 Convention* (Washington, D.C.: AFL-CIO, 1994), 118–20.

[6] Stephen Franklin, "Unions Regain Democratic Zeal, Support Clinton," *Chicago Tribune*, October 7, 1992.

[7] Ibid.

[8] AFL-CIO, *Report to the 1993 Convention*, 119; David J. Sousa, "Union Politics in an Era of Decline" (Ph.D. diss., University of Minnesota, 1991), 315.

[9] McGlotten is quoted in Kevin Salwen, "Labor Unions Prepare Lobbying Effort for Clinton Health-Care Overhaul Plan," *Wall Street Journal*, March 3, 1993; McEntee is quoted in John Judis, "Can Labor Come Back?" *New Republic*, May 23, 1994, 29; Kourpias is quoted in Michelle Levander, "AFL-CIO Has Clinton's Ear," *San Jose Mercury News*, October 5, 1993.

[10] Charles Lewis et al., *The Buying of the President* (New York: Avon Books, 1996), 70.

[11] Fred Barnes, "Hard Labor," *New Republic*, February 22, 1993, 13–15; John E. Mulligan and Dean Starkman, "An F.O.B. and the Mob," *Washington Monthly*, May 1996, 11–16.

[12] Lewis, *Buying of the President*, 70. See also Robert B. Reich, *Locked in the Cabinet* (New York: Alfred A. Knopf, 1997), 175–76.

[13] Clinton is quoted in Levander, "AFL-CIO Has Clinton's Ear."

[14] Bruce J. Schulman, "Labor Secretary for a Post-Industrial World," *Los Angeles Times*, December 20, 1992.

[15] Robert Reich, speech at the AFL-CIO Convention, October 26, 1995 (AFL-CIO press release).

[16] "Labor Letter," *Wall Street Journal*, February 23, 1993.

[17] Kirk Victor, "Point Man," *National Journal*, August 19, 1995, 2094.

[18] Stephen Franklin, "Unions Overlook Clinton Stand on NAFTA for Marriage's Sake," *Chicago Tribune*, October 11, 1993.

[19] Joseph C. Goulden, *Meany: Unchallenged Strong Man of American Labor* (New York: Atheneum, 1972), 303. For comments on the small number of labor appointments in the Truman administration, see David Plotke, *Building a Democratic Political Order: Reshaping American Liberalism in the 1930s and 1940s* (Cambridge: Cambridge University Press, 1996), 245.

[20] A cogent discussion of this activity in terms of "rent-seeking" can be found in Barry T. Hirsch and John T. Addison, *The Economic Analysis of Unions: New Approaches and Evidence* (Boston: Allen and Unwin, 1986), chap. 9.

[21] Barbara Sinclair, "Trying to Govern Positively in a Negative Era," in *The Clinton Presidency: The First Appraisals*, ed. Colin Campbell and Bert A. Rockman (Chatham, N.J.: Chatham House, 1996), 92.

[22] Ibid., 94.

[23] AFL-CIO, *Executive Council Report to the AFL-CIO Convention, 1993* (Washington, D.C.: AFL-CIO, 1994), 129.

[24] M. Stephen Weatherford and Lorraine M. McDonnell, "Clinton and the Economy: The Paradox of Policy Success and Political Mishap," *Political Science Quarterly* 111 (1996): 427. See also the discussions in Elizabeth Drew, *On the Edge: The Clinton Presidency* (New York: Touchstone, 1994); Reich, *Locked in the Cabinet*, 104–5; and Bob Woodward, *The Agenda: Inside the Clinton White House* (New York: Simon and Schuster, 1994).

[25] "Washington Wire," *Wall Street Journal*, March 5, 1993.

[26] Kirkland and McGlotten are quoted in Salwen, "Labor Unions Prepare Lobbying Effort."

[27] AFL-CIO, *Executive Council Report to the AFL-CIO Convention, 1995* (Washington, D.C.: AFL-CIO, 1995), 90.

[28] Haynes Johnson and David S. Broder, *The System: The American Way of Politics at the Breaking Point* (Boston: Little, Brown, 1996), 520.

[29] Sinclair, "Trying to Govern," 114.

[30] Jonathan Rauch, *Demosclerosis: The Silent Killer of American Government* (New York: Times Books, 1994), 89. See also Frank R. Baumgartner and Jeffery C. Talbert, "Interest Groups and Political Change," in *The New American Politics: Reflections on Political Change and the Clinton Administration*, ed. Bryan D. Jones (Boulder, Colo.: Westview Press, 1995), 106.

[31] Paul Starr, "What Happened to Health Care Reform?" *American Prospect*, no. 20 (1995): 25. For similar views, see E. J. Dionne, Jr., *They Only Look Dead: Why Progressives Will Dominate the Next Political Era* (New York: Simon and Schuster, 1997), 120–30.

[32] Theda Skocpol, *Boomerang: Clinton's Health Security Effort and the Turn against Government in U.S. Politics* (New York: W. W. Norton, 1996), 91.

[33] Eric Schmitt, "Labor and Business Fight for Senate Vote on Wage," *New York Times*, July 8, 1996.

[34] *Congressional Quarterly 1996 Almanac*, vol. 52 (Washington, D.C.: Congressional Quarterly, 1997), 7–8; Reich, *Locked in the Cabinet*, 316–19. See also the discussion in Margaret Weir, "Wages and Jobs: What Is the Public Role?" in *The Social Divide: Political Parties and the Future of Activist Government* (Washington, D.C.: Brookings Institution, 1998), 294–95.

[35] Clinton is quoted in "Unions Using 'Raw Muscle' against NAFTA, Clinton Says," *San Jose Mercury Tribune*, November 8, 1993.

[36] Clinton is quoted in "Clinton Attacks Labor on NAFTA," *Chicago Tribune*, November 8, 1993.

[37] Donahue is quoted in "NAFTA Will Cost Clinton, Union Says," *Chicago Tribune* Wire Service, November 22, 1993.

[38] Kirkland is quoted in Walter Galenson, *The American Labor Movement: 1955–1995* (Westport, Conn.: Greenwood Press, 1996), 137.

[39] Thomas L. Friedman, "Clinton, Kirkland Try to Mend Fences," *New York Times*, December 11, 1993.

[40] Christina Del Valle, "Big Labor and Big Bill: One Big Happy Family Again," *Business Week*, February 28, 1994, 48.

[41] *Congressional Quarterly 1993 Almanac*, vol. 49 (Washington, D.C.: Congressional Quarterly, 1994), 178–79.

[42] David R. Mayhew, "The Return to Unified Party Control under Clinton: How Much of a Difference in Lawmaking?" in Jones, *The New American Politics*, 119.

[43] Walsh is quoted in Salwen, "Labor Unions Prepare Lobbying Effort."

[44] Quoted in Kirk Victor, "Friend or Enemy," *National Journal*, November 5, 1994.

[45] Wilhelm is quoted in Gwen Ifill, "Hemmed In, Clinton Risks Union Fight," *New York Times*, November 9, 1993.

[46] Ibid.

[47] See Herbert R. Northrup, "The Dunlop Commission Report: Philosophy and Overview," *Journal of Labor Research* 17 (1996): 1–8.

[48] Quoted in Richard Rothstein, "New Bargain or No Bargain?" *American Prospect* 15 (1993): 35–38.

[49] AFL-CIO press release, January 9, 1995.

[50] See the comments in Leo Troy, "Sacred Cows and Trojan Horses: The Dunlop Commission Report," *Regulation: The Cato Review of Business and Government* (website: http://www.cato.org/pubs/regulation/reg18n1b.html).

[51] AFL-CIO, *Executive Council Report to the AFL-CIO Convention, 1995*, 52.

[52] See Rothstein, "New Bargain or No Bargain?"

[53] Kirk Victor, "Try, Try Again," *National Journal*, July 9, 1994, 1623–26.

[54] Thomas J. DiLorenzo, "The Dunlop Commission Report: Implications for Small Business and the Economy," *Journal of Labor Research* 17 (1996): 108.

[55] Summary of the Commission on the Future of Worker-Management Relations, *Final Report*, January 1995 (website: http://www.ilr.cornell.edu/library/e_archive/Dunlop/).

[56] *Congressional Quarterly 1994 Almanac*, vol. 50 (Washington, D.C.: Congressional Quarterly, 1995), 403.

[57] Catherine S. Manegold, "State Republicans Deal a Major Defeat to Labor," *New York Times*, July 13, 1994. See also Reich, *Locked in the Cabinet*, 149.

[58] Kassebaum is quoted in "Clinton Sides with Unions, Angers GOP," *San Jose Mercury News*, March 9, 1995.

[59] For analysis of the profound impact of America's unique institutional configurations on the nature of the labor movement, see Peter G. Bruce, "Political Parties and Labor Legislation in Canada and the U.S.," *Industrial Relations* 28 (1989): 115–41; Victoria C. Hattam, *Labor Visions and State Power: The Origins of Business Unionism in the United States* (Princeton: Princeton University Press, 1993); and William E. Forbath, *Law and the Shaping of the American Labor Movement* (Cambridge, Mass.: Harvard University Press, 1991).

[60] A brief discussion of Clinton's NLRB appointments can be found in James A. Gross, *Broken Promise: The Subversion of U.S. Labor Relations Policy, 1947–1994* (Philadelphia: Temple University Press, 1995), 387, 389.

[61] William B. Gould IV, *Agenda for Reform: The Future of Employment Relationships and the Law* (Cambridge, Mass.: MIT Press, 1993), 22.

[62] Kassebaum is quoted in Kirk Victor, "Ready, Aim, Fire," *National Journal*, September 10, 1994, 2081.

[63] Gould is quoted in Steven Greenhouse, "Labor Board Chief Takes Assertive Stance," *New York Times*, June 2, 1996.

[64] These and the following figures are from William B. Gould IV, "Three Year Report by William B. Gould IV, Chairman, National Labor Relations Board," *Labor Law Journal* 48 (1997): 175.

[65] Gould is quoted in Greenhouse, "Labor Board Chief Takes Assertive Stance."

[66] Quoted in ibid.

[67] Victor, "Ready, Aim, Fire," 2079.

[68] Gould is quoted in Greenhouse, "Labor Board Chief Takes Assertive Stance."

[69] Gould is quoted in Julie Kosterlitz, "Striking Out," *National Journal*, March 29, 1997, 614.

[70] The account that follows is derived from: Harold Meyerson, "Mother Jones Returns," *LA Weekly*, November 3–9, 1995, 18–23; John Judis, "Sweeney Agonistes," *New Republic*, Au-

gust 21 and 28, 1995, 23–27; and my own interviews with John Sweeney in 1990 and other AFL-CIO officials in the winter of 1997.

[71] Bureau of Labor Statistics, Department of Labor, press release, January 31, 1997 (website: http://stats.bls.gov:80/newsrels.htm).

[72] See Peter Kilborn, "Bringing Down Labor's Giant Leader: Union Presidents Recount 2-Year Plan to Unseat Lane Kirkland," *New York Times*, September 4, 1995.

[73] See Frank Swoboda, "Key Union Leaders Want Kirkland to Leave," *Washington Post*, January 28, 1995.

[74] Kilborn, "Bringing Down Labor's Giant Leader."

[75] Thomas Donahue to General Presidents, National and International Unions, memo, June 30, 1995 (copy in personal possession of the author).

[76] See the interview with Rosenthal in Elizabeth Drew, *Whatever It Takes: The Real Struggle for Political Power in America* (New York: Viking, 1997), 72–73.

[77] The figures that follow are from Jennifer Shecter, *Political Union: The Marriage of Labor and Spending* (Washington, D.C.: Center for Responsive Politics, 1997) (website: http://www.crp.org/Pubs/laborweb/laborindex.htm).

[78] Barnes and Cohen, "Divided Democrats."

[79] Drew, *Whatever It Takes*, 69–78.

[80] James Rowley, "Ickes: Labor Laid Elections Plans," Associated Press Wire Service, October 6, 1997.

[81] Quoted in Lloyd Grove, "After Years in Retreat, the AFL-CIO's Troops Have Mounted a Forceful Campaign," *Washington Post*, October 30, 1996; see also Phil Kuntz and Glenn Burkins, "Worried by AFL-CIO's Election Funds, Business Groups Ready Own War Chest," *Wall Street Journal*, May 10, 1996.

[82] Helene Cooper, "GOP to Rebuke Companies for Bipartisan Donations," *Wall Street Journal*, January 9, 1997. For the scale of business spending, see Drew, *Whatever It Takes*, 247, and Shecter, *Political Union*.

[83] See "Labor Targets," *Congressional Quarterly Weekly Report*, October 26, 1996, 3084.

[84] Gary C. Jacobson, "The 105th Congress: Unprecedented and Unsurprising," in *The Elections of 1996*, ed. Michael Nelson (Washington, D.C.: Congressional Quarterly, 1997), 159.

[85] Guy Molyneux, "The Big Loser in Election? It's Not Labor," *Los Angeles Times*, November 17, 1996; Adam Clymer, "Labor Flexes Financial Muscle to Raise Stakes against G.O.P. in Congressional Fights," *New York Times*, October 31, 1996.

[86] Steven Greenhouse, "Despite Setbacks, Labor Chief Is Upbeat over Election Role," *New York Times*, November 15, 1996.

[87] Molyneux, "The Big Loser."

[88] Sweeney is quoted in Frank Swoboda, "AFL-CIO Urges 'Soft Money' Ban, Other Campaign Finance Changes," *Washington Post*, September 23, 1997.

Conclusion: Organized Labor at the End of the Twentieth Century

[1] Until at least the year 2001, I plan to post occasional updates on the current political activities of unions at the following website: http://taylordark.com

[2] For a useful summary, see Sven H. Steinmo, "American Exceptionalism Reconsidered: Culture or Institutions?" in *The Dynamics of American Politics: Approaches and Interpretations*, ed. Lawrence C. Dodd and Calvin Jillson (Boulder, Colo.: Westview Press, 1994).

[3] See James G. March and Johan P. Olsen, *Rediscovering Institutions: The Organizational Basis of Politics* (New York: Free Press, 1989); Sven Steinmo, Kathleen Thelen, and Frank Longstreth, eds., *Structuring Politics: Historical Institutionalism in Comparative Analysis* (New York: Cambridge University Press, 1992); and the review essay by Peter Hall and Rosemary C. R. Taylor, "Political Science and the Three New Institutionalisms," *Political Studies* 44 (1996): 936–57.

[4] Steve Fraser and Gary Gerstle, introduction to *The Rise and Fall of the New Deal Order, 1930–1980*, ed. Fraser and Gerstle (Princeton: Princeton University Press, 1989), ix.

[5] Ibid., xi.

[6] Ibid., xix.

[7] David Plotke, *Building a Democratic Political Order: Reshaping American Liberalism in the 1930s and 1040s* (New York: Cambridge University Press, 1996), 1.

[8] Ibid., 1, 145.

[9] David Plotke, "Party Reform as Failed Democratic Renewal in the United States, 1968–1972," *Studies in American Political Development* 10 (1996): 252.

[10] Plotke, *Democratic Political Order*, 45.

[11] For like-minded observations, see Karen Orren and Stephen Skowronek, "Beyond the Iconography of Order: Notes for a 'New Institutionalism,'" in Dodd and Jillson, *The Dynamics of American Politics*, 320.

[12] Plotke, *Building a Democratic Political Order*, 61.

[13] See J. David Greenstone, *Labor in American Politics*, 2nd ed. (Chicago: University of Chicago Press, 1977), chaps. 8–10.

[14] Jill Abramson and Steven Greenhouse, "Fight over Trade Bill Showcases Labor's Growing Political Muscle," *New York Times*, November 12, 1997.

[15] See ibid.; Thomas B. Edsall and John E. Yang, "Clinton Loss Illuminates Struggle within Party," *Washington Post*, November 11, 1997; Kevin Galvin, "Labor Wins in Fast Track Defeat," Associated Press Wire Services, November 11, 1997; Peter Beinart, "The Nationalist Revolt," *New Republic*, December 1, 1997, 20–26.

[16] Hamilton is quoted in Bill Sammon and Jerry Seper, "Clinton, Teamsters in Cozy Alliance," *Washington Times*, October 1, 1997, and in Kevin Galvin, "Teamsters President Carey Testifies," Associated Press Wire Services, October 1, 1997.

[17] For a range of perspectives, see Paul Pierson, *Dismantling the Welfare State? Reagan, Thatcher, and the Politics of Retrenchment* (New York: Cambridge University Press, 1994); Morgan O. Reynolds, "Labor Reform: A Blip on the Radarscope," in *Assessing the Reagan Years*, ed. David Boaz (Washington, D.C.: Cato Institute, 1988); Larry Schwab, *The Illusion of a Conservative Reagan Revolution* (New Brunswick, N.J.: Transaction Books, 1991); Stephen Skowronek, *The Politics Presidents Make: Leadership from John Adams to George Bush* (Cambridge, Mass.: Harvard University Press, 1993), chap. 8; and Immanuel Wallerstein, *Geopolitics and Geoculture: Essays on the Changing World-System* (Cambridge: Cambridge University Press, 1991), chap. 2.

[18] Theodore J. Lowi, *The Personal President: Power Invested, Promise Unfulfilled* (Ithaca: Cornell University Press, 1985), 58.

[19] Theodore J. Lowi, *The End of Liberalism: The Second Republic of the United States*, 2nd ed. (New York: W. W. Norton, 1979), 80.

[20] Ibid., 297.

[21] See Paul E. Peterson, "The Rise and Fall of Special Interest Politics," in *The Politics of Interests: Interest Groups Transformed*, ed. Mark P. Petracca (Boulder, Colo.: Westview Press, 1992). For a contrasting view, see Jonathan Rauch, *Demosclerosis: The Silent Killer of American Government* (New York: Random House, 1995).

[22] Or, as Stephen Skowronek would put it, we are in a period marked by the "waning of political time," in which presidential initiatives to dislodge preexisting political and institutional commitments are far more difficult to sustain than they were in the nineteenth century or early twentieth century. See Skowronek, *Politics Presidents Make*, chap. 8.

[23] Marick F. Masters, *Unions at the Crossroads: Strategic Membership, Financial, and Political Perspectives* (Westport, Conn.: Quorum Books, 1997).

Postscript

[1] Alice Ann Love, "Labor to Rethink Alliances," Associated Press, May 26, 2000.

[2] Excerpts in David Rogers and Michael M. Phillips, "UAW Remarks Widen Democrats' Rift on China," *Wall Street Journal*, May 24, 2000.

[3] Rahm Emanuel, "Free Trade Is a Winner for Democrats," *Wall Street Journal*, May 23, 2000.

[4] The following section is based in large part on an interview with Steve Rosenthal, AFL-CIO political director, on Sept. 1, 2000 at AFL-CIO headquarters in Washington, D.C.

[5] More detailed discussion of the 1998 results can be found in Taylor E. Dark III, "Labor and the Democratic Party: A Report on the 1998 Elections," *Journal of Labor Research* 21 (2000): 627–640.

[6] Remarks of Al Gore, Vice President of the United States, at the 23rd Constitutional Convention of the AFL-CIO, October 13, 1999.

[7] Labor's role is exhaustively documented in David Magleby, ed. *Getting Inside the Outside Campaign: Issue Advocacy in the 2000 Presidential Primaries* (Center for the Study of Elections and Democracy, Brigham Young University, 2000) web site: ⟨http://www.byu.edu/outsidemoney/2000primary/index.htm⟩.

[8] Ibid.

[9] Mike Hall, "Mobilizing for Labor 2000," *America@Work*, April 2000.

[10] This belief, which AFL-CIO officials claim was supported by their own internal polling, fits well with recent political science research that demonstrates the efficacy of face-to-face voter mobilization; see Alan S. Gerber and Donald P. Green, "The Effects of Canvassing, Telephone Calls, and Direct Mail on Voter Turnout: A Field Experiment," *American Political Science Review* 94 (2000).

[11] Jonathan D. Salant, "Unions Gear Up for Fall Election," Associated Press, August 15, 2000.

[12] Robert Dreyfuss, "Rousing the Democratic Base," *American Prospect*, November 6, 2000.

[13] Steven Greenhouse, "Labor Tailors Its Vote-for-Gore Message, State by State," *New York Times*, November 2, 2000.

[14] Jim Suhr, "Unions Step Up Efforts for Democrats," Associated Press, October 27, 2000.

[15] Ronald Brownstein, "NRA, Unions Fight for Blue-Collar Voters," *Los Angeles Times*, October 22, 2000.

[16] All of the above figures are based on FEC data compiled by the Center for Responsive Politics: ⟨http://www.opensecrets.org/2000elect/storysofar/sectors.asp⟩

[17] "In the 'Cliffhanger' Presidential Election, Massive Mobilization and High Turnout by Union Members Made the Difference in Key States," AFL-CIO News Release, November 8, 2000.

[18] Ibid

Index